Nietzsche as Philosopher

Columbia Classics in Philosophy

Columbia Classics in Philosophy
Columbia Classics in Philosophy celebrates the longstanding
tradition of influential works from Columbia University Press.

Arthur C. Danto, *The Philosophical Disenfranchisement of Art*,
with a foreword by Jonathan Gilmore
John Rawls, *Political Liberalism*, Expanded Edition
Noam Chomsky, *Rules and Representatives*, with a foreword by
Norbert Hornstein

Note on the design: The material added to this edition is set in a
different typeface and with a different page design from the original
pages of *Nietzsche as Philosopher*, thus maintaining the integrity of
the first edition and distinguishing the added material.

Nietzsche as Philosopher

Expanded Edition

Arthur C. Danto

Columbia University Press   New York

Columbia University Press
Publishers Since 1893
New York   Chichester, West Sussex
Copyright © 2005 Arthur C. Danto

"Beginning to Be Nietzsche: On *Human, All Too Human*" was originally published as an introduction to Nietzsche's *Human, All Too Human: A Book for
Free Spirits*, trans. Marion Faber (University of Nebraska Press, 1996), ix–xix.
"Nietzsche's *Daybreak: Thoughts on the Prejudices of Morality*" was originally
published as "Thoughts of a Subterranean Man," a review of R. J. Hollingdale's translation of Nietzsche's *Morgenrote*, *Times Literary Supplement*
4148 (1 October 1982): 1074.
"Some Remarks on *The Genealogy of Morals*" was originally published in *Nietzsche, Genealogy, Morality: Essays on Nietzsche's* Genealogy of Morals, ed.
Richard Schacht (Berkeley and Los Angeles: University of California Press,
1994), 35–48.
The preface to this volume and "The Tongues of Angels and Men: Nietzsche as
Semantical Nihilist" first appeared in German in Arthur C. Danto, *Nietzsche
als Philosoph* (Munich: Willhelm Fink Verlag, 1998)

Library of Congress Cataloging-in-Publication Data

Danto, Arthur Coleman, 1924–
    Nietzsche as philosopher / Arthur C. Danto.—Expanded ed.
        p.   cm.—(Columbia classics in philosophy)
    Includes bibliographical references and index.
    ISBN 0–231–13518–1 (cloth : alk. paper)—ISBN 0–231–13519–X
(pbk. : alk. paper)
        1. Nietzsche, Friedrich Wilhelm, 1844–1900.   I. Title.   II. Series.

B3317.D3 2004
193—dc22

                                                          2004056186

To the memory of my parents, Samuel B. and Sylvia Danto

Contents

Acknowledgments

Nietzsche as Philosopher grew out of a long essay on Nietzsche, originally written as a contribution for *A Critical History of Western Philosophy*, edited by D. J. O'Connor, and published in 1964. The authors were not historians of philosophy so much as philosophers who, for one reason or other, had some particular interest in a figure from the past. It was a moment when analytical philosophers had begun to think of the canonical texts of our discipline as something more than nonsense, which meant that the largely iconoclastic views of philosophy, militantly espoused by logical positivism, were at last losing their charm. I was invited to contribute to the O'Connor volume by the general editor of the series in which it appeared, Paul Edwards, largely because my philosophical credentials passed muster and because I was the only one he happened to know who met that criterion and also seemed to know anything about Nietzsche. Admittedly, I did not know a lot—but I had read Nietzsche as an undergraduate at Wayne University in Detroit with Marianna Cowan, who later published a superb translation of Beyond Good and Evil. I accepted the invitation chiefly out of brashness and wrote the essay in Rome. I had moved there from the south of France, where I had completed a draft of my first major book, *The Analytical Philosophy of History*. As it turned out, my essay was too long, but Edwards offered me a contract for a book on Nietzsche if I would agree to shorten the article. *The Analytical Philosophy of History* and *Nietzsche as Philosopher* were published in the same year, 1965.

A recent study by the Italian scholar, Tiziana Andini—*Il volto Americano di Nietzsche* (The American face of Nietzsche)—addresses the singular quantity of writings on Nietzsche that American philosophers produced in the second half of the twentieth century; she speculates that Nietzsche answered to something deep in the American grain. What I can claim credit for, I think, is that my book opened Nietzsche up for young analytical philosophers, for my effort had been to show that Nietzsche had written boldly and imaginatively on the very questions that defined analytical philosophy as a movement—questions in the philosophy of science, of language, and of logic—and that he was not some marginal kook who stood for something alternative to philosophy as we understood it. My book showed that it was possible to write on Nietzsche without losing ones philosophical credibility. One could in at least this one case have one's cake and eat it too. And this secured an intellectual annuity for the book, which has remained part of the growing literature it helped validate at the beginning and to which I contributed from time to time with essays on this or that aspect of Nietzsche's thought.

When my wonderful German publisher, Axel Kortendeick—alas now dead—raised the question of a German translation of *Nietzsche as Philosopher*, I proposed that it appear together with these supplementary writings. The result was that readers of *Nietzsche als Philosoph* (Wilhelm Fink Verlag, 1998) had access to a broader picture of my thought on Nietzsche than was easily available in English. I cannot say how grateful I am to Wendy Lochner, the philosophy editor at Columbia University Press, for welcoming the suggestion of bringing out a new edition that would incorporate this added material. There is no way in which I could rewrite a text that reflects that moment, nearly forty years ago, in the history of contemporary philosophy. But the book continues to be read and taught in the growing number of courses and seminars devoted to Nietzsche, and since it is part of the history it has helped shape, and since I still stand by its interpretation of its subject, nothing much could be gained by tweaking it to deal with the criticisms it has naturally generated: no response is a response in its own right. The added materials, meanwhile, enrich the reading of Nietzsche's writing from the perspective the book first opened.

I would like to acknowledge here some of the philosophers who have not only contributed to the history Dr. Andini traces but have in one way or another engaged my subsequent reflections on Nietzsche. These include Maudemarie Clark, Kathleen Higgins, Robert Solomon, Alexander Nahamas, Bernd Magnus, and Richard Schacht. The short note on Nietzsche's "Artistic Metaphysics" was delivered as a response to an excellent presentation by Birgit Recky, of Hamburg Universität, at a session, organized by Paul Guyer on "Ethics and Aesthetics," at the 2003 meeting of the American Society for Aesthetics.

Preface to the Expanded Edition

A few years before the killings at Columbine, a group of youths in Pearl River, Mississippi, embarked on a rampage of murder and brutality, inspired, according to their leader, by the philosophy of Friedrich Nietzsche. The aggressors did not describe themselves as "Supermen" but as "thinkers," set apart from the "herd" who did not understand them—parents, teachers, and insufficiently responsive girls, to whom they felt themselves entitled to teach a hard lesson. As I followed the accounts in the *New York Times*, I thought of how dangerous Nietzsche—as the prophet of the Superman, the critic of herd morality, the self-styled Antichrist—still can be for turbulent minds who discover in him someone, finally, who understands their value, sees into their hearts, knows their hurt, tells them they are beyond good and evil, and licenses their will-to-power. Despite the effort by intellectuals of the last four decades to transform Nietzsche into a benign presence—a hermeneutician, a deconstructionist, a literary artist, a feminist—his vivid images and incendiary language can still arouse muddled youths to gun down girls who spurn them, stab their nagging mothers, or torture animals to demonstrate their unflinching strength. The fact that he is universally acknowledged a great philosopher lends a certain authority to the ferocity of his injunctions and his scary menu of permissions.

One might wonder if the spontaneous effort on the part of the learned community, to interpret Nietzsche's writings through various systems of postmodern thought might be an artful measure of penning him, like the

Minotaur, within labyrinths it is hoped he cannot escape. Alas, as Pearl River shows, the Minotaur, now and again, gores his way out for a night of blood and horror before allowing himself to be led back into the seminars, the colloquia, the commentaries, the readings, in which he seems somehow safe and even caring. And as Columbine demonstrates, the lowered threshold of adolescent rage answers to causes deeper and wider in contemporary culture than anything Nietzsche can be held responsible for.

Like the Minotaur, however, Nietzsche is a fusion of disparate parts—a subtle philosophical critic of the austere concepts to which gifted thinkers devote entire lifetimes and an intemperate prophet, the vehemence of whose voice carries over into his philosophical investigations. On the other hand, the same philosophical blood flows through the different parts, which makes it difficult to mute his characteristically strident claims. Had the Pearl River "thinkers" consulted a standard encyclopedia, they would have found their vision corroborated: Nietzsche is the "German philosopher," who "passionately rejected the 'slave morality' of Christianity for a new heroic morality that would affirm life. Leading this new society would be a breed of supermen whose 'will-to-power' would set them off from the 'herd' of inferior humanity." These teachings, which flooded European consciousness as the twentieth century began, seemed to many to be supported by what they knew of his philosophy, more narrowly considered: that philosophy is autobiography, that language is arbitrary, that truth is a lie, and that logic is merely the way a certain species thinks, with none of the certainty or necessity once felt to belong to it. Anton Chekhov entertained a fantasy of meeting Nietzsche by chance, on a train or a steamer, where they would discuss through the night their agreements and differences. As a scientist, Chekhov wrote, in the somewhat moralistic idiom with which evolution was discussed at the time, that "Nature is doing everything in her power to rid herself of all weaklings and organisms for which she has no use." But, as a doctor, Chekhov was committed to serving the weak and hence struggled against Nature's ruthless and indifferent pruning. So there was a certain felt inconsistency between his thought and practice, which Nietzsche might have helped him resolve. Nietzsche had an inverted reading of this Darwinist gloss on evolution and survival, holding, roughly, that morality and compassion interfered with the workings of Nature, with the result that the "weaklings," united under religion, survived. The only hope for humanity accordingly lies in reversing the "unnatural" survival of the unfit, and he set himself the task of reversal through a destructive critique of morality that rested on a deep critique of scientific knowledge. That is the connection between the monster's disparate parts. So one cannot, as it were, dismiss the fierce ranting of the prophet as incidental to Nietzsche's system. It is rather, like his inverting of Darwinism, that the sharp critiques of science, the perspectivism, the invention of a novel theory of truth, the refined analyses of language, the pyschologization of logic and the trivialization of mathematics are enlisted to rewrite a universe in which the strong can come into their rightful ascendancy over the weak.

There are not therefore, two distinct Nietzsche's—one tough and the other tender. There is not one Nietzsche who addresses graduate students of semantics and another who calls out to the rednecks who feel themselves philosophers through the mere fact that they are able to read him. But that makes it all the more urgent to expose *his* thought to the kind of critique he used as a weapon against so many bodies of philosophical thought—to use against him the weapons he taught us to wield. The intellectual joys of dealing with the philosophical subtleties of a great analytical thinker, as I deem Nietzsche to be, is enhanced by the sense that in doing so, one is disarming one of the most dangerous moral voices of modern times. Such was the spirit in which *Nietzsche as Philosopher* was written.

My strategy was to circle the enemy in two different ways. One of them was to demonstrate that Nietzsche really was a philosopher in the precise sense that he contributed, brilliantly and with the originality of genius, to the questions which define philosophical inquiry, and hence that his writings do not establish him as a counterweight to academic philosophy—or as a philosopher for those who lack the patience for philosophy. He is as much a philosopher in the received sense by which we admire the leading figures in the major departments in which the discipline is taught to aspiring professionals. My other strategy was to apply Nietzsche's philosophy to his own philosophy, in the hope of disarming the rabid Nietzsche and neutralizing the vivid frightening images that have inspired sociopaths for over a century. Admittedly, Nietzsche's writings will continue to be read by those who do not feel the need for commentary. Still, one does what one can. The only recourse for a philosopher is to elaborate an anti-Nietzschian philosophy from within Nietzsche's philosophy itself. Philosophy itself, after all, is a maze. If one could engage Nietzsche in the endless disputations about truth and meaning with sharp but decorous philosophical colleagues, who would not think of using their destructive analyses to frightful purposes, what better way could there be to keep him out of harm's way? The Nietzsche who emerged "as philosopher" from my book was an unfamiliar Nietzsche, addressed as contributor to the central issues of analytical philosophy. The book helped canonize him as philosopher while damping the fires of his ruthless if inspired harangues. Before *Nietzsche as Philosopher* appeared, it was common to read him out of the history of philosophy by saying that he was not really a philosopher—or not a "real" philosopher—but a metaphysician whose nonsense was redeemed by the lyricism of his language. Whatever else it did, my book gave Nietzsche philosophical credibility, admittedly in a far narrower philosophical culture than he would have recognized, that of professional philosophers in a discipline that had become technical and logical, as it had in the Anglo-American academic world, whose philosophy departments it dominated. The book introduced him as a new colleague to my admired peers.

I confess that I failed to appreciate a further mode of disempowerment when I composed this strategy and wrote the book that executes it. This would be to treat his texts as *literature*. "Poetry," W. H. Auden wrote, "makes nothing happen." If one could treat the texts as literature, broadly understood, a space within reading would open up, deflecting readers from taking his interpretations and injunctions literally and urging them to attend instead to the poetry of his expression. In part my oversight was due to the belief that his books lacked, to a far greater degree than they do, any larger unity than collections of aphorisms and short essays allow. I went so far as to claim that it scarcely mattered where in his many volumes a given passage might be located. I thought the style was in the language rather than the structure of the writings and that the minimalist structure of externally conjoined passages might have an explanation through the circumstances of his illness. At one point it occurred to me that within a few weeks, Van Gogh cut off his ear and Nietzsche went spectacularly mad in the Piazza Carlino in Turin—and I marveled that the most advanced painter and the most advanced philosopher in Europe should have trespassed into insanity at nearly the same moment. Both were infected by a form of syphilis, and I wondered whether there might be further symptomatic parallels in the way they produced their work. One such parallel, I speculated, lay in the fact that Nietzsche was able only to write in short bursts while Van Gogh, especially in the period leading up to his self-aggression, had a certain attention deficit that expressed itself in work that had to be done quickly, like drawings and oil sketches. Such a view, if sound, would support the thesis that the single aphorism would be the unit of philosophical expression for Nietzsche. But I have since come to appreciate that the books have a structure more cohesive than mere conjunctions of passages could be, with enough textual architecture to qualify as literary works. It seemed accordingly that it would be of great value to write essays on his main texts from this perspective, and I have accordingly rethought *Truth and Lies for an Extra Moral Point of View*, *Human All-Too Human*, *Morgenrote*, and in a much more sustained and probing way, *The Geneaology of Morals* in the essays here published in conjunction, for the first time, with the integral text of *Nietzsche as Philosopher*. These at least point the way, brilliantly taken by Alexander Nahamas, to an ideal work—*Nietzsche as Poet*—referring not to the actual rather lame verses he inserted into his books but to the books themselves, taken as literature. It would be wonderful to have the time and leisure to write in the same vein about *The Birth of Tragedy*, *Thus Spake Zarathustra*, *Beyond Good and Evil*, and his brief masterpiece, *The Twilight of the Idols*. But these essays perhaps suffice to establish the claim that granting their claims as literature, the underlying philosophy remains as it is represented in *Nietzsche as Philosopher*.

So these essays do not quite amount to the dramatic about-face I am credited by friendly critics with having made. Robert Solomon, in a recent study of Nietzsche, declares that I have renounced the earlier book. Bernd Magnus, in *Nietzsche's Case: Philosophy as/and Literature* compares two statements by me, written twenty years apart. The first was my somewhat careless claim that none of Nietzsche's books interestingly "presuppose an acquaintance with any other. [So] his writing may read in pretty much any order, without this greatly impeding the comprehension of his ideas." I still, I am afraid, believe that. None of the textual discoveries, such as they are, seem to me greatly to penetrate the system of ideas I tried to establish in *Nietzsche as Philosopher*. When, for a celebration of Nietzsche's 150th birthday, I delivered a lecture on Nietzsche as what I called a semantical nihilist—meaning that the world, having no structure other than what we impose upon it, cannot underwrite the truth of our propositions so that, as he liked to say, "everything is false," a literary scholar in the audience observed that I seemed not to have changed my mind about anything in the twenty five years since my book's publication. I still have not. Certain excesses excepted, I have not changed my views on Nietzsche as philosopher at all. I still feel that in all essential respects, the literary and hermeneutical discussions of Nietzsche's philosophy have made little difference in how his *philosophy* is structured. And I am enough convinced of the systematicity of philosophy to believe that the system in its entirety is visible in Nietzsche's earliest works.

Magnus contends that "the truth as Nietzsche saw it requires a certain relation to the text, one in which Nietzsche's polysemantic metaphors are not perceived as distractions but are instead thought to be required by the very thought itself, indeed may perhaps be said to *be* the thought itself." From the strategic perspective of disarming Nietzsche, I enthusiastically applaud the idea of transforming his prose into the metaphors that convey it, letting literary interpretation combine with philosophical analysis to interpose a defensive shield between it and at least his more vulnerable readers. But I am certain that Nietzsche meant what he said in the literal way the terrorists of Pearl River High School recognized. He would not have wished his thought to be relativized to a metaphor and turned from exhortations into tropes. He wrote clearly and pungently and ornamented his texts with brilliant images, the better to prepare the mind for receiving the sharp and pointed messages it was his prime intention to plant into the flesh of the soul. When one lays out the propositions, they stand on their own. The philosopher was in the employment of the prophet.

I am not quite so naive as to believe the Minotaur will never again burst out of the labyrinth he himself showed me how to build—but neither can I think of a more justified philosophical task than, by turning his arguments back against themselves, to blunt his language. How often, after all, does a philosopher, acting in the line of duty, actually help save lives?

Arthur C. Danto
NEW YORK CITY, 2004

Preface to the Morningside Edition

arthurdantist, n. One who straightens the teeth of exotic dogmas.
"Little Friedrich used to say the most wonderful things before we took
him to the arthurdantist."—Frau Nietzsche
—DANIEL DENNETT AND KAREL LAMBERT, *THE PHILOSOPHICAL LEXICON*

From one of the innumerable *pensions* in which he passed the
restless years of his forced retirement from the University of Basle, and during which he composed the amazing texts which house his philosophy,
Nietzsche wrote to his psychological collaborator and amatory rival Paul Rée
of having met a remarkable fellow guest: the editor of what Nietzsche identified as "the most prestigious philosophical journal of the anglo-saxon
world." In high excitement, Nietzsche informed Rée of the great interest this
personage expressed in their work, and of how anxious he was to publish
something of it. The guest, by comedic happenstance, was Croom Robertson, the editor of *Mind,* even then a periodical of singular austerity and rig-
orous logical address. Nietzsche and the editor of *Mind*! It was one of those
cruel ironic encounters of polar opposites which Max Beerbohm fantastically
depicted in a delicious genre of his invention: Charles Darwin and the Arch-
bishop of Canterbury, say, or—to underscore the absurdities of incommuni-
cation with more contemporary possibilities—Simone Weil and the editor of
Gourmet, Ti-Grace Atkinson and the editor of *Playboy,* or Che Guevara and
the editor of *Forbes*; caricatures of what organizers of conferences solemnize
as "dialogue." And I can picture poor Mr. Robertson, riveted by an Etonian
politeness to the conventions of the common-table, interposing "How fascinating!" or "Come now!" as his partner, through his eccentric moustache,
declaims, over the potato soup and the sauerbraten, of the Superman, the
Eternal Return, the origins of tragedy in the Dionysiac orgy, slave morality, and

the Blond Beast. "You must by all means send us something, Mr. Nietzsche," I can hear him stammering as he makes his grateful departure after a desperate change of itinerary.

I came across this letter to Rée in the course of reading through Nietzsche's correspondence one spring in Rome, having just finished writing *Analytical Philosophy of History*, and beginning to think about the present book. It was a project of highest priority for me, once returned to New York, to examine the relevant volumes of *Mind* to see if, by a spectacular oversight, the Nietzsche bibliographies had neglected an extraordinary item. There was, of course, nothing by him, and I lack the archival enterprise to find out whether Nietzsche indeed submitted a manuscript—though it is amusing to draft an imaginary letter of rejection in correct if stilted German. Nietzsche would hardly have been capable at the time of casting his thoughts into the regimented etiquette of the standard journal article. Yet, *question de style* apart, as a philosopher, his interests and those of Mr. Robertson's sober readers were not so hilariously at odds as my cartooning implies, and in retrospect it seems to me as though my effort in this book is that of a third guest at the *Gaststatte*, patiently translating into one another's idiom the seemingly incommensurate preoccupations of these two ill-matched diners thrown together by the malevolence of chance. The pages of *Mind* would have been one of the forums in which what we think of today as analytical philosophy took shape, with its central teaching that the problems of philosophy are *au fond* problems of language, however heavily disguised. But just this, I came to believe, was Nietzsche's own view, that the structures of language determine what are the structures of reality for those whose language it is, and that the deep order of the world, so sought by philosophers of the past, is but the cast shadow of the deep order of their grammar. He went on from there, of course, to pose the startling thesis that a change in human reality cannot be expected until there is a change in language—that we shall not get rid of God, as he says in *Beyond Good and Evil*, until we get rid of grammar—and he polemicized in favor of that change by submitting the realities of his tradition to the most devastating criticism it had ever sustained. The demolition of idols, the moral arson, the brash defacement of sacred writ by brilliant graffiti, brought him notoriety and enthusiasm—alas too late to slake his thirst for recognition. But beneath it all, and giving it a point and basis, was a philosophy of language so novel for its time that neither his contemporaries nor he himself fully perceived it for what it was. It took an independent development of contemporary philosophy to render it logically visible. Thus Nietzsche as philosopher, as I would seek to explain him to Croom Robertson and those who came after him and worked in the spirit of his celebrated journal.

Not long after the book appeared, I had a nice discussion about it with Lionel Trilling, in one of those impromptu chats which compose the charm of street life at Columbia, the two of us carrying bags of groceries from the B & B Market. "Your book," he said just as we finished, "has the snottiest title I ever saw." Whole libraries of arrogant redundancies realized themselves in an instant's fantasy: *Picasso as Artist, Notre Dame as Cathedral, Lenin as Revolutionary, Trilling as Critic.* . . . And of course he was right: the title was intended to be (mildly) offensive. But until then it had seemed to many that Nietzsche had been manhandled into the history of philosophy for want of an obvious alternative space to store him in. But his presence there was deemed anomalous and possibly wrong. "Nietzsche isn't really a philosopher," I had been assured by an esteemed senior colleague. And there were those disposed to believe that if he was a philosopher, no one before him could really have been that, since none did quite what he did— he philosophized with a hammer, went mad, barked up every wrong tree in Christendom, wrote stunning prose. Or he was thought of as almost everything except a philosopher. So I wanted to show that whatever else he was or was not, he was certainly a philosopher in just the way that everyone who is one is one: that he thought systematically and deeply about each of the closed set of questions which define what philosophy is, and that he gave serious, original, and coherent answers to them all. Whatever else he was, he was a philosopher. The title—and of course the text—was an effort to rescue this man for my own discipline from all those poets, politicians, potheads, and photographers from Princeton. There were lots of Nietzsches. He belongs to the histories of philosophy, opera, ideology, and hermeneutics; to the chronicles of loneliness, madness, and sexual torment. Mine is the philosopher.

Of course, it is an exercise in "arthurdanture," and some may feel the bite is gone when straightened. My own view is that the things he says are more interesting than the things Frau Nietzsche—who was anyway not much of a philosopher—thought so much of. And they have the extra fascination of perhaps being true, in whatever way it is that philosophy is true. I have thought enough of Nietzsche's theories to have exploited them in my own subsequent philosophical work. But further confession is unseemly in a preface and in any case, as Nietzsche wrote in another letter, this time to Jacob Burckhardt, *Alles Persönliche ist eigentlich komisch.*

A.C.D.
BROOKHAVEN AND NEW YORK CITY
OCTOBER, 1979

Preface

The vocabulary of philosophy is much less technical than the layman might suppose; many of its words are from the common lexicon of everyday, ordinary speech. Thus, the distances between the philosophical use of these terms and their usual employment in daily communication might seem negligible to the nonphilosopher, who had expected, perhaps, words more recondite or exotic. Accordingly, he might think to apply sentences, which make a philosophical use of a word, to situations, where the ordinary use of that word is called for. When this occurs, however, tensions always arise. The philosophical sentence sometimes seems insanely irrelevant in contexts where the mere *words* have an otherwise unexceptionable application; and the ordinary sentences have an almost comic impertinence when inserted in philosophical discussion. Suppose, for example, a man is pinned under a log and complains that he cannot get free. It would be absurd to reply to him that none of us can, because we live in a deterministic world. It would be just as absurd as for a dentist to direct us to seek nirvana—a general surcease from the suffering of the world—when we merely complain of a toothache. Or for an arch seducer to remind a reluctant maiden that the Bible enjoins us to love our neighbour. It is difficult to get the two sets of uses to mesh harmoniously; perhaps it is impossible.

Nietzsche's philosophy is often expressed in sentences which sound such dissonances when taken in conjunction with ordinary language, and some of his most celebrated utterances acquire their pungency through the stresses and strains of using the same word simultaneously in a wide and a narrow context. His style of writing and philosophizing, in part, was to dilate and then suddenly to circumscribe the meaning of a word, although he likely was not always aware that he was doing so, and was at times as misled by what he wrote as his puzzled readers must have been. He would take a word, which had a restricted usage, and begin to give it a far wider application, using it now to describe things that had never been seen as falling within the meaning of that term before. Then, having immensely widened the scope of the word, he would force it back into the context from which it was originally taken. The context is then charged with an overload of conceptual energy it was not made to withstand. The effect was not always felicitous. Old words used in new ways in old contexts sometimes exploded into absurdity or silliness. But at times the sentence would attain a singular intensity and induce a creative distortion in the structure of our understanding. Because he was given to self-dramatization, Nietzsche liked to speak of himself as philosophizing with a hammer. His purpose was in part to crack the habitual grip on thought in which language holds us, to make us aware of how much our minds are dominated by the concepts from which we can hardly escape, given the rules our language follows. Then, realizing the conventional nature of our language, we might try to create fresh concepts and so whole new philosophies. The violent chemistry of subtle linguistic incongruities yielded a prose that was sparkling and explosive at its best, and a means to the liberation of the human mind. Men had to be made to understand that everything was possible if they were to be moved to try anything at all, Nietzsche felt, and his philosophy, therefore, is one of total conceptual permissiveness. The concepts he attacked had to be the most basic ones, the piers, so to speak, which supported the entire ramified networks of human ideas, piers sunk so deep in the human psychology as scarcely to be acknowledged. It is for this that he is entitled to be called a philosopher.

Nietzsche was more than a critic of concepts and a word-tormenting anarchist. He tried to construct a philosophy consistent with the extraordinary openness he felt was available to man, or at least a philosophy that would entail this openness as one of its consequences. In the course of his piecemeal elaborations he touched on most of the problems that have concerned philosophers, and he discussed them interestingly, and even profoundly. If one takes the trouble to eke his philosophy out, to chart the changes in signification that his words sustain in their shiftings from context to context and back, then Nietzsche emerges almost as a systematic as well as an original and analytical thinker. This task, however, is not a simple one. His thoughts are diffused through many loosely structured volumes, and his individual statements seem too clever and topical to sustain serious philosophical scrutiny. Nietzsche seems distrustful and almost officially defiant of philosophic rigor, and he has, in fact, often been the thinker *de choix* of men who find academic and professional philosophy too circumspect or meticulous for their bold and bohemian tastes. Moreover, Nietzsche's not altogether undeserved reputation as an intellectual hooligan, as the spiritual mentor of the arty and the rebellious, and, more darkly, as the semicanonized proto-ideologist of Nazism, has made it difficult even for philosophers to read him as one of their own. For this reason I have written a book which treats of Nietzsche merely as a philosopher, whose thought merits examination on its own, in- dependent of the strange personality and the special cultural circumstances of its author. Only now and again, when a special historical explanation seems called for, will I include biographical or historical information.

Nietzsche has seldom been treated as a philosopher at all, and never, I think, from the perspective, which he shared to some degree, of contemporary analytical philosophy. In recent years, philosophers have been preoccupied with logical and linguistic researches, pure and applied, and I have not hesitated to reconstruct Nietzsche's arguments in these terms, when this was compatible with the aim of making a book available to the general reader. This may precipitate some anachronisms. However, because we know a good deal more philosophy today, I believe it is exceedingly useful to see his analyses in terms of logical features which he was unable to make explicit, but toward which he was unmistakable groping. His language would have been less colorful had he known what he was trying to say, but then he would not have been the original thinker he was, working through a set of problems which had hardly ever been charted before. Small wonder his maps are illustrated, so to speak, with all sorts of monsters and fearful indications and boastful cartographic embellishments!

Nietzsche cannot be regarded as having been an influence upon the analytic movement in philosophy, unless in some devious, subterranean way. Rather, it is for the movement to reclaim him as a predecessor. It is, however, not too late for him to become an influence. I hope that this volume will not only make clear his philosophy but also help to introduce his arguments and contentions into the context of discussion and interchange which is where philosophy lives.

In one of his cautionary aphorisms on good style—he prided himself as a stylist and master of language—Nietzsche warned against citations from other writers. In disregard of this warning, I shall quote the warning itself: "An outstanding quotation can cancel out whole pages, and even the entire book, for it seems to call out in warning to the reader 'Watch out! I am the precious stone—and everything about me is lead, dull and worthless lead.'" Unfortunately, I must quote amply from Nietzsche, to document rather than to ornament my argument. This cannot be avoided. The translations, despite a merely adequate German, are my own, although I have benefited immensely from the superlative translations of Marianna Cowan, Francis Golffing, Walter Kaufmann, and R. J. Hollingdale, and from the efforts of the zealous translators who produced the edition of Nietzsche's collected work under Dr. Oscar Levi in the early years of this century. I have used my own translations because not all of the writings I cite have been translated by any one person, and it is stylistically important to have Nietzsche speak with a single voice, even if it is a voice I have given him. Also, except for Professor Kaufmann, few translators have been professional philosophers, and often it is necessary to use the same English word for what are only synonymous terms in German, in order to make clear that the same idea is involved; or to use, of all the variants available to the translator, that one which most closely strikes the required philosophical tone. Finally, even if I had used translations by others, I should have had to translate at least one-third of the passages I cite, for these come from the *Nachlass*, the unpublished notes, which have not truly been translated into English at all. I make heavy use of this material, in which we see Nietzsche in the laboratory, as it were, experimenting with this or that idea which echoes only obscurely in the published work. Had he retained his sanity, quite feasibly a good deal of this would have found its way into his books. There have been some celebrated tamperings with the *Nachlass*, which I shall speak of later. But I feel reasonably safe in using it, for his editors, so far as I have been able to determine, had not the slightest interest in philosophy and were concerned primarily in distorting biographical detail or underscoring attitudes which, though they have had a certain scandalous notoriety, are only tenuously connected to the main philosophical architecture of this writer.

Introduction to Nietzsche's thought is but one of the debts I must acknowledge to Mariana Cowan, in whose course at Wayne University I first read this philosopher. Mrs. Cowan conveyed a contagious intelligence and a will to examine the writer himself which is seldom encountered among Nietzsche enthusiasts. Although my own philosophical interests became increasingly analytical, I have never since read Nietzsche without feeling the lightness and exhilaration which are the effect of superlative intellectual vitality upon one's spirit; and I have never found Nietzsche démodé or naïve or impossible, but always stimulating and quickening. Yet I should never have written this book had it not been for Professor Paul Edwards, to whom I, together with many other philosophers, owe a special debt for his energetic and imaginative editorial leadership in philosophical publication today. Professor Edwards proposed that I write the essay on Nietzsche for D. J. O'Connor's *A Critical History of Western Philosophy* (New York: The Free Press of Glencoe, 1964), and then encouraged me to undertake this present work. For his advice and help, I am immensely indebted. The bare structure for this book may be found in that essay, although the material has been reworked completely. The few pages which I have transferred bodily—mainly the central argument in my discussion of Eternal Recurrence—are here reprinted through the kind permission of the Free Press. This volume was written during the summer of 1964, while under a grant from Columbia University's Council for Research in the Humanities. I am grateful to that body for its generosity and confidence. Some ideas have been discussed with James Gutmann, Arnold Koslow, Richard Kuhns and Sidney Morgenbesser, each of whom made improving suggestions.

A.C.D.
NEW YORK CITY
SEPTEMBER, 1964

Nietzsche as Philosopher

Words strain,
Crack and sometimes break, under the burden,
Under the tension, slip, slide, perish,
Decay with imprecision, will not stay in place,
Will not stay still.*

—T.S. ELIOT

BURNT NORTON, V.

Neue Wege gehe ich, ein neue Rede kommt mir;
müde wurde ich, gleich allen Schaffenden, der alten Zungen.
Nicht will mein Geist mehr auf abgelaufnen Sohlen wandeln.

—FRIEDRICH NIETZSCHE

ALSO SPRACH ZARATHUSTRA, II, i.

ONE
Philosophical Nihilism

I

NIETZSCHE's books give the appearance of having been assembled rather than composed. They are made up, in the main, of short, pointed aphorisms, and of essays seldom more than a few pages long; each volume is more like a treasury of the author's selections than like a book in its own right. Any given aphorism or essay might as easily have been placed in one volume as in another without much affecting the unity or structure of either. And the books themselves, except for their chronological ordering, do not exhibit any special structure as a corpus. No one of them presupposes an acquaintance with any other. Although there undoubtedly was a development in Nietzsche's thought and in his style, his writings may be read in pretty much any order, without this greatly impeding the comprehension of his ideas. The vast, disordered mass of his posthumous writings was shaped into volumes, and given a name, by his sister Elizabeth Förster-Nietzsche, who was the self-appointed executrix of his literary estate. Yet there is little, if any, *internal* evidence that they were put together by hands other than his, and it would be difficult even for a close reader to tell the difference between those works he saw through the press and those pieced together by his editors. Exceptions must be made in the case of *The Birth of Tragedy*, perhaps, and of *Thus Spake Zarathustra*, for the former exhibits a conventional unity and develops a main thesis, while the latter acquires a certain external structure by having each segment pose as a homiletic uttered by Zarathustra. In neither book is there an ordered development, however, or a direction of argument or presentation. They may be entered at any point.

The thoughts expressed in these essays and aphorisms have the same disjointed appearance as do their literary embodiments. Taken individually, they are bright and penetrating—"full of thorns and secret spices"[1]—but read in any number, they tend to cloy and to repeat one another, with much the same barbs being flung, over and over, at much the same targets. The first glimpse of the sea, the first sound of the surf, can intoxicate and quicken the spirits, but this feeling dissipates when the experience is prolonged; and waves, which after all resemble one another to a striking degree, soon became indistinguishable, and lose their identity to us in some general flux and monotonous roar. One soon becomes fatigued with Nietzsche as a writer, as one might with a landscape of diamonds which end by dimming one another's brilliance. With no structure to sustain and direct the reader's mind, the books, once entered, must soon be set down, and one's experience with them is either of isolated illuminations that do not connect with one another or of a blur of light and noise.

The aphorisms first impress the reader as commentaries upon and jibes against contemporary morality, politics, culture, religion, and literature by a jaundiced, irritated, destructive, and unforgiving person—a clever crank with a certain abused literary gift and a long list of private peeves, more the sort of person who writes letters to the editor than a constructive thinker. They would strike the casual reader as infused with a certain conventional profundity and an amateur, erratic kind of learning: philosophers, religious figures, historical episodes, literary works, musical compositions are mentioned, a few words are said about them, and the subject quickly changes. One has the sense of dealing with a self-taught eccentric, hardly a college professor, or a scholar trained in the exacting discipline of German philology, or, for that matter, a philosopher in any save the most perfunctory sense of the term. Those fine and subtle distinctions, the circumspect marshaling of argument, the cautious and qualified inferences which are the hallmarks of professional philosophical writing are conspicuously absent. Nor does one hear that dispassionate, austere tone that philosophers affect. There is, instead, the shrill, carping, at times almost hysterical, voice of the chronic malcontent and pamphleteer.

Nietzsche's writings, for the most part, make no heavy demands on his readers' intelligence or learning. The points appear clear and direct, the targets large and obvious, and the language is lucid if inflamed. They have been taken up joyfully by an audience led to believe that philosophy is difficult, but who find, through Nietzsche's accessibility, that either philosophy is easier than they had thought or they are cleverer than they had believed. It is perhaps for the same reason that philosophers have been reluctant to count Nietzsche as one of themselves. Reference is made, here and there, to darker and more puzzling doctrines: the doctrine of Eternal Recurrence, of *Amor Fati*, of the Superman, the Will-to-Power, the Apollinian and Dionysiac phases of art. Here, perhaps, Nietzsche speaks as a philosopher in a somewhat narrower sense. But these doctrines do not give the sense of fitting together in any systematic and coherent way, nor do they, either individually or as a group, fall readily under one or another of the convenient and unavoidable headings with which we identify philosophical ideas. They do not seem to be solutions to what we would acknowledge as philosophical problems. If, indeed, Nietzsche's philosophy is to be found here, then that philosophy appears as a conjunction of disparate teachings, once again an assembly rather than a construction, composed of idiosyncratic speculations, unsupported, ill-digested, and unfit for location within that context of philosophical analyzing in which the philosophical critic or historian feels at home. His corpus seems an odd, incongruous page in the history of official philosophy, a *non sequitur* inserted into the standard histories of the subject almost as a result of belonging even less obviously in other histories. Even here it is an obstacle to be gotten round rather than part of the flow of thought or a stage on a narrative way from Thales to the present. He seems to belong to philosophy *faute de mieux*. But then Nietzsche felt that he had made a clean break with official philosophy; if it is true that he hardly fits with the subject he so often impugned, so much the worse, he would have said, for philosophy. If there is an irony, it is that he is considered part of the history of what he hoped to destroy.

For his philosophy there seems, not surprisingly, to be no ready name like Idealism or Realism or even Existentialism. At times he spoke of his philosophy as *Nihilism*, a title which, in view of what I have said about his books and style and thought, seems almost bitterly suitable, suggesting negativity and emptiness. If, however, we have any wish to understand him, we must divest his Nihilism of both these connotations and come to see it as a positive and, after all, a respectable philosophical teaching. I shall take Nihilism as the central concept in his philosophy, and through it I shall try to show the connections, altogether systematic, among those exotic doctrines that otherwise loom so blankly out of the surrounding aphorisms and frantic obiter dicta. I shall even endeavor to show that these obiter dicta are neither the surface nor the substance of what he had to say, but rather illustrations and applications of certain general principles to particular cases. Finally, I hope to locate these general principles in the main philosophical tradition, as proposed answers to the same problems that have occupied the best attention of philosophers throughout the ages.

II

There exists no place in which this system—as I shall prematurely regard it—appears in Nietzsche's writings. This is due, in part, to his singular lack of architectonic talent, a failing shown not only in his philosophical writings but also in his musical compositions. Nietzsche had a certain flair for improvisation at the piano and he had a high regard for himself as a composer. He shares with Rousseau the distinction of having a place in the history of both philosophy and musical composition. But, according to one critic, his musical works show, as a chief defect, "the lack of any real harmonic definition or melodic continuity despite the recurring motifs."* His fugues "after brave beginnings . . . soon degenerate into simpler textures, and there are numerous violations of the canons of part writing without compelling reason."† Even in a

* F. R. Love, *Young Nietzsche and the Wagnerian Experience* (Chapel Hill: University of North Carolina Press, 1963), p. 20.
† *Ibid.*, p. 21.

late and ambitious work, "short motifs dominate, and with the total absence of a more spacious melody or a compelling logical structure, the pieces never gain sufficient momentum to become convincing."* These critical judgments on his music might apostrophize his literary productions as well. There is nothing in them of that organizing intellect, that architectonic feeling for structure which Kant's writings, for example, exhibit to an almost supererogatory degree. They are, indeed, like improvisations on marginal philosophical themes, abrupt impromptus.

Quite apart from this incapacity, it is not unreasonable to suppose that the system itself was never fully explicit even in his own awareness; or, if it was so, this would have been toward the end of his productive period when he was engaged in other projects, not knowing that he would not have the time and clarity to write it down. In a late letter to Georg Brandes—the first scholar to lecture on Nietzsche's thought—written in what seems to have been an exceptionally sunny period in his life, Nietzsche says that he has enjoyed, for an entire week, a few hours of energy each day which enabled him

to see my entire conception from top to bottom, with the immense complex of problems lying, as it were, spread out beneath me, in clear outline and relief. This demands a maximum of power which I scarcely any longer hoped were mine. It all hangs together, for years it had all been on the right track, one builds one's philosophy like a beaver, one is necessary without knowing it.[2]

Few writers in philosophy, and certainly few great ones, built up their systems scrap by scrap, as Nietzsche's metaphor perhaps correctly suggests that he did. A philosophical system does not ordinarily grow by accretion. Yet it may be possible for a philosophical thinker to analyze topically, and in a piecemeal fashion, for a period of time without realizing that the topics are connected and the solutions, without his knowing it, support and even require one another. He will then have eked out a system undeclared to himself, unless, as Nietzsche suggests, a synoptic moment is granted

* *Ibid.*, p. 70.

him during which the unity of his thought becomes revealed. He might then discover, as though spectator to his own activities, what he had been up to all along, there having been an unrecognized systematic necessity between statement and statement which he had not heretofore discerned. It does not follow, of course, from the fact that he was unconscious of creating a system that he was creating a system unconsciously, that the system itself lay, as we have come sometimes to think of these matters, in the writer's unconsciousness, hidden in the subterranean recesses of the creative mind, revealing itself only at the last. Rather, I believe, we can account for these achievements by appealing to two distinct facts.

The first is the systematic nature of philosophy itself. In the character of the philosophical discipline, there is no such thing as an isolated solution to an isolated problem. The problems of philosophy are so interconnected that the philosopher cannot solve, or start to solve, one of them without implicitly committing himself to solutions for all the rest. In a genuine sense, every philosophical problem must be solved at once. He may work piecemeal at isolated problems only insofar as he accepts, if only tacitly, a system within which to conduct his inquiries. However, if from the beginning he offers what proves to be a novel answer in philosophy, this will introduce, as it were, distortions throughout his conceptual scheme, and these tensions must sooner or later be felt by any sensitive mind. Nietzsche's writings were taken up with philosophical problems. It is difficult to determine the order in which he addressed these problems. And his structural incapacities made it difficult for him to think protractedly or to hold a problem in his mind until it yielded to a solution. The fact remains however, that philosophy as such is architectonic, and imposes an external regimen upon its least systematic practitioners, so philosophers are systematic through the nature of their enterprise. One finds this exemplified repeatedly in pre-Socratic philosophy.

The reader who is familiar with the grand outlines of an author's thought may turn to his *juvenilia* and discover there an amazing portentousness. He will encounter phrases and ideas anticipating themes in the mature works which, had they never been written, would have left these *juvenilia* without any interest whatsoever.

Indeed, we should perhaps never have found in them what, having the later corpus, we are so impressed to learn were already present in the youthful mind. This is no less so with Nietzsche. In his writings from the early 1870s we come upon ideas which echo throughout his later work, almost as though they were all contained here. In fact, it is the late works which echo in these earlier ones. There is doubtless a continuity in any writer's thought, but in part the continuity is to be attributed to his readers, who look back to the early writings with the late ones in mind. They see them as the author could not have seen them when he wrote them, for he could not have known his own unwritten volumes. There is a unity in a man's life if only in the sense that we cannot think of a life as other than unified.

This brings us to the second fact. We are apt to attribute to an author's unconscious what is in fact our own knowledge, which he could not have been conscious of because it has to do with facts which lay not in the depths of his mind but in the future. Had his later writings been different, we should perhaps have been as forcibly struck by themes to which we are in fact blind as we are by those we find so impressively precocious. These go unremarked because of the retroactive unification that historical understanding imposes. So the unifying forces of historical intelligence work together with the systematizing dynamisms of philosophical thought to produce a coherent structure in a writer's works (his literary style and methods of composition notwithstanding), quite independently of whether he ever was able to express it as such, for himself or anyone else.

To say that the system I wish to discuss was truly Nietzsche's raises some complicated questions concerning the integrity of the history of philosophy. He is not among us to avow it as his own, and he did not, perhaps because he could not, vouchsafe us the coherent, internally necessary vision he reported to Georg Brandes. Yet, by his own admission, he must have been unaware of this system, supposing it to be his, while it was emerging through the accumulation of aphorisms, and so he could not, through that entire time, have *intended* his work to be taken in this way. The system I offer must be appreciated as a reconstruction, to be understood as one must understand any theory; that is, as an instrument for unifying and explaining a domain of phenomena—in this case the domain of an individual's writings. I shall use texts as scientific theorists employ observations—to confirm my theory at this point or that. I am reasonably confident that, in at least a loose sense, this theory has a certain predictive power; that is, it allows us to know more or less what Nietzsche is going to be saying. It will enable us to find our way through the domain it is meant to order, or so I hope. There may, of course, always be theories incompatible with this one but nevertheless compatible with all the same facts that appear to support mine. Then mine shall prove to be only an alternative system, and I should be pleased enough if another system, equally coherent with the one I think I have found, were to be laid out. For this would be to acquiesce in the view that Nietzsche's philosophy is systematic (regardless of which system we ascribe to him) and hence to take a stand against the claim that he was some other, more spontaneous and irrational sort of thinker.

There is of course a further possibility that facts unknown to us—in this instance, texts so far undiscovered—may one day turn up which will quite invalidate my interpretation. One must run such risks in philosophical as well as in scientific theorizing. Here and there, in addition to references to his system, we find sketches and projections for a final systematic statement of his philosophy. None of these, to present knowledge, materialized. Madness intervened in 1889, after which Nietzsche wrote nothing; he lived mutely through the twilight of the eleven years remaining before his other death. But the sheer mass of his posthumous writings—the *Nachlass*—together with his seeming total inability to impose any but the most external form upon his work, virtually guarantees that there would have been no integrating systematization even if he had retained his mind. The vastness of the *Nachlass*, together with the size of his published work, guarantees something else. Once Nietzsche was rendered helpless through insanity, his person as well as his work and reputation became the charge of his sister. The editorial liberties which she and others took with the unpublished (and even some of the published) work went from scandal to scandal. "The life and work of Nietzsche is the most heavily falsified phenomenon of modern literary and intellectual history."* Distortions, omissions, spurious additions, and false structures disfigured the corpus; only now, through the most patient philological work, are these being refined out, and the texts, the letters, and even the chronology of Nietzsche's life being restored to their true order. One must concede the enormity and, from a scholarly point of view, the utter immorality of these falsifications. Yet I believe that the restorations will little affect the philosophy we may find in Nietzsche's work now or when it is purified. Elizabeth Nietzsche mainly induced falsifications concerning her relationship to her brother; her wish was to secure a certain image of herself as confidante and first understander of her brother's darkest thought. She tampered here and there to save her brother's good reputation as she saw it, and to make him appear at times in advocacy of doctrines he in fact contemned. These were never philosophical doctrines; in fact she had barely a child's comprehension of philosophical ideas, and would not have known one to distort it. Even if her meddlings (and those of Peter Gast and yet others) were vaster than we now imagine, they would have almost negligible consequences when spelling out Nietzsche's philosophy. It is precisely in this respect that the loosely federated aphorisms, fragments, and essays stand Nietzsche for once in good stead. His message appears over and over again, so much so that from any random sample of his writings the entirety of his philosophy can almost be reconstructed.

There is a theory that our memory is stored in protein molecules, of which in each of us there is an immense number. These molecules have the remarkable property of idempotency—of exactly reproducing themselves. According to this theory, the same messages are stored in various places throughout the body, so that, should one part be destroyed, the possibility remains that our

* E. F. Podach, *Friedrich Nietzsches Werke der Zusammenbruchs* (Heidelberg: Wolfgang Rothe Verlag, 1961), p. 430. Podach tells an incredible story of counterfeiting and editorial malfeasance. See also Karl Schlechta, *Der Fall Nietzsche* (Munich: Carl Hanser Verlag, 1959); and Richard Roos, "Les Derniers Ecrits de Nietzsche et leur Publication," *Revue Philosophique* (1956), pp. 262–287, and "Elizabeth Förster Nietzsche ou la Soeur Abusive," *Études Germaniques* (1956), pp. 321–341.

memory will stand intact and we will persist integrated with ourselves. The prodigality and idempotency of the protein molecules might almost be taken as a providential piece of insurance against the destruction of the self. Nietzsche's extravagantly numerous, yet oddly repetitive aphorisms, dealing with much the same problems in much the same way, seem to me to have had much the same result. New writings may be found and old ones restored, but it is difficult to suppose they will furnish us with a philosophy different in any essential respect from the one we may find by carefully examining what we have.

III

"Nihilism" connotes negativity and emptiness; in fact, it denotes two bodies of thought that, although distinct from Nietzsche's, nevertheless bear it some partial resemblance. The Nihilism of Emptiness is essentially that of Buddhist or Hindu teaching, both of which hold that the world we live in and seem to know has no ultimate reality, and that our attachment to it is an attachment to an illusion. Reality itself has neither name nor form, and what has name and form is but a painful dreaming from which all reasonable men would wish to escape if they knew the way and knew that their attachment was to nothingness. Life is without sense and point, there is a ceaseless alternation of birth and death and birth again, the constantly turning wheel of existence going nowhere eternally; if we wish salvation, it is salvation from life that we must seek. This Oriental pessimism, articulated in Europe in the philosophy of Arthur Schopenhauer, is based upon a set of metaphysical views which, as we shall see, are closely akin to theses that Nietzsche advanced as his own. He sought, he tells us, "to get to the bottom of the question of [European] pessimism and liberate it from the half-Christian, half-German narrowness and stupidity in which it has finally presented itself to our century."[3] He did not, however, draw the same consequences which Schopenhauer and the Oriental philosophers did, and Nietzsche adds that whoever had analyzed pessimism "has perhaps just thereby, without really desiring it, opened his eyes to behold the opposite ideal: the ideal of the most world-approving, exuberant, and vivacious man."[4] Part of what we must clarify, then, is the manner in which Nietzsche was able, on the basis of a metaphysical Nihilism of the most uncompromising sort, to justify an attitude toward life which, in its affirmativeness, was in every respect discordant with the Nihilism of Emptiness: his "new way to 'Yes.' "[5]

The Nihilism of Negativity, as I shall call it, is exemplified in the movement properly known as Nihilism, which flourished in the latter decades of the nineteenth century in Europe, especially in the 1850s and 1860s in Russia, and which found its most respectable expression in Turgenev's *Fathers and Sons* (1861). Russian Nihilism was essentially a negative and destructive attitude against a body of moral, political, and religious teachings found or felt by the Nihilists to be confining and obscurantist. As against their elders, Nihilists claimed that they believed in nothing, though what this specifically meant was that they held in total discredit the beliefs, tastes, and attitudes of their elders and those in current authority. "Nihilism in the St. Petersburg style—i.e., belief in unbelief to the point of martyrdom for it, shows always, and above all, the *need* for belief. . . ."[6] In actual fact they believed, in an uncritical and wholesale manner, in a crudely materialistic interpretation of science. It was basically in the name of science that they proclaimed, as invalid, the principles they inveighed against. But inasmuch as their understanding of science was filtered through a version of materialism which they mistook for science itself, or which, if more sophisticated, they took to be the only attitude compatible with and justified by science, there was an undeniable component of belief, indeed of faith, which interpenetrated their nihilism and rendered it halfhearted. The nineteenth century, in its way, was as much an age of faith as was the twelfth century. Almost any European thinker of this epoch appears to us today as a kind of visionary, committed to one or another program of salvation, and to one or another simple way of achieving it. It was as though the needs and hopes which had found satisfaction in religion still perdured in an era when religion itself no longer could be credited, and something else—science, education, revolution, evolution, socialism, business enterprise, or, latterly, sex—must be seized upon to fill the place left empty and to discharge the office vacated by religious beliefs which could not now sustain. And so it was with Nihilism. It was not so much a matter of science driving out faith as of one faith replacing another. The hope for a better dispensation in another life was replaced by a psychologically indistinguishable hope for a better dispensation in this one, for a sound and scientifically based set of institutions which would come about, almost inevitably, once the old orders and the vested interests were swept away together with the ideas which protected and supported them. This was recognizably the ideal of the Enlightenment, of course, but expressed a century later with a certain drama and violence, in part, perhaps, because it now had become the ideology of the youthful and disenfranchised sons in rebellion against their fathers. There is something touchingly adolescent in the attitudes expressed through the person of Bazirov in Turgenev's book. But it is scarcely an exaggeration to say that the Nihilist movement, its historical consequences notwithstanding, scarcely advanced a step beyond Bazirov's "I do not believe in anything"; his "A decent chemist is twenty times more useful than any poet"; or his views, as unintentionally caricatured by a peasant who puzzlingly thought him to be saying that "You and I are frogs."

Nietzsche was not less but more negativistic than his Nihilist contemporaries (though he was not part of that movement in any sense whatsoever), and he is celebrated, attacked, or applauded for his bitter denunciations of many of the same traditions, beliefs, and institutions which they explicitly repudiated. His Nihilism, nevertheless, is not an ideology but a metaphysics, and in no respect is his difference from the Nihilists more marked than in his attitude toward science. Science he regards not as a repository of truths or a method for discovering them but as a set of convenient fictions, of useful conventions, which has as much and as little basis in reality as any alleged set of fictions which might be thought to conflict with it. It, no more and no less than religion, morality, and art, was an instance of what he termed Will-to-Power, an impulse and a drive to impose upon an essentially chaotic reality a form and structure, to shape it into a world congenial to human understanding while habitable by human intelligence. But this was its *sole* justification, and any imposed form which worked to the same purpose would be equally justifiable, content counting for less than function—counting, indeed, for nothing at all. Science, in a sense of truth which I shall elaborate on in a later chapter, is not true. But in the sense in which it is not true, neither is anything else; and relative to this theory of truth, which was his, Nietzsche must say that he did not, because in metaphysical honesty he could not, believe in anything. His was accordingly a deep and total Nihilism, from the vantage point of which the contest of the Russian Nihilists with their declared ideological enemies was but an instance in the struggle of wills, a struggle for power and form which, as Nietzsche saw it, characterizes human life everywhere and always and, in a sense, was the single characteristic he was prepared to ascribe to the universe at large, which he saw as an eternal strife of will with will.

Both of the non-Nietzschean forms of Nihilism derive from much the same attitude. Each believes that there *ought* to be some order or external purpose in the world. The Nihilism of Emptiness, Schopenhauer's Nihilism, presupposes an outlook, become habitual, "in accordance with which purposes are established from without."[7] This Nihilism expresses a disappointment that there is no such purpose when, in fact, the state of mind that demands that there be one ought to be overcome. With its overcoming, the grounds for pessimism and despair are disqualified. Man transcends his chagrin at the niggardliness of the Good Fairy when he comes to realize that there is no Good Fairy to be either generous or miserly. Russian Nihilism, meanwhile, is typical of thought that derives from the same habit just mentioned, that there is an external authority to whom or to which we must appeal in order to determine the purpose of life: "having learnt not to believe in one authority, [it] sought to find another"[8]—in this case Science. But men find it difficult to function in this world without supposing one or another external source of authority and significance, "if not God or Science, then Conscience, Reason, Social Instinct, or History," conceived of as "an immanent spirit with a built-in purpose, to which one may surrender."[9] It is a general tendency of the human mind, which, to Nietzsche, is ultimately a disastrous disposition, to imagine, and to seek to identify a purposive armature, a basis for significance, in the world itself, something objective to which men may submit and in which they may find a meaning for themselves. The Nihilism of Emptiness, as a mood of thought and as a psychological condition, arises in direct consequence of the realization, or suspicion, that really there is no such thing to be found, no world order in which we ourselves are integral parts, and such that our entire value derives from being related to it in determined ways. Perhaps we then, as the Buddhists, write off the entire thing as a dream and seek no longer to be bothered by what has no substance. Or, like so many philosophers and visionaries, we invent, in compensation, "a world which lies beyond this one, a true world,"[10] in contrast with which *this* world is completely disvalued. But once man attains a realization that the alleged real or true world is of human provenance, created in response to certain unfulfilled human needs, a fabrication which is philosophically unjustified if psychologically comprehensible, then he achieves the final form of Nihilism: a disbelief in any world alternative and metaphysically preferable to this one. At the same time, he regards this world as the only one, however unstructured and purposeless it may be, and however valueless.

The feeling of valuelessness is attained when one apprehends that the general character of existence must not be interpreted with the concept of "purpose," of "oneness," or of "truth." . . . The world fails to have in the plenitude of happenings any overarching unity; the character of existence is not "true," is *false*. . . . One has no longer any ground to persuade himself of a *true* world . . . In brief, the categories "purpose," "oneness," and "being," with which we give a value to the world, are now withdrawn by us—and the world now looks valueless. . . .[11]

The claim that the world is valueless [*wertlos*] is not to say that it has some low value in the scheme of values, as when we say, of something, that it is of little worth or none, but rather, it is not the kind of thing of which it logically makes sense to say either that it is worth little, or that it has such and such a higher value. Values have no more application to the world than weights do to numbers: to say that the number two is weightless is not to say that it is *very light*, but that it is senseless to assign it any weight at all. This would be Nietzsche's view. Strictly, it follows that the world has no value from the fact that there is nothing in it which might sensibly be supposed to have value. There is neither order nor purpose, things nor facts, nothing there whatever to which our beliefs can correspond. So that all our beliefs are false. This (we must later determine what reasons he has for this spectacular claim) he regards as "the extremest form of nihilism—the insight that every belief, every taking-for-true [*Für-wahr-halten*], is necessarily false: because there is no *true world* at all."[12] In the end, we shall see that this is a highly dramatized rejection of the Correspondence Theory of Truth.

Nietzsche's unbridled claims in behalf of this extreme Nihilism are plainly in need of considerable clarification before we can so much as raise the question responsibly as to whether there is any compelling reason for endorsing them. In this first chapter I wish only to emphasize the way in which Nietzsche's Nihilism has little to do with the ordinary political connotations of the term, and that by "Nihilism" he had in mind a thoroughly disillusioned conception of a world which is as hostile to human aspirations as he could imagine it to be. It is hostile, not because it, or anything other than us, has goals of its own, but because it is utterly indifferent to what we either believe or hope. The recognition and acceptance of this negative fact should not lead us to "a negation, a no, a will to nothingness." Rather, he felt, it is an intoxicating fact to know that the world is devoid of form and meaning, encouraging, if anything, "a Dionysian *yes* [*Ja-sagen*] to the world as it is, without exceptions, exemptions, or deductions."[13] To be able to accept and affirm such a view he thought required considerable courage, for it meant that we must abandon hopes and expectations which had comforted men, through religions and philosophies, from the beginning. For the attitude he felt he could and we should adopt, he provided the formula of *Amor Fati*—loving one's fate, accepting, without palliative or protection, the results of a most thoroughgoing critique of philosophical and scientific ideas, seen as fictions, the products of some human need for security; and then endeavoring to live in a world impervious to these needs, to say Yes to the cosmic insignificance, not only of oneself and of human beings generally but also of life and nature as a whole.

This Nihilism (which in succeeding chapters I shall spell out in some detail), finds its culmination, or so he believed, in the obscure doctrine of Eternal Recurrence, a view that the world repeats itself infinitely and exactly, the same situations in which we now find ourselves having already occurred an infinite number of times. These will happen again, without end, exactly as they always have and as they are happening now. Nietzsche took an immense and not altogether readily understandable pride in having discovered this doctrine, which he considered both as a serious scientific truth and, more importantly and even less plausibly, as the only genuine alternative to the view that the world has or can have a goal or purpose or final state.[14] If each state of the world (insofar as we may speak so of anything as structureless as he appears to claim the world to be) recurs infinitely, then no state can be a final state, and in the nature of things there can be neither progress nor regress, but always the same thing repeated. So the fate which he encourages to accept and indeed to love is made considerably more difficult through this purposeless repetitiveness of the universe *in toto*:

Let us think this thought through in its most fearful form: existence, such as it is, without sense or goal, but inevitably recurrent without a finale in nothingness: the Eternal Recurrence. That is the extremest form of nihilism: nothingness ("meaninglessness") forever![15]

Nietzsche's philosophy is a sustained attempt to work out the reasons for and the consequences of Nihilism as I have briefly sketched this doctrine here. Enough has been said, pending some further support and some refinement of statement, to justify to some provisional degree the claim I have made that there is some systematic interconnection among some of his leading ideas: Nihilism goes with *Amor Fati*; and that goes with the Eternal Recurrence; and that, as I shall show in due course, goes with the doctrine of the *Übermensch*. Nietzsche's critique of other philosophies rests upon a psychological thesis that each metaphysical system ever advanced was due, in the end, to a need to find order and security in the world, a position where the mind might "repose and recreate itself."[16] Each system provided, accordingly, a consolatory account of things in which this might be possible. Nietzsche was persuaded that all such views were false. The problem then was to exhibit their inviability, determine why people should have thought them viable, and then go on to ask how it might be possible to go on living in the full recognition of the inviability of every possible religious and metaphysical assurance.

The picture that results from his psychological–philosophical analyses is that of human beings trying continually to impose an order and structure upon an unordered and senseless universe so as to preserve their sense of dignity and importance. It is their prejudice that, somehow and somewhere, there must be a reason for it all, and that there *cannot* be any truth in what Nietzsche advances as the correct (if one may speak of correctness here) view of things as "change, becoming, plurality, opposition, contradiction, and war."[17] There is then no true, rational, orderly, permanent, or benign universe for us. Our entire mode of thinking, he believed, is based on the assumption that there is such a universe; it is far from simple, accordingly, to work out a form of thought adequate to the nullity of things as they are: a total revolution in logic, science, morality, and in philosophy itself would be demanded. Nietzsche sought to achieve at least the beginning of such a revolution, but I shall begin with the diagnostic part of his philosophy, the germ of which is to be found already in his earliest significant writing, embodied as the celebrated distinction between Apollinianism and Dionysianism in his *The Birth of Tragedy*. Human thought, because it has heretofore required form and structure, has always been Apollinian. But reality is formless and Dionysian, and the problem for him was whether one could significantly achieve a Dionysian language with which to express Dionysiac thought.

TWO

Art and Irrationality

NIETZSCHE occupies an assured place in the history of aesthetic theory. His early book on the birth of tragedy stands as an acknowledged, if puzzling, classic in the skimpy canon of this least advanced field of philosophical inquiry and speculation. His enthusiasts are typically those who, like Nietzsche at the time the book was written, maintain a high and sometimes exalted view of the arts. In his case, partly in consequence of certain biographical events and partly as a result of a natural philosophical development, he came in time to attach decreasing value and importance to art. He perhaps never quite liberated himself from that febrile, demonized image of the artist that was a cliché in the milieu he inhabited and which the composer Richard Wagner, with whom he was at one time connected, personified almost to perfection. Indeed it was his disillusionment with Wagner as man and artist that led to his later deflationist attitude toward artists and hence toward art itself, for it was never easy for him to separate a product from the character of its producer. The original disenchantment with Wagner was in part caused by Nietzsche's subscription to a concept of art which Wagner simply could not live up to, as perhaps no human being could; one might put the best light on this by saying that Nietzsche was prepared to abandon a philosophical theory in the light of recalcitrant fact. But the rupture with Wagner is a complicated episode in the biographies of both men, and the psychology available to us is too crude to explain everything that happened, even supposing we were clear (as we are not) about all the relevant historical facts. I do not propose to follow any chronological order in my exposition of Nietzsche's philosophy, nor do I intend to relate it in any special way to events in his life. My concern is with the reasons for rather than the causes of his doctrines. Yet any discussion of his artistic theories must perforce be restricted to his earliest period of genuine productivity—when he was a young professor at Basle, brooding on the art and philosophy of the ancients, and when his sympathies with Wagner were profound and uncontaminated and, to a measure, reciprocated by the composer himself. Even in this bright period of his life, the dominant philosophical preoccupations of his mature thought were present and insistent, and though the immediate subject of his interest was art, the logic of his ideas already had a wider implication.

I

Philosophers occasionally raise a question concerning the cognitive import of art. For it is sometimes thought, or hoped, that in addition to the commonly acknowledged modes of achieving positive knowledge of the world—through sense experience and scientific investigation—art provides us with a special way of attaining to perhaps a special class of truths; and these are said to have as great a claim to objectivity as any other. Art, together with its escapes and pleasures, has been thought to yield intellectual benefits as well, of possibly a very high order, conducting us to factual insights perhaps not otherwise accessible to (mere) human cognition. Because it has always been the task and prerogative of philosophers to assess claims concerning knowledge, there exists a philosophical literature devoted to the question of whether cognitive claims that are urged on behalf of art (and derivatively of artists) might justifiably be honored. The radical character of Nietzsche's thought, even in its first significant expression, may be seen in the fact that he is indeed prepared to allow that art has no less a claim than sense or science to objective truth. But this is because neither sense nor science can make any stronger claim to truth than art. Neither art itself nor the avenues ordinarily credited with conducting us to truth regarding the objective world lead us, in fact, to the truths they promise. There *is* an analogy to be found between art and cognition (so-called) regarding both their provenance and function: each consists in illusions, the illusions of science and sense making life possible, the illusions of art making it bearable.

Nietzsche's reasons for these highly skeptical conclusions consist in certain epistemological analyses, rather like those often urged later by Bertrand Russell, according to which our perceptions are said not to resemble their causes, so that the language we employ, learned in connection with the having of perceptions, does not describe the world as it really is. Language rather describes— insofar as, in Nietzsche's view, we may think of language as descriptive at all—the illusions we *take* for reality. At this point Nietzsche was supposing that there might be an order or structure in the world which we were incapable of capturing. Yet, given his ideas concerning the origin and function of our language, we could not say what the world might in fact be like, even if, *per impossibile*, we were in a position to experience whatever causes our perceptions. We plainly could not apply *our* terms to *these* causes. But I shall consider these epistemological topics later.

Art consists in fresh illusions, while "truth," which we contrast with it (as we contrast art with nature, fiction with fact), consists in stale illusions, illusions so worn with use that they have come, with time, to be accepted as expressing the rock-bottom facts of the universe. The difference between (so-called) fact and (so-called) fiction is virtually quantitative, that being taken as fact which has been repeated a sufficient number of times. In a precocious essay, written in 1873, although only posthumously published, Nietzsche asks the old, cynical question, What is truth? It was to be a question that occupied him throughout his entire philosophical life, and the answer that he gave it here, apart from its rhetoric and to some extent apart from the reasons he advanced in its favor, was one that he never saw fit to modify in any essential respect.

What then is truth? A mobile army of metaphors, metonymies, anthropomorphisms, a sum, in short, of human relationships which, rhetorically and poetically intensified, ornamented, and transformed, come to be thought of, after long usage by a people, as fixed, binding, and canonical. Truths are illusions which we have forgotten are illusions, worn-out metaphors now impotent to stir the senses, coins which have lost their faces and are considered now as metal rather than currency.[1]

Our primitive mode of contact with the world is essentially as artists, as more or less unwitting makers of images and metaphors, transforming rather than reproducing our experiences, themselves transformations and not duplications of their causes and objects. But metaphors, through time and use, become resolved into concepts, and concepts elaborated into systems, and ultimately these "edifices of concepts exhibit the rigid regularity of a Roman columbarium."[2] One must, he acknowledges here, vastly admire the architectural genius of mankind which builds "an infinitely complex cathedral of concepts [Begriffsdome] upon shifting foundations and flowing waters, so to speak."[3] But this admiration must be restricted to the structuring genius of the collective human intellect, not to its capacity for discovering truth in any conventional sense of the term, because, at bottom, our concepts are the residue of metaphors, and the architecture of our conceptual structure is "anthropomorphic through and through and contains not a single point which is 'true-in-itself,' objective and universal, apart from man."[4] We dwell in a structure we have built for ourselves, and could not for a moment survive as recognizably ourselves "outside the prison walls of these beliefs."[5]

An acknowledged *true* idea is but one which is enshrined in the conceptual columbarium that is the "cemetery of metaphors." A *false* idea is an unenshrined or "live" metaphor, a deviant image. We cannot, therefore, contrast metaphors with other utterances in the ordinary way, the difference between metaphors and nonmetaphoric utterance being only a matter of relative location within a system of concepts—not a difference between fact and fancy. But then (on this analysis), neither can we contrast poet with scientist nor either with the plain man. The statements of the one are quite as inadequate to the way things are as those of the other, today's common sense and scientific orthodoxy being yesterday's metaphor, cooled, so to speak, and hardened into fact. Notice, however, that metaphors here are spoken of as linguistic expressions for *experiences*, not for things, so there are routine and deviant experiences. The linguistic utterance or expression of a deviant experience must, in the nature of the case, be either metaphorical or unintelligible relative to a linguistic scheme worked out to accommodate routine experiences. This almost guarantees that expressions of deviant experiences will border on unintelligibility. From such experiences or, as he calls them, *Intuitionen*, there is "no regular way into the domain of ghostly schemata, of abstractions"—

There are no words for these, and either man is mute before them, or speaks in loud forbidden metaphors, or in unheard of combinations of ideas, in order at least to respond creatively to the present powerful intuition by mocking at, and shattering, the old conceptual scheme.[6]

It is with this idea that Nietzsche turns in a direction tangential to the Kantian theses which so plainly inform this youthful effort. Kant proposed, and indeed pretended to have proven, that experiences must, as a matter of course, conform to the shape imposed upon them by a fixed set of concepts and categories which are the conditions for experience to be intelligible. We know things not as they are in themselves but as they are presented to us and shaped by the a priori armature of the logic of experience. Whether Kant allowed that there are not and cannot be any experiences which fail to conform to our categorical structure, or only that such experiences, if there are any, would be incoherent, is a hard point in Kantian exegesis. Nietzsche's account differs from this in a number of ways. He does not contend, as Kant seemingly does, that a certain determined set of concepts lies inherent in the human mind and is invariant as to differences between human beings. Rather, Nietzsche sees conceptual schemes as varying from society to society and possibly, assuming one could survive outside a society, from person to person. There are various ways of ordering experience, ours being only the way which has worked out for us, having nothing immutable or sacrosanct or necessary about it. Moreover, there is always the possibility that some of our experiences might fail to fit the scheme with which we work. These we cannot express in the language made available to us by our society, for, by hypothesis, they are deviant. But we can at least employ language expressively and artistically, responding to these experiences in the same way that the framers of our language responded to experiences which, as things turned out, became standard under the conceptual scheme of our society. There is no reason to suppose that these experiences, deviant under this structure, may not become standard under another, so that language which is deviant here and now may sometime and somewhere else be plain speech.

Deviant speech and deviant experiences are dangerous in two distinct ways. They are dangerous to society insofar as they pose any threat to the conceptual scheme so long ago worked out, so easy and so comfortable, with which we have housed ourselves in the shifting world. They are also dangerous to the individual to the extent that he is led outside the precincts marked off as safe by the culture he will have absorbed. Nevertheless, it is an open possibility that one may escape, not, to be sure, from ideas to reality itself, for that is permanently closed to us, but from one set of ideas to another. It is always at least possible to build a world upon the basis of one's intuitions, however difficult this may prove in execution; even though there is no general exit from our conceptual prison, save momentarily through art or through the intuitions which can become art, we have some choice as to prisons, and so we enjoy a limited conceptual freedom.

These notions, first introduced in *Concerning Truth and Falsehood in an Extramoral Sense*, were in essence to remain with Nietzsche always. He saw himself, increasingly so, as an outsider, hence as an artist, and hence as a danger to himself and to society: I am not a man, he came to say in his late moments of self-dramatization which heralded the supervention of madness, I am dynamite.* But even before this it gave him an altogether exultant

---

* From a letter, written in 1888, to a possible translator for an English edition of his work. This would undoubtedly have been Helen Zimmern, the translator of Schopenhauer, whom he knew from his summers at Sils Maria. Cited by Ernest Newman, in *Life of Richard Wagner* (New York: Knopf, 1946), chap. IV, p. 597. Enough letters from this period just before the *Zuzammenbruch* survive in which similar wording is used. To Strindberg he wrote on December 7, 1888, "I am strong enough to break the history of mankind into two bits." The next day he wrote Gast regarding *Ecce Homo* that "It blasts, so to speak, the history of man in two pieces—highest superlative of dynamite!"[7] He had been called dynamite in a rare sympathetic review which appeared in a Swiss newspaper in September, 1886. He was pleased beyond measure when the journalist said "Here is dynamite!" and he mentions this note of appreciation in his letters of the time.

view of himself and his activities, and it created for him an image of himself as a singularly adventurous and audacious person as, self-dramatization notwithstanding, he truly was, if only intellectually. It also gave him a hopeless feeling that any set of metaphors he might formulate would be misunderstood by the society in which he lived and, at the very best, would degenerate into stale "truths" in any new society they might help make possible. They would yield concepts different from the ones he contested, but they would be no less binding, if successful, and no more true. "An anti-metaphysical world-view—but an artistic one," he wrote of himself in the *Nachlass*[8]; but of his own thoughts he wrote ruefully, in the last section of *Beyond Good and Evil*, "You have taken off your newness, and some of you, I fear, are ready to become truths: so undying do you already look, so heart-breakingly decent, so dull!"[9] Either way, then, he saw inevitable failure for himself. But of this too, more later.

There are two types of man, he suggests to us in this essay on truth,[10] the rational and the intuitive man [*der vernunftige Mensch und der intuitive Mensch*], who fear intuition and scorn rationality respectively. Yet the difference between them is not ultimate, but only relative to some given scheme of concepts. Rationality is the destiny of any intuition that survives, and intuition is the source of any rationality that prevails. Nevertheless, artistic (or intuitive) activity is conceived of here as the basic exploratory activity of man, in which an effort is made to say what cannot after all be said in the language we have available to us except metaphorically, even if acceptance and descriptiveness catch up with it finally. It is only through intuitions that our conceptual scheme may ever be modified or possibly even overthrown and replaced. It is in this sense that Nietzsche wrote in his preface to *The Birth of Tragedy*, which was flatteringly dedicated to Wagner, that art is a metaphysical activity and "the highest human task." In a later preface to a later edition, he qualified this claim, and conceded that his "whole artistical metaphysics might be taken as arbitrary, fantastic, and empty."[11] As we shall discover, apart from the stress it puts upon art as such, it is very like the mature view which he saw it, in this preface, as having prefigured.

II

It is not difficult to be critical of this account. For one thing, it might be readily objected that the claim that *every* sentence is metaphorical verges on meaninglessness. It is one thing to say that some sentences, deviant under a given scheme, are metaphorical relative to sentences which are standard under that very scheme. If one thus defines *metaphor*, however, then if every sentence is metaphorical, each sentence is deviant, which is absurd. Moreover, if we do not have some sentences to be counted as straight declarative utterances with which to contrast others (by plain semantic criteria and grammatical rule) as metaphorical, it is difficult to see what we any longer can mean by metaphor at all. Nietzsche, I think, might reply along the following lines: Metaphors are sentences which, at the very least, are never literally true; no sentence ever is literally true of what it is about; hence, every sentence is to some extent metaphorical. In practice (if not in rhetoric) it makes little difference if we say that no sentence is literally true or, as he was later and more sweepingly to declare, that every sentence is literally false. The question is only whether our language allows us to get on in life, and if it does this, little more can be demanded of it. The demand that in addition it be literally true is a philosophical not a realistic or practical demand. The one-to-one correspondence between sentence and fact, sometimes entertained as the ideal relationship between an ideal language and the world it isomorphically mirrors, is more than will ever be required or, as he would later have said, more than is theoretically possible. To show this will require a closer analysis of Nietzsche's philosophy than I have so far given. But it is worth noting, for the moment, that he nowhere specifically asks what a literally true sentence would be like. To this extent his notion of metaphor, supposing metaphors to be sentences which contrast with literally true ones (and metaphors are not necessarily false because they are metaphors), is ill-defined. But he could have replied that *we* have no clear idea ourselves what literal truth would look like (what, after all, are the queries about ideal language, the *form* of sentences and of facts?), and *we* get on well enough with our notion of metaphor. The quest for a clear characterization of truth and metaphor is something we must undertake together.

One might slyly suggest that Nietzsche's general proposition has semi-paradoxical consequences. Let us grant his idea that a metaphor is but a concrete image used in place of a concept,[12] that metaphorical thinking is nonconceptual thinking, and that we have, in whatever way, adjusted ourselves to the idea that all of language is metaphorical. To say that all sentences are metaphorical entails that the thesis itself is metaphorical, hence not literally true, hence *literally* false. So, if he is right, he is wrong. I believe Nietzsche would have acknowledged this criticism, and underscored it. He wrote self-consciously under the persuasion that language has inherent limitations and that literal truth is, for deep reasons, never to be attained even superficially. He then could ask only that men try his way, and see whether it did not enable them to get on in the world by means of it. Using deviant expressions and deviant ideas, he wrote, to some degree, as an artist; his work, at its best, was an instance as well as a discussion of artistic activity. Human activities, the conceptual systems which men fabricate out of a primordially poetic rapport with experience, rise, are modified through art, and fall. They are, like the universe itself, according to his interpretation of the teaching of Heraclitus, a work of art, a creation of Zeus: "A becoming and a passing away, a building up and tearing down without any moral additive: the world is the play of an artist and a child, in perpetual innocence."[13] But, one might press, discounting these poetic notions, is it not entailed by his thought that all activity is artistic, a transformation of experience through metaphor and analogy, image and illusion? So that art, properly speaking, is itself only an instance of art in this extended sense? Again, I think Nietzsche would have conceded this consequence. Indeed, it is exactly here that he might have pointed in indication of his most radical insight.

In ordinary language, certain activities are termed artistic and certain objects are termed art-works. The artist then is a person distinct from others, as art-works are objects distinct from other objects. To speak of everyone as an artist, and everything made by men as art-work, is to stretch this concept to the point of ultimate debasement. It is this way with concepts which often generates philosophy, however. A certain activity, conventionally distinguished from the rest, is said to be more like these other activities, or these others more like it, than conventional thought permits us to suppose. To then say that these other activities just *are* this activity which they importantly resemble is to use language dramatically. It introduces tensions of the sort we would recognize if someone were to say that all infants are logicians or all women are men. The purpose of this flagrant usage (which is metaphorical) is to demolish barriers, to emphasize similarities that had been overlooked, and, more important, to draw attention to the real nature of the activity or thing which was typically contrasted with the activity or thing it is now said to *be*. Nietzsche frequently uses language this way. It gives a certain pungency to his writings and exemplifies one of his methods for attacking the conventional structure of thought. It is shown, for example, in his claim that all language is metaphorical. Meanwhile, it presupposes the precise concept which is under attack, for the latter specifies the model he is using to fit things to. He did, in fact, think of artistic activity as being more widely exhibited than the rules for the word "artistic" commonly permit us to say; however, it is precisely artistic activity narrowly construed which he takes as *paradigmatic* for the entire range of activity now declared to be artistic. We all are artists all the time but—to protract the image—some of us are hacks and some of us original, which is what his distinction between reason and impulse, here at least, comes to in the end.

"Art," then, has both a wide and a narrow use in Nietzsche's writings, and the wide use takes its meaning from the narrow one. Because we know what artists in the narrow sense distinctively do, we are able to see how we, in other activities, are artists as well. Nietzsche thus means to claim that our original and most fundamental involvement with experience is artistic and transforming, that we spontaneously seek to express, in images and apposite cadences, the way in which we feel and perceive the world. He speaks of a "primal faculty of human fantasy" [*Urvermögen menschlicher Phantasie*] through which the human individual functions essentially as "an artistically creating subject" [*als kunsterlisch schaffendes Subjekt*].[14]

This singularly interesting idea is not deeply exploited by Nietzsche, but it is perhaps not difficult to see what he might mean by our *Urvermögen*. It seems, for one thing, unnecessary to teach a child how to play in an imaginative way with such things as sticks, or for the child to say that a certain stick "is" a horse. Or, one can give a child an array of geometrical shapes and ask which of them is *him*, and he will invariably give some answer, never rejecting the question as meaningless, however aware he doubtless is that he "is" no more the octagon he identifies as himself than the stick he "rides" upon is a horse. It is exceedingly difficult to understand how, on most theories of teaching language, anyone ever should be taught this use of *is*. Certainly it could not be taught via ostensional acts, for that is the way in which the meaning of words in their straightforward use is allegedly taught, and *this* use is not straightforward but imaginative.

A chief difficulty, however, and one which seems to me seriously to affect Nietzsche's entire account, is that there is a plain sense in which the imaginative use of *is* logically presupposes mastery of the straightforward use. A child who calls his stick "horse" but who holds it to his shoulder and cries "Bang!" has not an overactive fantasy but an underdeveloped knowledge of horses. We *may* say the child imagines a horse is a gun. But this is only a way of saying he is mistaken, not that he is imaginative; for a genuine exercise of imagination is not regarded as a way of being mistaken. In effect, then, a child must know something about the real behavior of horses before he can play imaginatively with play horses, and fantasy takes flight only upon the sturdy wings of standard usage and genuine knowledge. If this is so, it is hard to see how language could have *originally* been imaginative. Indeed, one's spontaneous response to an experience, say with a noise, would be more by way of giving a *name* to that experience than responding to it musically, because nothing counts as a poetic response if nothing counts as a prosaic one. Imaginative usage, in presupposing ordinary use, seems almost to entail the sociological thesis that there could be artists in a society only after there were sober, productive citizens. If, sociologically, a society consisting solely of poets is impossible, so would be a language which was only poetic. Perhaps, then, we do not have quite the liberty with the concepts of art and imagination which Nietzsche assumed in moving to his wider conception of art and artistic activity. The first sentences ever uttered simply could *not* have been metaphors. Well, he might have replied, they could not have been literal descriptions either. This will hardly help him support his positive contention: metaphors and straightforward uses are conceptual interdependencies.

III

We have been concerned up to now with artistics in the sense in which there is an alleged capacity for minting metaphors that may later wear down into concepts and come to be taken as truths. Our transforming *Urvermögen* is that which has, together with custom, generated those truths out of which our world is shaped. But I suggested earlier that Nietzsche saw art not so much in terms of providing truths but as enabling us to bear with the truths we countenance. Art was said to be what makes life supportable. This brings us to the narrower sense of "art," and to another strand in the complex concept of art which Nietzsche, sometimes to his own confusion as well as to that of his readers, was employing. In addition to supplying the metaphors out of which our conception of the real world first springs, art (in the narrow sense) creates for us another world alongside the real world—an art world, as we might call it—into which we may from time to time escape, finding respite and repose from the pains and struggles of existence, if only for a suspended moment. This was a very Schopenhauerian idea of art; Schopenhauer felt that in the contemplation of beauty, in nature, in painting, and especially in music, man turned away from suffering in a healing intuition of eternity.

Art of course is not the only mechanism of escape available to us. There are, to mention two others that Nietzsche particularly cites, fantasy and drunkenness. In consonance with his generalized conception of artistic activity, Nietzsche speaks of dreams and intoxication as artistic, or at least as ways of satisfying certain urges which call for art. "In the production of the fair illusions of the dream sphere, every man proves himself an accomplished artist."[15] It must almost certainly have been the fact of dreaming—the spontaneous production of images in the absence of any causes which these images resembled—which suggested to Nietzsche the *Urvermögen*, the primitive artistry of man. In the narrow sense of art, meanwhile, there are two chief kinds of art that correspond to the primitive modes of escape which dreaming and intoxication illustrate: Apollinian art, which is like dreams, and Dionysiac art, which is like drunkenness. Nietzsche asserted that the evolution of art is due to the interactions between these distinct modes of artistic expression;[16] *The Birth of Tragedy out of the Spirit of Music* (1872) was an attempt to write a philosophical history of Greek art in just these terms.

Apollinian art and Dionysian art are exhibited, respectively, in painting and in music, in "Vision and in the Orgiastic."[17] These are expressions of conditions which, in normal [nonartistic] life are "prefigured, only more weakly, in dreams and intoxication."[18] The German word here translated as "intoxication" is *Rausch*, which has connotations of ecstasy and transport and is less narrowly connected with *alcoholic* states than is our word. Alcoholic drunkenness is drunkenness with alcohol as its *cause*, but it is the state of drunkenness, rather than its cause, in which Nietzsche is interested. We can be transported into the same state in other ways, through dancing, sexual intercourse, and participation in religious activities, for example.

A certain analogy can be sustained between dreaming and painting, if we are prepared to think of dreaming as the production and contemplation of images. "The objects which appear to us in dreams," Descartes wrote in the *First Meditation*, "are, as it were, painted representations"; if we introduce *imaging* as a word which means only the production of images, then dreaming and painting would be instances of imaging. Again, daydreams, or fantasies, are ways of manipulating the images we produce in such a manner as to gratify certain emotional requirements without having to make the adjustments and concessions or to take the risks required were we to seek satisfaction of them in reality. Freud, as is well known, sought to explain the phenomenon of dreaming with reference to the mechanism of wish-fulfillment. In analogy with fantasies, by means of a novel or a play, we live vicariously through sequences of episodes and adventures without our having to *do* anything—enjoying unearned experience in the security of theater or study. Finally, art, no more than fantasy, can impose itself upon us as reality itself: to cross this line is to lapse into pathology.[19] Descartes would not have dared to say he *was* dreaming, for that, he said, would be madness. One derives benefit from dream or from art only so long as one preserves a sense of the reality with which they contrast. Indeed, art and dream alike will throw into relief the rawness, asperity, and insecurity of the real world which we have, for a moment, turned our back on in order to find a certain fleeting peace. Thus each makes life "possible and worth living."[20] Parenthetically, a well-adjusted, happy person would, one might think, require neither art nor fantasy, and, if Freud were right, he whose every wish had been fulfilled would never have dreams. If the Greeks were as healthy and sunny a people as legend has painted them, they would not have required art, at least not Apollinian art. So one must infer that they were not so harmonized with the world as all that. This is precisely what Nietzsche is going to argue.

Drunkenness [*Rausch*] might again be diagnosed as a mechanism for fleeing reality, but there is a difference between fantasy and drunkenness. When a man indulges himself in fantasy, he turns away from the world, and enters a private space more congenial to his feelings, needs, and wishes. By contrast, a drunkard is often one who has set out not so much to forget the world as to forget *himself*, to "let himself go," to overcome rather than emphasize the boundaries between himself and other things, which grow blurred as the intoxication heightens until, at the orgiastic climax, they are blotted out entirely. It is in such moments that mystics achieve union and celebrants attain communion and lovers touch the pinnacle of joy.

Apollinian art as such (and here we depart from the analogy) is exemplified by pictorialization, the depiction of things and scenes. It is at once a shaping and an individuating art, giving form and clarity of contour to the contemplated images of its audience. Dionysiac art is less easy to characterize except in opposition to this, dissolving contours and breaking forms down, *dis*individuating. It is exemplified in lyric poetry and music, as its opposite is in sculpture and painting. But it would be a mistake to identify either of these art forms with specific artistic genres, largely because the distinction will reappear within each genre. Thus there is room (as we know today) for a Dionysiac painting; music, after all, originally had Apollo as its patron deity; and Nietzsche recognized a kind of Apollinian music—"a rhythm of waves beating the shore, a plastic art."[21] Even Greek tragedy, which Nietzsche characterized as the fusion of the two—"an Apollinian embodiment of a Dionysiac intuition and impulse"[22]—is only this in the tragedies of Aeschylus and possibly of Sophocles; Euripides is specifically indicted for having expunged from his works all the Dionysiac elements, making of them instead a fusion of Apollinian and *Socratic* forms. So Apollinian and Dionysiac are not even exhaustive aesthetic predications.

It is too glib to identify Nietzsche's pair of artistic categories with rationality and irrationality. Dreaming is, after all, no more a rational activity than is dancing, nor is music—which was put on a footing with mathematics by the Greeks themselves—less rational than poetry. If there have been fewer mad logicians than poets, this will be because there have been more poets than logicians. As we shall see, rationality in art is opposed to both the Nietzschean types. Notice, especially, that Dionysianism cannot simply be identified with self-abandonment, ecstasy, frenzy or madness, except insofar as art is able to induce these states in its audience. First, the term has application primarily to *art* and nothing is art which does not hold together, follow some rules, give some shape to space or sound.* Second, Nietzsche distinguishes plainly between *barbaric* and *Hellenized* Dionysianism.

---

* Nietzsche again neglected these considerations in his own musical compositions. He sent his *Manfred Meditation* to Hans von Bülow, Wagner's conductor and a great admirer of *The Birth of Tragedy* (as all Wagnerians would have been, of course). The musician was not impressed. "Is it," he wrote, "by intent that you persistently defy every rule of tonal connection, from the highest syntax down to the lowest spelling? . . . You should master the musical language: a frenzied imagination, revelling in reminiscences of Wagnerian harmonies, is no sort of foundation to build upon." Bülow to Nietzsche, July 24, 1872. Cited in Newman, *op. cit.*, p. 324. Bülow advises him that, if he perseveres in music, he might best stick to vocal music. Words, after all, already give structure which mere sound cannot.

Throughout the range of ancient civilization . . . we find evidence of Dionysiac celebrations. . . . The central concern of such celebrations was complete sexual promiscuity, welling over all ties of family, and their rules and prohibitions. The wildest bestialities of nature were unchained until that horrifying mixture of cruelty and lust, which has always seemed to me the true witches' brew, was attained. . . .[23]

The Greeks were no different in this regard from the other ancient peoples nor, in Nietzsche's view (later expressed in *The Genealogy of Morals*), from the rest of humankind in taking a special pleasure in the spectacle of suffering and the cruel infliction of pain.

The Greeks, who were the humanest men of ancient times, have in themselves a streak of cruelty, a tiger-like joy in destruction . . . a trait which must terrify us when, with the tame conception of modern humanity, we encounter it in their entire history and mythology.[24]

Greek art, of course, was often a celebration of warfare, and the Greek hero saw in combat itself, as well as in its rewards, the best of lives while "the whole Greek world exulted in the *Iliad*'s scenes of fighting."[25] Nevertheless, of Homer (an Apollinian artist par excellence, for epic poetry is paradigmatic of this mode of art) Nietzsche writes:

We are already, through the extraordinary artistic clarity, the quietness and purity of delineation, lifted above the sheerly material amalgamation: its colors appear, through an artistic illusion, lighter, milder, warmer, its men better and more sympathetic in this colored, warm illumination.[26]

If, however, we "step backward into the pre-Homeric world, [we encounter] night and horror, the offspring of a fantasy habituated to the monstrous."[27] So Homeric art, and Apollinian art in general, transform to some extent these impulses to cruelty and the destructive energies; in a similar way the Dionysiac excesses of the non-Hellenic world were taken up and transformed into art, so that the advent of Dionysianism into Greece became "an aesthetic event." Even so, Dionysiac art "conveys an undertone of terror," and stimulates a dim memory of "the times when the infliction of pain was experienced as joy, and a sense of supreme triumph elicited cries of anguish from the heart." Still, *it was art*, even if "Apollinian consciousness was but a thin veil concealing from the Greeks this [barbaric] Dionysiac world."28

The Greeks apparently were never the serene spirits that the Hellenists once thought them to have been. Prey to these gusts of aggression, they were, according to Nietzsche, sensitive to suffering to an extreme degree. Throughout the cultural expression of that people there is an undertone of pessimism and of fear which Nietzsche, if not the first to have detected, was surely the first to have seen as a problem. He wanted to know how we would reconcile the bright picture of this ancient people with the black hints, frequent enough if we look for them in their myth and poetry, that life is suffering and the world alien and dreadful. Silenus muttered that the best good for man was never to have been born, and the next best thing to die quickly. The entire edifice of the Greek pantheon, the *Zauberberg* of gods who stand aloof from the charging terrors of existence, is a projection, Nietzsche says, of Greek fears and a consolation for them. Only through their vision of a set of beings superior to the sufferings attendant on life "could life have been endured by a race so hypersensitive, so emotionally intense, so uniquely capable of suffering."29

Greek art, like Greek religion, was then a contrivance for coping with and finally accepting life instead of its abbreviation or extinction. The idea here is one quite central to Nietzsche's thought, and it has application to all of culture, not to the Greeks alone. Art, religion, philosophy, morality, and indeed whatever gives a form to experience, are, in the end, a response to suffering and must be understood as a means for making life possible and tolerable and for overcoming the death wish (if we may call it so) which is released by the sense for suffering.* Greek tragedy was then a solution to rather than a celebration of suffering; Apollinian culture was required in order "to overthrow a population of titans and to kill monsters, and by means of powerful and pleasurable illusions to triumph over the frightening depths of their apprehen-

* The transformation was sufficiently successful to transform death from the second highest good to the greatest evil. *Cf.* Achilles' underworld lament or Sappho's brilliant "If death were a good thing, the gods themselves would die."

sion of the world and their susceptibility to suffering."[30] Nietzsche adds, at the end of his book, "What suffering these must have endured to produce such beauty!"[31] The psychological assumptions underlying this analysis are complex and dubious, of course, quite apart from any questions of its truth to the facts of the genesis of Greek art. I am indicating now only that the discussion in *The Birth of Tragedy* was a striking application to a single case of a general and ramified theory which will emerge in the course of later exposition.

IV

Dream life and waking life are often invidiously contrasted, not least frequently by philosophers, for whom the difference between these states is the difference between illusion and veracity. From the time of Descartes there has been an unremittent investigation into the question of whether it is possible to prove in any way that what we presently entertain in experience is not illusory, and that what appears as solid to us, and real, is not instead insubstantial phantasm. But even plain men, who seem able and ready to draw a distinction which philosophers have despaired of justifying, regard dreams as interruptions of their real lives, and they have, in their languages, no expression more suited to emphasize the relative unreality of certain episodes than "dreamlike" or "nightmarish." The real business of life is conducted in the intervals between dreams. "Although," Nietzsche wrote, "of the two halves of life— the dreaming and the waking half—we hold the latter to be the more important and privileged, more worthy, and the only one which is really lived, I might, in obvious paradox, maintain the opposite."[32] What Nietzsche means by this arch, elusive statement is that any experience which is intelligible to us is already, and in the nature of the case, an illusion, created by the human *Urvermögen* which gives form to experience, this form answering to nothing in the world itself. "Closed in by and constituted out of [such illusions], we must find ourselves nonexistent";[33] inasmuch as "empirical reality" has no ultimate existence anyway, being our own creation, Cartesian anxieties are somewhat superfluous. The question as to whether we experience reality or suffer illusion is gratuitous, and the difference which vexes us is between illusion pure and simple, which is what our waking life is, and illusions within illusion, which is what dreams are. If the former is a response to some original need for illusion, the latter is an even higher satisfaction of it, and so dreams within life must be, by our own implicit criteria, more valuable than the dream in which life itself consists.[34] But this explains the value men set upon art, since art, like dream, meets this need more gratifyingly.

In saying that experience is illusory, Nietzsche means, at some points, only that temporal, spatial, and causal concepts have application to it or, to put it another way, that we perceive things in space and time.[35] Apollinian art adheres to the *principium individuationis*, but so, in effect, do we all in distinguishing thing from thing. Insofar as we do this, we are imposing form upon what Nietzsche calls, with a Teutonic pompousness not found in his later writings, the *Primal Oneness* [*Ur-einen*]. It is the mark of Dionysianism that it seeks to rend the individuating meshwork of temporal and spacial individuating and to restore the *Ur-einen* to its *Einheit*. Dionysiac art, specifically dithyrambic music, is allegedly free of image and concept, and it celebrates the undifferentiated oneness stained and delineated by Apollinian superimposition: "Music symbolizes a sphere which is both earlier than appearance, and beyond it."[36] Nevertheless, this counter-Apollinian art, quite as much as its rival, provides solace and reassurance in its own way:

Dionysiac art, too, would persuade us of the eternal pleasure of existence—only we must seek for this not in appearance but behind it. It makes us realize that whatever comes into being must be ready for its painful dissolution, and it compels us to gaze into the terror of individual existence, but not be immobilized with fear: a metaphysical comfort takes us, for a moment, out of the continual drive of changing form.[37]

Attic tragedy, as I have said, was analyzed by Nietzsche as a fusion of these two forms of art, an amalgam of image and music, individuating and disindividuating at once. I must analyze, if only briefly, this famous thesis, not so much for its intrinsic interest but for the reverberations it sets ringing in his later philosophy. There are, I suppose, historical doubts as to the veracity of the theory, but he was at least as much concerned that what he said be psychologically correct and adequate to the nature of art as he understood it—"not an imitation of, but a metaphysical supplement to nature, raised up alongside it in order to overcome it."[38] Hence it is a shallow view that *tragic* art is an imitation of real tragedy. And why should we require such imitations, "life being sufficiently tragic already"? It is by means of tragic art that we are to transcend and not just dramatically duplicate the tragedies of existence itself. We must remind ourselves here of the exalted office which Nietzsche, in this period, would assign to art.

His discussion commences with a query concerning the origin and purpose of the tragic chorus. He speaks sharply against the theory that the chorus is an "ideal spectator"; first, because a spectator (and certainly an "ideal" one) should be able to distinguish art from reality, when in fact the chorus seems often to participate in the action itself; second, because the chorus antedates drama as such, and as the concept of spectator is logically correlative with the concept of drama, there hardly could have been audiences before there were spectacles.[39] "Tragedy was originally chorus only, and not drama."[40] His own account is exceedingly difficult to follow, but it seems to come more or less to this, if I have understood him here at all. Just as dreams and fantasies are sometimes thought to enable certain energies within us to be discharged harmlessly and vicariously, as it were, without any of the destructiveness or terror which might result if they were permitted free discharge in real life, so the impulses that erupted into the shattering excesses of the old Dionysiac rites could be disarmed and rendered harmless, if they could be similarly discharged in some proxy manner. The tragic chorus, the ancient chorus of satyrs, was an artistic substitute for the Dionysiac rite as the dream is an imaginary substitute for an aggressive act. One could participate in this chorus, achieve the sense of unity, the dissipation of individuality which was the state of transport attained at the climax of the wild rites, but with none of the consequent or instrumental cruelty. It was in this sense that the Greeks made an aesthetic event out of the Dionysiac celebration. The public, in whose presence this choric transformation of a beastly ritual was enacted, related to the chorus in much the same way that a dreamer stands to his dream: the aesthetic relationship would indeed be a waking dream.

The public at the Attic tragedy found itself in the chorus of the orchestra, so that fundamentally there was no distinction between audience and chorus. Rather, everything was one transcendant chorus of dancing, singing satyrs, and of those who allowed themselves to be represented through these satyrs. An audience of spectators, as we know it, was unknown in Greece.[41]

There was an internal relationship, accordingly, between public and chorus, with therapeutic benefits:

The Greek *Kulturmensch* felt himself raised up in the presence of the satyr chorus . . . so that whatever separated man from man weakened before an overwhelming sense of unity leading back into the heart of nature. . . . With this chorus, the deep Hellene, so uniquely sensitive to the most profound and exquisite suffering, consoled himself . . . he was saved by art, and through art was saved for life.[42]

In the earliest stages of this remarkable artistic transmutation there was no dramatic action; the chorus simply enacted the celebration of the god Dionysus. It was enough that the god's presence be felt or dramatically implied, but at some point (perhaps in response to a demand of the Apollinian impulse that had always characterized Greek expression) the idea of representing the god was evolved; hence, the chorus was given a focus and drama, in "the strict sense," was born. With the explicit representation, the feelings of the choric group—active and passive, dancer and public —were directed to a specific image, an illusion within an illusion, and hence once more like a dream. The result was Greek tragedy as we know it, "the Dionysiac lyric of the chorus and the Apollinian dream world of the scene."[43]

The first "image" would have been of Dionysus himself, thus introducing a split within the heretofore unified choric group between god and celebrant. Later heroes of tragedy were but *personae*, masks, of this god. In time, image encroached upon lyric, dialogue replaced music, the chorus became less and less necessary and more and more a mere stage convention, standing as an odd barrier between audience and dramatic action and making the performance stylized and unreal. In Euripides' plays, its role and function were already long forgotten, and the chorus is merely vestigial. This increasing Apollinization of the tragic form, as we might call it, should perhaps be taken as the natural direction of evolution in Greek art, but Nietzsche, in fact, felt that Euripides killed tragedy. This requires some explanation.

Euripides, as Nietzsche characterizes him, was essentially a rational man, genuinely puzzled by what to him were irrational factors in the drama of his predecessors. So might we be by ritual residues in some current practice which have long outlived the circumstances that gave rise to them. They are allowed to continue as the result of inertia or sentiment, but rationally they no longer have justification and might as readily be eliminated as not. It was Euripides' disposition to dislike whatever was "ambiguous and subterranean" and to excise "every powerful, original Dionysiac element from tragedy and to rebuild it, purified and new, upon the foundation of non-Dionysiac art, morality, and outlook."[44] But not, as it turned out, upon Apollinian foundations. Euripides was but a mask through which a new force was expressing itself. This was Socrates. The antagonism within Greek art was henceforward between Dionysiac and Socratic forces.[45]

V

Nietzsche is so often taken to be the apostle of impulse and unreason that it is worth dwelling on the opposition between Dionysianism and Socratism. Nietzsche quite plainly blames the triumph of Socratism for an artistic catastrophe of huge dimension: the death of tragedy through the spirit of reason, if we may pun an antithesis to the title of his book. Specifically, this meant the emergence of an ideal of artistic naturalism, and the leading principle of this he termed *aesthetic Socratism*: "In order for something to be beautiful, it must be sensible [*verständig*]."[46] In light of this, Euripides must have esteemed himself "the only sober poet among the drunk ones," for his drama alone was free of anything irrational and incomprehensible, making perfectly clear what was happening in the action and why, so that the audience, their rational curiosity satisfied, might respond to the rhetorical pathos of the hero, upon which Euripides exercised his main lyrical gifts. He prided himself on knowing what he was doing, assured that without self-awareness one is certain to go wrong. Socrates, in the *Republic*, asks whether, even if he is right, his being so counts for anything if he does not know *why* he is right: he may be like a blind man who has found the right road by accident. Translated into *aesthetic* Socratism this becomes, "Whatever is to be beautiful must be conscious [–ly done]."[47] Euripides' plays are rational structures, rationality having replaced Apollinian image as, in Nietzsche's early theory of knowledge, concepts replace metaphor. These dramas are set pieces for theatrical emoting, "fiery emotions taking the place of Dionysiac transport." All ice and fire, the tragedies are the "counterfeits"[48] of true art.

Socrates' mistrust of the poets is of course well known. It was, in part, their seeming incapacity to give reasons for what they did that constituted his animus toward them. It struck him as odd and almost immoral that men who so spontaneously and sub-rationally produced their writings (as they themselves claimed) should be taken as the mentors of Greek youth, their works regarded as manuals of moral instruction. Socrates was astounded to discover that not only artists but statesmen and others "pursued their calling by instinct without a true and certain insight."[49] Condemning whatever arose solely out of instinct, Socrates, in parity, was required at once to condemn the art and ethics of his age: "Wherever his probing glance fell, he saw failure of understanding and the power of false opinion. He inferred from this a deeply perverse and blamable state of affairs."[50] He became the hero of a special art form, the Socratic dialogue, in which the hero is the dialectician. Out of these dialogues evolves the idea that "between virtue and knowledge, as between belief and morality, a necessary and demonstrable connection must exist";[51] and as "the dialectical hero of the Platonic drama, [Socrates] is closely allied with the Euripidean hero who must justify his action through argument and counterargument." The *essence* of tragedy "can only be interpreted as a manifestation and symbolization of Dionysiac conditions, a tangible representation of music, the dream world of intoxication."[52] This essence "was destroyed" through the abolition of the chorus and the insertion of dialectic in explanation of action.

Nietzsche regarded Socrates as having created a turning point in the history of mankind as well as having caused the decline of Greek tragedy. Both characterizations of his achievement are interconnected. Tragic art in Attica was a response to the pessimistic view the Greeks originally had of nature, enabling them to live through transforming their anxiety. But Socrates, oddly, intended the same end, or at least effected it. He originated the view that the universe is intelligible through and through, and that by means of the rational acquisition of knowledge men might be freed "even from the fear of death."[35] Tragedy, then, no longer was required, because its function could be discharged as well by rational science. Despite the artistic (or anti-artistic) consequences of Socratism, Nietzsche expresses an almost unqualified admiration for its rational achievement. Suppose, he asks, that human energies had not gone toward the pursuit of knowledge but instead "for the practical, i.e., egotistical goals of men and nations." The result would have been,

in all probability, the weakening, through universal wars of annihilation, and the continual migrating of peoples, of man's lust for life. Suicide would have become so common that individuals sensitive to a last remnant of a sense of duty might, like Fiji Islanders, throttle parents and friends.[54]

[Such] wholesale slaughter out of pity is present wherever in the world art in some form—particularly as religion or science—did not appear as a prophylactic against barbarism.[55]

It is well to keep these exaggerated and dramatized claims in mind as we consider Nietzsche's philosophy. It is important to do so because neither here nor in any later work was Nietzsche ever hostile to rationality or to science, and he never regarded either of them as inimical to "life." On the contrary, humankind has an instinct for life but is unhappily susceptible to great suffering; the latter may prevail over the former unless it is shored up and protected against the otherwise overwhelming thrusts of existence against us. The contrast is always between suffering and exultation, between barbarism and civilization, and science, no *less* than art, is an instrument for the enhancement of life. He never opposed art in the narrow sense against art in the wide sense—the latter counting science as one of its forms.

The complaint against Socrates is directed only against his narrowness in regarding reason (science, logic) as the unique instrument of human delivery. Socrates contrasted rational with artistic activity similarly to the way in which we contrast veracity with illusion. But it is Nietzsche's deepest conviction that art and science are *together* illusory and must be judged and distinguished on an altogether different basis, in connection with their instrumental rather than their descriptive power, and in the service of life. In a somewhat Schopenhauerian passage, he writes:

It is an eternal phenomenon: the avid Will always finds a means, through some illusion spread over things, to anchor its creatures in life, and to coerce their perdurance. One man is captivated by the Socratic lust for knowledge and the illusion that through it he might heal the everlasting wound of being. Another man is seduced by the beguiling beauty-veil of art fluttering before his eyes. Yet another has the metaphysical solace that life eternally and indestructibly flows on beneath the whirl of appearances. . . . Whatever we call culture is composed of these beguilements; and according to the proportions of the mixture, we have a predominantly *Socratic*, or *artistic*, or *tragic* culture.[56]

At times, however, there is a fresh panic when one of these modes of protective illusion gives way and can be seen merely for what it is. This can occur even in science, which has its limits. Nietzsche is not very explicit about this in *The Birth of Tragedy*:

Every noble and gifted man . . . when he reaches the periphery of the circle of science and sees, to his horror, how logic here turns back upon itself and bites its tail, breaks through to a new form of experience—*tragic experience*—which requires, in order to be endured, the shelter and remedy of art.[57]

Art, accordingly, "is the necessary complement of rational discourse,"[58] even though "on a lower level, the zest for knowledge appears to be inimical to art, particularly to Dionysiac-tragic art."[59]

Nietzsche felt that he had discovered the role of reason as providing devices for navigating the fearful waters of life, and that, moreover, he knew the inherent limits reason was up against despite the optimistic claims it made, in Socratic spirit, on behalf of its ubiquity and power. In the period during which he was writing this book, he had already attained to a singularly skeptical view of our cognitive claims. Already he had before him the main outlines of the Nihilistic philosophy I sketched earlier, in accordance with which the world, in contraposition to an old empiricist idea, is in effect a blank tablet upon which *we* make imprints. At the same time, he was deeply impressed with the cultural possibilities of art, and Wagnerian art in particular. By combining these two elements of his mind, we might characterize his aim by paraphrasing a famous statement of Kant's: he found it necessary to deny knowledge in order to make room for *art*. His estimate of art soon declined, however, partly as a consequence of his disenchantment with Wagner and the Wagnerian program. But the disillusionment with Wagner was almost certainly contributed to by the composer's incapacity to live up to the high demands made upon art in *The Birth of Tragedy*—which was, ironically enough, written to supply an aesthetics as well as to find a historical precedent for the Wagnerian conception of art. In the end, Nietzsche was left with his own skeptical conclusions, and one might truly describe his intellectual activity from this point on as a quest for a philosophy to fill the space left empty by art. Although religion was a natural candidate, it was not an acceptable one. This philosophy came later, but his first response, after his relationship with Wagner went shipwreck, was to turn to the study of the natural sciences.

VI

Despite the continuing popularity of *The Birth of Tragedy*—it remains among Nietzsche's most frequently read, translated, and cited works—the volume was a failure on many counts. When he conceived and wrote it, he was on intimate terms with Richard and Cosima Wagner, spending academic holidays from his post in Basle at their estate in Tribschen, near Lucerne. Wagner was to Nietzsche the embodiment of genius, the artist, as he saw it, of a regenerated age and culture, just as Schopenhauer was to have been its philosopher. He himself would be its herald and theoretician. Wagner perceived the immense intelligence of his disciple, and he was genuinely pleased to have a mind of this high quality enlisted in his own cause which, in his total and disarming egoism, he never succeeded in distinguishing from the cause of civilization per se. No doubt there were tensions. Nietzsche fancied himself a composer as Wagner considered *himself* a philosopher, and the continual usurpation of each other's prerogative must have been galling to men whose vanities verged on megalomania. There must also have been erotic tensions, for Wagner was living out of wedlock with Cosima von Bülow (whose husband was Wagner's conductor), and Nietzsche was apparently attracted to "Ariadne," as he came to call her when he styled himself Dionysus. But she had just left husband and children to become chief Wagnerian of the day and bed partner to her deity, and she never saw Nietzsche save through Wagner's eyes. Nevertheless, relations were often enough idyllic, whatever there may have been beneath the surface, and they remained so until the festival of Wagner's music at Bayreuth in 1876.

Nietzsche spent little time at Bayreuth, although the precise circumstances of his sojourn there are exceedingly murky because of Elizabeth Nietzsche's subsequent meddling with documents and dates. It has been proven that some facts she cited as expressions of pain at Wagner's music refer instead to the headaches Nietzsche was severely suffering from at this time. Ernest Newman has shown decisively, I think, that Nietzsche actually could have heard very little of the music, and then only a bit of one rehearsal. Even so, Nietzsche had come primarily not to an aesthetic but to a cultural event, and in the mental frame of a prophet and not a mere music lover. "For us," he wrote in *Richard Wagner at Bayreuth* (1876), "Bayreuth signifies the morning consecration [*die Morgen Weihe*] to the battle . . . for righteousness and love amongst men."[60] He was interested as much in the audience as in the art, and indeed a criterion for the value of the art—which was to have been the rebirth of tragedy in the world[61]—must lie in the conduct and attitude of the audience. Unhappily, if predictably, the audience at Bayreuth failed to be one grand chorus of dancing, singing satyrs. Nor had they come to be consecrated in the great struggle for love and justice, through art, for the highest sacrifices.[62] Instead, they were simply people out for a good time. Anyone with 900 marks could gain admission; the audience was opulent, made up in at least as high a proportion of paunchy businessmen from the nearby Marienbad, and their wives in diadems and lavalieres, as it was of noble spirits. Wagner was elated, directing what must have seemed more like a circus rather than officiating, as chief priest, at a "jubilee of humankind over the secured togetherness and progress of humanity in general."[63] It was, in brief, human, all-too-human, at Bayreuth, and Nietzsche fled. The two men saw each other after this, but their sympathy had been irreparably ruptured. It became officially so, in effect, when, at the same time as Nietzsche sent Wagner his *Human, All-too-Human*, Wagner sent *him* a dedicated copy of *Parsifal*. In retrospect, Nietzsche spoke of the crossing of the two books as the crossing of two swords.[64] He found in Wagner's new Christianity and in his old anti-Semitism further causes for repudiating his erstwhile mentor. Of course, the celebration of chastity in *Parsifal*, now that he had outgrown a prudery which still had affected him at Tribschen, impressed him as life-denying. Whatever the case, *The Birth of Tragedy* failed as cultural-artistic prophecy.

It failed, too, in furthering Nietzsche's wildly idealistic program for reforming academic philology in Germany. He had hoped, he wrote to his former teacher, Ritschl, that the book might be a manifesto through which he would gain the allegiance of the younger generation of German philologists.[65] Ritschl dismissed the book as *geistreich Schwiemelei*, clever giddiness, and the reaction among academics was hostile enough. His friend Rohde wrote a favorable review, but Wilamowitz-Moellendorff attacked

it violently, and Hermann Usener told his students at Bonn that
the writer of such a book was "scientifically dead." Rohde and
Wagner wrote in Nietzsche's defense, but the details of the controversy are without relevance here, as Nietzsche's specific views
about the Greeks are irrelevant to the philosophy they illustrate.
Today we are prepared to accept them, but then we are in general
prepared to accept the notion that the mass of human behavior
is irrationally motivated. The importance and the influence of this
book do not consist in its antiquarian rectitude, even though
Nietzsche was convinced that he had said in it something historically true.

In time Nietzsche came to take a somewhat condescending
stance toward *The Birth of Tragedy*. In a critical preface, added
in 1886, he stigmatized it as an "impossible book":

badly written, ponderous, painful, its imagery wild and confused,
emotional, here and there sweetish to the point of femininity, uneven
in tempo, lacking a will toward logical sobriety, so self-assured that it
exempts itself from proof, is suspicious, indeed, of the very *propriety*
of proof. . . .[66]

He became, moreover, increasingly suspicious of many of its
central teachings. Yet his revisions in doctrine were modifications
rather than rejections. Although he never abandoned his concept
of Dionysianism, his conception of it changed to some extent.
For example, it no longer contrasted either with Socratism or
Apollinianism, but with Christianity, and it stood to the latter in
the antithesis in which (as he saw it) a life-affirming philosophy
stands to a life-denying one. Nietzsche indeed identified himself
(figuratively and, on the threshold of insanity, almost literally)
with Dionysus, and he saw Wagner and Schopenhauer as his exact
"antipodes":

Every art, every philosophy, might be seen as a means either as healing
and helping the growth or the decline of life. They always presuppose
sufferers and suffering. But there are two sorts of sufferers, those who
suffer from the overfullness of life, who will a Dionysiac art and a
tragic insight into and outlook onto life—and those who suffer from
an impoverishment of life. *These* long for rest, stillness, smooth waters

or intoxication [*Rausch*], convulsion, stupefaction. The revenge upon life itself—the most voluptuous sort of intoxication for such impoverished ones! Wagner and Schopenhauer alike correspond to this twofold need. They deny and revile life, and are, therefore, my antipodes.[67]

A striking feature of this late utterance (1888) from *Nietzsche Contra Wagner* is the separation of Dionysianism from *Rausch*, which had, in the first formulations, been virtually its criterion. Indeed, Nietzsche had long since come to see in this intoxication, and in the pursuit of it, a pronounced danger. He had sought already in *Daybreak* [*Morgenröthe*] (1881) to offer a psychological analysis of *Rausch*. Men who attain to moments of such ecstasy are typically led to contrast with these the ordinary stretches of their lives, felt, naturally enough, as letdowns and valleys. But then they are apt to think that they are only truly themselves in these few emotional moments which punctuate ordinary life; as a result they look upon ordinary life, and whatever reinforces it, as hostile to the attainment of their true selves. "Humanity," he writes, "owes much of its evil to these fanatical intoxicates"

for they are the insatiable sowers of the weeds of discontent with themselves and with their neighbors, of contempt for their age, and the world, and, above all, they are world-weary. . . . Moreover, these fanatics implant, to their utmost power, the belief in *Rausch* as the belief in life itself. A fearful belief! As savages are rapidly corrupted by firewater, so mankind has become, slowly but fundamentally, corrupted through the intoxicating feeling caused by *intellectual* firewater, and through those who keep alive the craving for it. Perhaps mankind might be destroyed through it.[68]

This is of course much exaggerated, but for our purposes it is sufficient to mark a qualification on the idea of *Rausch*.

Nietzsche also began to take on the distrust toward the artist which he had criticized in Socrates. "With regard for the truth," he said, "the artist has a weaker morality than the thinker":

He does not wish to be deprived of his sparkling, penetrating interpretations of existence, and he resists simple, sober results and methods. He appears to strive for the higher divinity and significance of man when in fact he simply does not wish to surrender the most effective premises of his art. . . . He thus holds the perdurance of his own sort of creativity as more important than scientific surrender to the true in whatever form.[69]

Whole sections of *Human, All-too-Human*, written after the break with Wagner, are attacks on and depreciations of the artistic type of person. The artist is but a child "arrested at the point where he was first overcome by the artistic impulse" and it is his mission to "make mankind childlike."[70] He would like indeed to "lighten the lives of men"—but in fact "heals and smooths only temporarily, and holds man back from working toward a genuine betterment of his condition."[71] Art "makes the face of life endurable by throwing over it a veil of cloudy thought."[72] It makes us long for religion and "at such moments, our intellectual integrity is put to the test."[73] Art induces a retrograde effect because, when it gets a grip on us, we are put into that frame of mind which prevailed when art flourished best: "we spiritualize nature and detest science."[74] It presupposes an ignorance of our true inner condition: "Art is for neither physicians nor philosophers."[75] The overevaluation of the artist and the underevaluation of the scientific man "are but puerilities of reason."[76] Regarding tragedy itself, "people only want to be moved a bit and have a good cry."[77] And, finally,

It is not without deep sorrow that one perceives how artists, in every age, have, in their highest flights, glorified precisely those ideas which we now know to be false. They are the extollers of the religious and philosophical errors of mankind.[78]

The best that can now be said of art is that it does get us sometimes to take pleasure in existence and to "regard human life as of a piece with Nature." This indeed has become part of our make-up, so that "even after the disappearance of art, the intensity and diversity of the joys for life which it has planted in us would still demand satisfaction. The scientific man is the further development of the artistic man."[79] But we are in a new era, having lived through the "twilight and afterglow" [*das Abendrot*] of art. It has served its purpose and exhausted itself as a viable institution.[80]

What remains, after all this, of *The Birth of Tragedy?* Nietzsche came to see, with the historical and systematic vision granted us when a philosophy has evolved through a man's work, that the problem to which the book was addressing itself was none of what it had failed in. It was, he saw, a philosophical essay, having to do only superficially with Greece and Wagner, intoxication and art, the birth and demise of tragedy. Rather, he wrote in 1886,

I should say today that it was the *problem of science* itself—science for the first time grasped as problematical, as questionable. . . . The question to which this presumptuous book was the first to venture upon was—*to view science through the lens of art, and art through the lens of life.*[81]*

To "see through the lens of life" means, for Nietzsche, to appreciate the role human practice plays in the furtherance and enhancement of life. Science, like art, turned out to be illusory, a fabric of our own construction, so that in contrasting the one with the other we were only contrasting illusion with illusion, neither yielding truth. But "All of life rests upon appearance, art, illusion, optics, the necessity of error and the perspectival."[82] This is a second basic idea in Nietzsche's system. We score the blank surface of reality with the longitudes and parallels of concepts, but the concepts and ideas are ours, and they have not the slightest basis in fact. This is his doctrine of Perspectivism. By his later declaration it was a central idea in this early book, and, unlike the other ideas it more famously contained, it was never repudiated by him.

* The German word *Wissenschafft* I have translated as "science," although our word has more the meaning of *Naturwissenschafft*, or "natural science." Although *Wissenschafft* generally designates any discipline of scholarship, not merely the natural sciences, it would too narrowly interpret Nietzsche's intent to translate this as "scholarly investigation" (with Francis Golffing, for example). That would make the point too parochial and too vindictive somehow, and not really very philosophical. The contrast is with art and science in a general way, not with art and just scholarship.

THREE

Perspectivism

I

NIETZSCHE held a view of human beings in accordance with which we have, for whatever reason, evolved into creatures "so delicate, sensitive, and suffering, that we have need of the highest means of healing and consolation."[1] He is not of course referring merely to modern men, for the diagnosis applies equally to the Greeks, no less "delicate children of life" than ourselves. The evidence for this claim, he would say, is to be found in the plain and patent need, apparently felt in every age and culture, for religious and metaphysical solace and for some assurance, upon some high authority, that life is not without meaning nor we without value. How else are we to account for the pertinacity of these extraordinary systems of belief than through their power to assuage? The need itself persists, however, even after these are discredited; although he felt that we cannot any longer accept either religious or metaphysical assertions in intellectual conscience:

How gratefully we would exchange the false assertions of the priests . . . for truths which were as healing, calming, and as beneficial as these errors! Philosophy can only oppose them with metaphysical illusions (at bottom just as untruthful).[2]

Art, which may have provided a substitute soporific, fails to provide the shelter we demand for ourselves; even in its highest exemplifications art can exacerbate the metaphysical hunger of a man who thought he had put behind him all such consolations:

How strong the metaphysical need is, and how difficult nature makes our departure from it, may be seen in this, that even in the free spirit, who has cast metaphysics aside, the highest workings of art can easily sound a tone from some string which has long been mute—even if it has been torn out. . . .[3]

In this way "Art makes heavy the thinker's heart." These throwbacks to one's precritical past try our intellectual integrity, and if we are to find salvation and surcease, it must derive from elsewhere than in religion, art, or metaphysics.

For a time, in what sometimes is known as his second or "Positivistic" period, Nietzsche entertained the possibility that science might answer such questions as we can meaningfully ask, and that, if through anything, "through science one really does approach the real nature of the world and a knowledge of it."[4] Moreover, he thought it at least possible that science might become an adequate substitute for the religions it replaced intellectually and the art of which it was a further development:

Can science awaken such faith in its results? In fact, science needs debate and distrust as its closest companions. Yet in time, the sum of unimpeachable truths—which is to say, those that have survived all the storms of skepticism and all reductive analyses [Zersetzungen] —will have become so great . . . that men might decide to ground "eternal works" upon them.[5]

Science, then, might give a meaning to life, and we need not, in virtue of having renounced metaphysics and religion, abandon all hope for the benefits these unquestionably provided to men. Metaphysics sought to identify solid, indubitable foundations for knowledge, detecting the ultimate "furniture" of the universe and the bases of cognition and valuation. Religion was concerned with the eternal salvation of the soul. Science, more circumspectly, through testing and trying, might yet sustain the hope of something as enduring and immutable.

He considered himself at this time to be practicing a science. With a vanity characteristic of him in every utterance about himself and his work, he called it "the greatest triumph of science."[6] This was the *science of the origins of thought*. One proposition put forward by this discipline was that religion, metaphysics, morality, and art rest on errors and originate in fear. One need not, accordingly, take seriously the claims advanced by their advocates, and one renders them sterile by showing how the problems and solutions to which they gave rise ever came about. This was a methodological device he employed constantly:

Directly the origins of religion, art, and morals have been so described that one can explain them without having recourse to metaphysical concepts either at the beginning or along the way, the strongest interest in [metaphysical problems] ceases.[7]

The chief problem in philosophy, as he saw it, was not to try to provide solutions to the questions that have divided philosophers down the ages (for which all the main positions possible are known) but rather to show how these quarrels might have arisen. Once this is clear, it no longer seems interesting or important to try to solve the problem on its own terms. To Nietzsche a philosophical problem is a question not to be answered but to be overcome; it is through science, especially the science he believed himself to have developed, that this is to be done.

This antimetaphysical, proscientific, therapeutic view of philosophy has a decidedly contemporary ring to it (i.e., the contemporary philosophy of but a few years ago), however little Nietzsche himself may have contributed to these recent attitudes. Throughout his intellectual life he remained a *soi-disant* scientist—a mixture of "historian of thought," psychologist, and even speculative physicist. He regarded his peculiar notion of the eternal recurrence as "the most scientific of hypotheses" and believed he had found scientific support for it. The spirit of scientific investigation never ceased to impress him as uniquely favorable not only for achieving knowledge but also for furnishing an atmosphere of dryness and clarity within which a man of genuinely intellectual conscience might function:

In those who give to science only a passing glance, in the manner of women and, sadly, of most artists too, the strictness of its discipline, its inexorability in small matters as in great, its rapidity in weighing, judging, rejecting, produce a feeling of dizziness and fright. The most difficult demand, the one which especially frightens them, is that one's best is to be done without reward or distinction, but rather as among soldiers. . . . The severity of science is like the form and etiquette of the best society: it threatens the uninitiated. But he who is accustomed to it may live nowhere else save in this light, transparent, powerful, and electric air, in this *manly* air. . . . In this clear, strict element he has his power whole: here he can fly![8]

Nietzsche's volumes are filled with such sentiments. "It is the mark of a higher culture to esteem more highly the little, unapparent truths, established by strict method, than the dazzling, happifying errors, which metaphysical and artistic epochs give rise to."[9] Nevertheless, science was not immune to the corrosiveness of his analysis, and he became increasingly persuaded that science, *as well as* its cultural rivals, rested on errors, accepted (as it has to) fictions which it took for truths and metaphors which it honored as description. "One must not talk about science as the blind speak of colors, *against* science in the manner of women and artists ('Ach! This wicked science,' sigh their instinct and modesty, 'it always gets underneath!')"[10] But, he goes on, the belief that science tells the only truths, much less tells the truth at all, is a naïveté. Indeed, as with the alternative modes of thought he supposed he might replace with science, the question became for him whether one could deny the basic propositions of science and still manage to survive. This was the problem, essentially, of viewing science "through the lens of life."

It is important to recall that in *The Birth of Tragedy* he had already spoken of religion and science as forms of art. "Metaphysics, religion, moralities, science—all of these are the offspring of the will to art, to falsehood, to flight from truth, to the denial of 'truth.' "[11] This of course was "art" in the wider sense. Science, like art (in the narrow sense), is creation or invention rather than discovery—a thesis which, whatever we might think of it, was hardly typical of the crude Baconian conception of science that for so long had been assumed to be the correct description of what science is and ought to be. It does not follow that we are to judge science aesthetically, any more than, in fact, Nietzsche was concerned to judge even art (in the narrow sense) that way. The criterion was always and only whether any of the structures which science exemplified enhanced and facilitated life. More than this, he felt, one could not claim, and more than this one should not need. To demand that science be true is to expose oneself to question whether "truth" means anything more than the facilitation of life. Nietzsche, as we shall see, advanced a pragmatic criterion of truth: p is true and q is false if p works and q does not.

Let us turn to Nietzsche's peculiar form of skepticism, which is not only central to his thought but also exceptional in the extremes to which he carried it. I but anticipate these extremities by saying that no distinction which we make, even the plainest distinction between thing and thing, has the slightest basis in reality. There are no distinctions between things because the concept of thinghood is itself already a fiction. That there are no distinctions Nietzsche would have termed a Dionysiac insight. But it would not have been an insight we could live with for very long. To attach a value to life is derivatively to attach a value to whatever makes life possible. Here the concept has some worth. It is important to note that this is the only criterion he would allow; whatever system of ideas fails to meet this test must be ruthlessly, if regretfully, torn away. It is always healthy, he thought, to remind ourselves that our ideas are arbitrary structurings of chaos, and the question is not whether they are true but whether we should believe them, and why. His answer was always put in psychological terms; in fact, for him every problem reduced to a problem of psychology.

II

Philosophers and plain men alike are inclined to believe that there is an objective order in the world, which is antecedent to any theories we might have about the world; and that these theories are true or false strictly according to whether they represent this order correctly. The conception of an independent and objective world structure, and the conception of truth which states that truth consists in the satisfaction of a relationship of correspondence between a sentence and a fact, are views which Nietzsche rejects. Indeed, he attached an importance to the overcoming of these views far in excess of what most philosophers—who might otherwise suppose the Correspondence Theory of Truth to be wrong, or unclear, or the belief in an objective world order to be suspect, or unjustifiable, or unwarranted by evidence—could believe this matter possibly to deserve. The typical philosopher would doubtless consider these questions to be of the most narrowly philosophical significance. But Nietzsche would take issue with them both in their contrast between a philosophical question and a commonsense one and in their implicit supposition that a philosophical theory could have no importance for the practical conduct of life.

The world of common sense in which the so-called plain man believes is a world made up of objects that are as they seem to be, are available for use and exploitation, and behave in conformity with laws so deeply embedded in the plain man's conceptual structure that he is hardly conscious of appealing to them and could not easily render them explicit. Philosophers have taken this world view more or less for granted. They have gone on to ask only whether there are in fact these objects, whether he who believes in science can accept this common-sense view, whether there might not be another world more real than this one and, if so, what connections there might be between this one and it. In taking the common-sense world as a *fait accompli*, philosophers have adopted a special stance—"setting themselves before life and experience . . . as though before a painting which is once and for all time unrolled." But they have, Nietzsche suggests, overlooked the possibility, and the significance of recognizing the possibility, that:

This painting—which we call human life and experience—evolved gradually, and is indeed still in process of evolving—and should not therefore be regarded as a fixed quantity. . . . We have, through millennia, gazed into the world with blind inclinations, passions, and fears; with moral, religious, or aesthetic demands; and have so wallowed in the bad manners of illogical thought that the world has become amazingly variegated, fearsome, rich in spirit and meaning. It has acquired color, but we were the colorists. The human intellect has allowed the world of appearance to appear, and exported its erroneous presuppositions into reality. . . .[12]

The world of common sense (impugned as the world of mere appearance by some philosophers, as the world of sheer illusion by others) is altogether the achievement of the human mind, not something, so to speak, which was found by it. "What we now call the world is the result of errors and fantasies, which, in the total development of organic being, gradually emerged and interbred with one another, and have been bequeathed to us as the accumulated treasury of the entire past."[13] So common sense is an *interpretation* (as Nietzsche will call it), not something with which interpretations contrast. It has had its origins, like any interpretation of the world, in irrational impulses, in fears and hopes and wishes, and it is to such extent indistinguishable, save in content, from any system of metaphysics. Common sense, indeed, is metaphysics made routine, just as, reminding ourselves of an earlier analysis, concepts are metaphors gone flat.

Nietzsche sustained a complicated attitude toward common sense. It was a tissue of errors and false beliefs, an interpretation only, without the slightest correspondence to reality. This sounds much like the typical philosophical repudiation of the world of sense and habit with which thinkers since Parmenides and Plato have been identified. Nietzsche goes on to say that relative to any *other* interpretation we are obliged to say that common sense is true. "Truth is that sort of error without which a particular class of living creatures could not live."[14]

"Truth": this means, in my way of thought, not necessarily the opposite of error but, in the most fundamental cases, only the position of different errors relative to one another. Perhaps the one is older and deeper than the other, and hence uneliminable because an organic being of our sort cannot live without it. Other errors, meanwhile, do not tyrannize over us as conditions of life . . . [and] can be laid aside or contradicted.[15]

Any attempt to reject common sense in favor of some allegedly more adequate scheme of things will not work. Rather, any such scheme will be false if common sense is "true" and it is incompatible with common sense. But then it would be "false" only in a sense determined by Nietzsche's characterization of "truth": it would be simply a set of errors with which our kind of organic creature could not survive or, less dangerously, which we could survive without. In the interests of life and survival, we are constrained to affirm the body of beliefs which passes for common sense and reject whatever conflicts with this. We could not defend it on any other grounds, and certainly not on the basis of its truth, if we take "true" in a more conventional sense of expressing what is the case. For in *that* sense nothing is true and everything is false.

Nietzsche proclaims time and again that everything is false. He means that there is no order in the world for things to correspond to; there *is* nothing, in terms of the Correspondence Theory of Truth, to which statements can stand in the required relationship in order to be true. In this regard, common sense is false and so is any other set of propositions false. But should that other set conflict with common sense, then it is false in another regard, having to do with the conditions of existence which we have worked out for ourselves over a long period of time. Any other system is inimical to life and to us, and must be combatted. It is a mistake to say that the problem of truth is exclusively of philosophical import. It is of most *vital* significance to get it right. Many systems of thought have claimed to be true, and indeed exclusively true, to the real nature of the universe. Often, in East and in West, these systems, as part of their contention, have adopted the view that the world in which we seem to live is but a world of appearance, of illusion, of mere phenomenality; and that all of our beliefs, which are based in this seeming world and have reference to it alone, are false in any more ultimate respect. If we seek for truth, we must then turn our back on this world (so-called) in favor of another world more real, the existence and nature of which are described through the system of thought that now demands our allegiance. This other world may be the noumenal world, the kingdom of heaven, Nirvana, Brahma, the universe of pure Forms, or what you will. Insofar as metaphysicians demand that, as a price for a different world, we turn our backs on this one, they are, Nietzsche insists, demanding that we turn our backs on life. Even though this world is made by us, and has certainly no more substance than any proposed alternative, it is the one in which we are able to live. In the interests of life we must attack these blandishing metaphysics. Nietzsche believed this to be a matter of the utmost immediate importance, which perhaps helps explain his prophetic and therapeutic fervor and tone. In themselves, philosophical problems were aberrations of the mind, insoluble and silly. Their importance lay in their threat to life; and behind each one was a will to impose its own order. As elsewhere, the strife within philosophy is a strife of will against will. Nietzsche's arguments will prove very analytical at their best, but it would represent him and his view of philosophy badly to think of him merely as an analyst.

III

It has become fashionable in recent times to defend common sense in philosophy and to reject philosophical doubts addressed toward its most entrenched beliefs. Nietzsche is not a defender of common sense in quite this way. The would-be opponents and deprecators of the categories of common sense are shown merely to have no better grounds for claiming authoritativeness than it has, while common sense itself is shown to have no basis at all in reality and not the slightest claim to truth. It is but one of a number of possible interpretations of the world, as Euclidean geometry (to use an illustration unavailable to him*) is but one of an infinite number of possible geometries. The question sometimes arises as to which of these geometries correctly describes the geometry of the physical world; a Nietzschean answer would be that not one of them does, for the world has no geometry to describe. So with philosophies, including that of common sense. There is no real world structure *of* which each of these is an interpretation, no way the world really is in contrast with our modes of interpreting it. There are *only* rival interpretations: "There are no facts [*Tatsachen*], only interpretations."[16] And accordingly no *world in itself* apart from some interpretation—"As though there would be a world left over once we subtracted the perspival!"[17] We can-

---

* Not chronologically, of course. In fact, Nietzsche read Riemann, and used the idea of a finite space as one of the "scientific" bases for his doctrine of Eternal Recurrence. But the logical implications of alternative geometries would have been clear only to someone sophisticated in the structure of axiomatic systems, and especially with the notion of the independence of axioms and the idea of models. He of course was aware of none of this.

not even speak of these interpretations as "distorting" reality, for there is nothing that counts as a veridical interpretation relative to which a given interpretation could distort: or *every* interpretation is a distortion, except that there *is* nothing for it to be a distortion of. To revert to the analogy with geometries, if we *decide* that Euclidean geometry is "true," this will be because it has worked for us for a long time as an instrument in surveying, triangulation, and other metrical activities. More we cannot say: "Euclidean space is a mere idiosyncrasy of a specific kind of animal, and is only one among many others."[18]

The doctrine that there are no facts but only interpretations was termed *Perspectivism*. To be sure, we speak of seeing the same thing from different perspectives, and we might allow that there is no way to see the thing *save* through a perspective and, finally, that there is no one perspective which is privileged over any other. These would be logical features of the concept of perspective itself. The only difficulty here is in talking about the "same thing" on which these are distinct perspectives. Certainly we cannot say what *it* is except from one or another perspective, and we cannot speak about it as it is in itself. "We cannot establish a fact *an sich*," Nietzsche wrote in an unpublished note, "and it is perhaps nonsense [*ein Unsinn*] to wish to do so."[19] We can meaningfully say nothing, then, about whatever it is on which these are perspectives. We cannot speak of a true perspective, but only of the perspective that prevails. Because we cannot appeal to any fact independently of its relation to the perspective it is meant to support, we can do little more than insist on our perspective, and try, if we can, to impose it on other people. Common sense constitutes one perspective among many. And it, no less than the others, seeks to impose itself where it can: it is the metaphysics of the masses or, as Nietzsche will say, of the *herd*.

We cannot speak of a perspective, of course, without relating it to the conditions of existence of the one whose perspective it is. "The world that we have not reduced to terms of our own being, our own logic, our psychological prejudices and presuppositions, does not exist as a world at all."[20] Thus the world is in fact only a "relation-world: it has a different aspect from every point, its being is essentially different at every point." But one cannot say that the world is then the sum of these perspectives: "for these in any case are altogether incongruent."[21] This means, then, that the only world we can significantly speak of is the world from where we are. Consequently we cannot, save as an abstract possibility, speak significantly of another world, and certainly not of one that could be intelligible to us, given the conditions under which we have evolved this one.

It is true that there might be a metaphysical world: the absolute possibility of this is hardly to be disputed. . . . But one can do very little with this bare possibility, much less hang happiness, salvation, and life from so slender a thread. For concerning the metaphysical world nothing could be said except that it would be a different world, but an inaccessible and incomprehensible one. Even should the existence of such a world be proven, this would be still the most irrelevant knowledge of all.[22]

Our perspective, which is common sense, has grown up over time and is not to be lightly set aside "for our whole humanity depends upon it."[23] Through science it may be refined here and there, but only slightly, and the chances are that "we can never break the strength of these primitive habits of thinking." All we are able to do is explain how they may have arisen and go on affirming them anyway, knowing their ancestry and falsity, realizing that "errors regarding life are necessary for life."[24] Nothing alternative to this, even if possible (there must be other possible perspectives; it makes no sense to speak of "the only perspective") could be viable, at least not for us, constituted as we are. Ours, if a fiction, is a useful and necessary one. One apparently can oppose it only with other fictions which would be superfluous or malignant. Still, there remains the possibility—a dangerous one—that if we were differently constituted, a different perspective might be ours. Philosophers had heretofore turned away from common sense, but in a spirit abnegative toward life. Would it be possible—and this was a main question in Nietzsche's philosophy—to turn away from common sense and the perspective of the herd though in the *name* of life? Can we, having once seen all perspectives as false, including any we ourselves might impose, still go on inquiring?

Recalling that *tragic* suffering is due to the perception that life is devoid of meaning and that the world is only emptiness, Nietzsche asked:

Does our philosophy not verge upon tragedy? Does not [our] truth become hostile to life and to betterment? A question seems to weigh upon our tongue and not wish to make itself heard: whether one can consciously remain in falsehood. Or, if one must, whether death might not be preferable. . . . The whole of human life is sunk deep in falsehood. The individual cannot draw it up out of this pit without becoming angry with his past for the deepest reasons; without finding his present motives, such as honor, absurd; and without opposing, with scorn and disdain, the feelings which press toward future happiness. Does there really remain only one way of thinking open to us, one which entails despair as a personal result, and a philosophy of dissolution as a theoretical one?[25]

He thought not. He thought it would be possible to face the emptiness without succumbing to it, and his philosophy is an attempt to show how this is to be achieved. It would be premature to try to say what his entire philosophy endeavors to express; for the moment it is enough to see the complicated polemic situation in which his queries seemed to place him. He had at once to criticize common sense (the philosophy of the herd) and to defend it against all the traditional philosophical and religious criticisms. This is one reason why his writing is difficult for the casual reader to follow. He wants to know where Nietzsche stands, and to this a simple answer cannot be given.

But other things are also likely to puzzle the reader. There seems somehow to be a basic inconsistency in Nietzsche's use of the word "truth." He writes, for example, "There is no pre-established harmony between the pursuit of truth and the welfare of mankind."[26] But "truth" had been defined specifically in terms of what was useful to the welfare of mankind. Since Nietzsche opposes the harmful and the useful, *Nutzen und Nachteil*,[27] what is false is what is harmful if the useful is what is true. One can call common sense into question not in the name of truth but in the name of falsehood, unless one has in mind a different sense of "truth." Nietzsche actually did not keep apart the use of "true" or "truth," for which his own theory of truth specified the rules, and a more ordinary sense of these terms which enabled him to speak from an extraperspectival standpoint *about* perspectives, declaring all of them false. Although he had developed a pragmatic theory of truth, he often spoke in an idiom more congenial to the *Correspondence* Theory of Truth which he was trying, not always and perhaps not ever in the awareness that he was doing so, to overcome. The inconsistency is not in his thought so much as in his language. Like many innovators, he was not quite sure of the theory he invented, or perhaps that he had even invented a new theory. So the reader finds odd dissonances in his writing, somewhat like architectural disharmonies in a transitional church, where the style being groped toward has not yet emerged, and the architect might not even be sure that he is groping toward a new style at all.

This leads us to a further difficulty. Nietzsche's is a philosophy of Nihilism, insisting that there is no order and a fortiori no moral order in the world. Yet he sometimes wants to be saying what the world is like. The world is made up of points of origin for perspectives. He goes still further and sees these points as occupied by active powers, wills, each seeking to organize the world from its perspective, each locked in combat with the rest. This is the beginning of his notorious and utterly misunderstood doctrine of Will-to-Power. In the end, then, he too has his metaphysics and his theory as to what its structure and composition ultimately must be. If Nihilism depends in any logical way upon this view, then Nihilism is false or, if it is true, it entails the falsity of its own presuppositions and cannot be seriously asserted. There is a crucial tension throughout Nietzsche, between a free-wheeling critic, always prepared to shift ground in attacking metaphysics, and a metaphysical philosopher seeking to provide a basis for his repudiation of any such enterprise as he is practicing. Does Perspectivism entail that Perspectivism itself is but a perspective, so that the truth of this doctrine entails that it is false? Would this be what he spoke of in *The Birth of Tragedy* as logic turning round on itself and biting its own tail? Or is this only a seeming paradox, soluble somehow or other? I do not believe Nietzsche ever worked it out, although I am convinced he was aware of it. At the end of this study I shall try to suggest the outlines for dissolving the problem, if there can be any dissolution at all. But here it is enough only to suggest that there is a twofold sense of metaphysics, just as there is a double sense of truth and a narrow and a wide sense of art. Many of Nietzsche's more infuriating paradoxical utterances can be clarified if we recognize his shifts in the use of a term. When he uses the term "metaphysics" he often has in mind only a philosophy that speaks of a reality which is higher and purer than the one we are seemingly acquainted with through the senses. His critique of such philosophies is worth considering in some detail.

IV

Although he is often classed as an antirationalist, Nietzsche in fact opposes reason only when reason is opposed to life, or to whatever makes life possible. Like Hume, he considers that reason is or ought to be the slave of passion, even though rational structures have as one of their functions the transformation and sublimation of passions which, were they given complete license, would lead to barbarism. Philosophers, who have enjoined a life of reason, have often seen the body as the captive place for our higher faculties seeking release, and the passions as distractions from a higher vocation. Depreciation of the body motivates depreciation of the senses, and the opposition between sense and reason has its origin in this distrust. Such *theories* of reason, not reason as such, are the target for Nietzsche's antirational attacks.

Consider, for example, the slighting attitude taken toward the senses by the Eleatic philosophers or by Plato. The Eleatics were persuaded that reason informs us of certain truths which are altogether contrary to what sense experience shows. But it is self-contradictory to deny a *rational* truth. Sense, opposed then to rational truth, must be inconsistent. But no rational person would affirm an inconsistent proposition. Hence no rational person can accept propositions based on the senses. Plato notoriously propounded the thesis that the senses at best reveal a secondary order of reality. They give us grounds for beliefs only, but never knowledge—for knowledge can be only of what is truly real. Whatever strengthens or flatters the senses holds us captive amid appearances and unreality. Philosophers down the ages have acquiesced in this deprecation. Descartes dismisses all beliefs based on sense experience as corrupt at the source and seeks, instead, for some intuitable propositions, clearly and distinctly understood and known to be true solely by virtue of being so understood. Even empiricists, who denied that we had access to any truths *not* based on sense experience, were sufficiently in the shadow of the rationalistic tradition to take a dim, skeptical view of the scant, uncertain knowledge afforded us only by the senses. Empirical propositions were deprecated, even by empiricists, by applying to them criteria which have proper application only to rational propositions, and which empirical ones can only fail to satisfy.

Nietzsche's views on sense experience, and the manner of his empiricism, will appear as we go along. He was certainly never an empiricist in any reductive sense of that term, but he was convinced that reason could not seriously be accepted should it propose theses contrary to the senses' evidence—even though the relationship between our beliefs and sense experience is a complicated one. This was his attitude throughout, and not merely in his so-called positivistic phase. In the *Twilight of the Idols*, one of his last and best books, he writes: "We possess science today strictly insofar as we have decided to accept the testimony of the senses—to the extent that we sharpen, arm, and learn to think through them." He continues: "The rest is miscarriage and not-yet-science. I mean metaphysics, theology, psychology, and theory of knowledge. *Or else*: formal science, sign-theories: like logic and that applied logic, mathematics."[28]

This is a singular passage in many respects. It is a banality, among those who speak diagnostically about contemporary culture, to see two dominant philosophical trends in the present world—an irrationalistic one, represented in Existentialism, and a rationalistic one, represented in Logical Positivism and its outgrowths. I shall not concern myself with this characterization, however out of sympathy I am with those who suppose that it says something important or even true. I want only to emphasize that Nietzsche, who is so naturally taken as a predecessor of the irrationalistic tendency in contemporary philosophy, in his own writings exhibits attitudes toward the main problems of philosophy which are almost wholly in the spirit of Logical Positivism. To begin, there is a policy throughout his books to undermine rather than to refute philosophical claims, his point being that to refute one is often to accept another, when it is the *whole problem* together with its array of "solutions" which must be extirpated. This radical attitude anticipates the Positivistic dictum that the utterances of philosophers are neither true nor false but "nonsense," and the perennial problems which have exercised them are only "pseudo problems." Nietzsche says, concerning his own procedures and methods, that he puts metaphysical teachings "on ice": "One error after another is laid calmly on the ice—the Ideal is not refuted, it is frozen. . . ."[29] Second, Nietzsche employs here (though it would be an exaggeration to say that he always does so) the same criterion of meaningfulness famously advocated by the later Positivists. They contended that those propositions are meaningful which fall into one of two classes: propositions verifiable through sense experience, and propositions certifiably true (or false) by virtue of their meaning alone. Any sentence which is of neither class is "meaningless," and metaphysical propositions are in this last class. Nietzsche holds such a view of metaphysics, at least insofar as the latter pretends to furnish us with positive and even profound knowledge of the world. It is strictly nonsense: "The *Ding an sich* is worth a Homeric laugh, since it *seems* to be so much, to be *everything*, when really it is empty—empty of meaning."[30] But it is not enough, for him at least, to be content with showing metaphysics to be senseless: this is just a first step. That there should be metaphysics at all is something which requires explanation.

Nietzsche's affinities to analytical philosophy (and not merely the parochial theories of meaning in Positivism) are nowhere more evident than in his preoccupation with language. Common sense is after all expressed in ordinary language; in speaking the language we have learned from infancy, we are implicitly prescribing how the world is to be viewed and comprehended: "Every word is a preconceived judgment."[31] Through our speech we perpetuate errors of a philosophical order. Bertrand Russell once spoke of ordinary language as embodying the metaphysics of the New Stone Age. He contended that if we are to seek a more adequate philosophy, we must work out a new language, one which does not commit us from the start to judgments we are unaware of making. If philosophers have become more reluctant today to criticize ordinary language in just these revisionist terms, they are at least prepared to suppose that there is a philosophy (even the correct philosophy) embedded in the language we employ; some philosophers go further by saying that such philosophical problems as there are arise through deviations from the correct employment of words in specified contexts. It would of course be a distortion to suggest that Nietzsche anticipated the discussions which have so dominated philosophy in recent years. But he is unquestionably a predecessor. We shall see problem after problem attacked by him through reference to what he identified as misleading modes of expression—which happen to be the modes of expression everywhere employed. It seemed clear to him that men are seduced by the grammar of the language they speak, and implicitly believe they are describing the world when, in fact, the world as they conceive it is only a reflection of the structure of their tongue. "There lies hidden in language," he writes, "a philosophical mythology which breaks out at every moment, however careful one might be."[32] In a long passage, "Language as a Presumptive Science," he continues:

The importance of language for the development of culture lies in this, that through language men erect a world of their own alongside the real world, a position they hold to be so fixed that from it they hope to hoist the other world off its hinges and make themselves master of it. . . . Man really thought that in language he had knowledge of the world. The language-maker was not modest enough to realize that he had only given designations to things. Instead, he believed that he had expressed through words the highest knowledge of things.[33]

In general, whenever primitive man laid down a word, there he believed himself to have made a discovery. How different it really was! He had hit upon a problem, and thinking he had solved it, he in fact only raised an obstacle to its solution. And now, with every piece of knowledge one must stumble over stone-hard, everlasting words—and one would rather break a bone than a word.[34]

Although Nietzsche felt that men were beginning to recognize, if only dimly, that they "had propagated an immense error"[35] in taking language literally, he also suggested, characteristically, that "happily it is too late to reverse the development of reason, which rests upon this error."[36] It is fortunate because of the role that language has played in the economy of human survival (we are what we are because we think and speak as we do): "Error has made men out of animals."[37]

The specific role of language in the development of philosophy may be seen in the interconnectedness of philosophical concepts. These do not develop sporadically and on their own, but, he asserts,

> grow up in relationship to and in interconnection with one another, so that however suddenly and arbitrarily they seem to make their appearance in the history of thought, they nevertheless belong to a system much as do the members of the [species of] fauna in a given part of the earth. This is to be seen in the fact that the most diverse philosophers will surely fill out a definite ground-scheme of possible philosophies. A hidden something keeps them running in the same charmed circle, no matter how independent of one another they might feel themselves to be. . . . Their thinking is less a discovering than a recognizing, a recollection, a coming home to a distant, primeval mental condition, out of which these concepts first took their growth. . . . The amazing family resemblance [sic: Familien-Ahnlich-keit] of all Indian, Greek, and German philosophizing is simply enough explained. Precisely where there is a linguistic relationship, it is not to be avoided that, thanks to a common philosophy of grammar—I mean thanks to the unconscious domination and guidance through the same grammatical functions—everything is prepared in advance for a similar development and order of philosophical systems. For the same reason, the way seems closed to the possibility of a different interpretation of the world.[38]

It would seem to follow directly that any world view different from our own could not be expressed in any language with the same structure as ours. This will have some philosophically important consequences for Nietzsche's own thought. Meanwhile, we might underscore certain grammatico-philosophical elements of our linguistic family which impressed Nietzsche as being especially pernicious intellectually, however indispensable in practice. He sometimes wondered how men who speak in unrelated languages must construe the structure of the world.

The first element is what Nietzsche regards as virtually an inescapable tendency on our part to posit entities—to think in terms of *things*—and to regard the world as characterized by "unity, identity, permanence, substance, cause, thinghood, and being."[39] These notions, which are the stock in trade of conventional metaphysics, are due completely to our language:

Language, at its origin, belongs to an age of the most rudimentary form of psychology. We enter a realm of gross fetichism when we become conscious of the fundamental presuppositions of the metaphysics of language or, in plain words, of "reason." . . . I am afraid we shall not get rid of God until we get rid of grammar.[40]

Epistemologists have often been concerned with the assumption we all make spontaneously: that there are objects which continue to exist between our perceptions of them, and the existence of which does not depend upon anyone's perception. In making this assumption, common sense is asserting, implicitly, a philosophical proposition of the most audacious sort. Again, we spontaneously subscribe to the old doctrine of substances insofar as we think, or speak, of something "being the same" despite undergoing changes. We do not suppose that we are referring to different things when we say at one moment that something is green and sometime later say that it is yellow. We think, rather, that it is the very same thing which exists, *itself* unchanged, which is now one color and now another. We scarcely can help construing the world as made of permanent objects which are the subjects of change: "every word and sentence we utter speaks in its favor."[41] Nietzsche wishes to say that we are wrong, "There are no things: that is our fiction."[42]

This is not a fiction we could readily get along without, either in daily life or in science, the latter being a refinement of common sense in Nietzsche's view. "We operate with things which do not exist: with lines, surfaces, bodies, divisible times and spaces."[43] These concepts have a *use*. But they do not denote anything in the world; accordingly, sentences which make an essential use of them are not true because there is nothing for them to be true *about*. Such sentences, therefore, have no explanatory value, as Nietzsche uses the term "explanation"; that is, they are interpretations rather than genuine accounts of the world: "It has begun to dawn upon five or six persons that physics, too, is only an interpretation of the world and an arrangement of it (to suit ourselves, if I may say so!)—and not an explanation of it [though] it is taken as an explanation."[44]* The concept of the atom, for example, involves an essential reference to something that does not exist: "In order to comprehend the world, we have to be able to calculate; in order to be able to calculate, we require constant causes. But since no constant causes are to be found in reality, we invent some for ourselves, e.g., the atom. This is the origin of atomism."[45]

It is tempting to speculate that what Nietzsche has in mind here is what philosophers of science today discuss as "theoretical entities"—entities postulated by certain terms which play a highly systematizing role in the theories utilizing them, but which, if they denote any entities at all, denote unobservable ones. A much-debated question is whether these terms may be eliminated in favor of a purely observational vocabulary. The details of this issue are beyond the scope of this volume, but perhaps it will serve to locate Nietzsche's attitude on this point to say that he has in mind a far more sweeping thesis than the one which holds that theoretical entities, as defined in recent discussion, are fictions. Rather, *all* entities are in that sense theoretical, and any such reference to concrete particulars is fictive:

We have arranged a world for ourselves in which we might live, with the accepting of bodies, lines, surfaces, causes and effects, motion and rest, form and content. Without these articles of faith, no one now would be able to live! But this hardly constitutes a proof. Life is no argument. Among the conditions of life, error might be one.[46]

* The opposition is between *eine Welt-Auslegung und -Zurechtslegung,* on the one hand, and *eine Welt-Erklärung* on the other. This same passage, from *Beyond Good and Evil,* has a complicated reference to sense evidence, which I refer to later. The distinction between "interpretation" and "explanation" is obvious enough, and it is found throughout Nietzsche in one way or another. See, for example, *Daybreak,* p. 428.

These "articles of faith" are part and parcel of the structure of our thought, from its most practical to its most theoretical employment, in daily life and in science. Owing their origin to a primitive psychology, woven into the grammatical fabric of our language, "they have been inherited to become, finally, almost the condition of the human species."[47] Granting the empiricist thesis that reliance upon the senses is indispensable for knowledge, knowledge must be understood instrumentally, and we cannot truly accept the simple empiricist account of how our knowledge develops. "So much by way of retort," Nietzsche adds at the end of a discussion of language in *Beyond Good and Evil*, "to Locke's superficiality with regard to the origin of our ideas."[48] He does not, however, wholly endorse the Kantian revision of empiricism which holds that there are some propositions, not derivable from experience, which nevertheless are genuinely cognitive, and these—the synthetic a priori judgments—are inherent in the structure of the human mind, which could not operate intelligibly without them. Nietzsche concedes that *we* could not indeed think other than in conformity with them, given the manner in which we have developed:

It is time to replace the question of "How are synthetic a priori judgments possible?" with "Why is the belief in such judgments *necessary*?" We must understand that such judgments must be believed true, however false they are in nature, just in order that beings of our sort may be preserved. . . . We have no [other] right to them: on our lips they are plain falsehoods. But the belief in their truth is necessary as a foreground belief . . . belonging to the perspective optics of life.[49]

Nietzsche surmises that "innumerably many beings, who reasoned differently from us, have perished. Yet *they* might have been closer to the truth."[50] What he has in mind is something like this. Consider the generalization that all A's are B's. Unless an individual were sufficiently gross in his discriminations, so as to be able to overlook differences between things which he then regards as effectively the *same*, he could never have arrived at such generalizations. These indeed require abstraction. Nevertheless, he might have perceived each thing as it is (assuming that there are things), and so have been "closer to the truth." Yet to the degree in which his sensitivity inhibits his power to generalize, his chances for survival over his coarser fellows are poorer. *Their* inductive successes would be all the greater in proportion to their capacity to disregard individual differences. "Every hesitancy in drawing inferences, every propensity to skepticism, is already a great danger to life."[51]

This of course is a weird argument. Rationality depends upon our capacity for abstract thinking, and certainly there would be scant likelihood for survival should we actually perceive the world as sheer, undifferentiated flux. We are obliged "to invent signs and formulas, with the help of which we may reduce the swirling complexity to a purposeful, useful scheme."[52] Nevertheless, this general conceptual scheme is a tissue "of lies and frauds,"[53] taken (necessarily) as true. "What are mankind's truths? They are the *irrefutable* errors of man."[54] All our most fundamental concepts must be regarded merely as lucky hits in the struggle for life and power:

Through immense stretches of time, the intellect produced only errors. Some of these proved useful and preservative of the species. Whoever hit upon or inherited these fought the fight for himself and his descendants with greater success.[55]

V

Nietzsche does not weary of making sly points about the unreasonableness of reason, arguing, tongue in cheek, and by appealing to the principle of *a minori ad majus*, that the universe can hardly be very rational if the part of it consisting of *human* reason is as unreasonable as it is.[56] His more serious philosophical point is that we are going to find the universe rational, or logical, only to the extent that we have made it so through imposition: "The world appears to us logical, because *we* first *logicized* it."[57] As for logic itself, and mathematics (which he spoke of as applied logic), this too, for all its alleged purity, arose psychologically and has no basis in fact. This of course is hardly a dashing thing to say about logic, although the psychologism that underlies it would doubtless be contested today. But Nietzsche means to argue somewhat as follows: If there are no things, a fortiori there are no things which are equal to one another or identical with themselves. Yet the relations of equality and self-identity are essential in the elaboration of logical systems. When applied to the world, these systems virtually demand that what we apply them to should be entities, each of which is self-identical, and some of which may be equal to one another. Men then are misled into thinking there *are* such things. But, once again, this is not an unfortunate thing. If it were first known to men that there are "no precisely straight lines, no real circles, no metrics," then "mathematics would never have arisen."[58]

Philosophers, however, should know better:

Instead of seeing logic and the categories of reason as means for the purpose of arranging the world for our own use (thus "in principle" as useful falsehoods), it [philosophy] sees them as touchstones of truth, and believes it has to do with reality. In fact the criterion of truth is merely the biological utility of such a system of "in principle" falsehoods. . . . The naïveté consists in taking an anthropocentric idiosyncrasy as the measure of things, as a guide to the "real" and the "unreal."[59]

It is not this alone, however, that Nietzsche charges against the philosophers. It is that philosophy turns back *against* the common-sense world in the name of concepts which are presupposed by the world of common sense—and then declares the latter to be illusory. After declaring as real only what has "unity, identity, permanence, etc.," philosophy rejects the things of common sense—the "world of appearance"—because they fail to exhibit these traits. But in fact the very things repudiated are projections of the categorical traits they are said not to exemplify. Metaphysics has repudiated the common-sense world on its own terms, by erecting a supernumerary world which is only the conceptual skeleton of the world to which it is said to be superior and more real. Once this is seen, the notion of the "true world"—as distinct from the "apparent world"—is revealed as a *useless* and self-stultifying fiction. Because it is superfluous and useless "[it is] therefore a refuted idea. Let's get rid of it!"[60]

Once quit of the so-called "real world" we have nothing against which to contrast the "apparent world"; as the latter expression derives its only significance through a spurious contrast, it too is a spurious expression. "With the true world we have gotten rid of the apparent world too."[61] The only remaining problem is to see what motivates philosophers to turn against common sense, and this would take us ahead of our story.

Perhaps I should add a few words about a further and somewhat different contrast which is sometimes made between the so-called common-sense and the so-called *scientific* pictures of the world. Nietzsche was much concerned with this.

Many men, not only metaphysicians, have questioned the world as conceived of by common sense. Since Galileo, if not long before, it has been customary for scientists, whose discoveries sometimes conflict with the findings of plain men (by the "unaided senses"), to dismiss these findings as having to give way before an allegedly more justifiable conception. The heliocentric theory, the theory of evolution, psychoanalytical theory, the concept of the curvature of space, the fourth dimension, the electronic theory of matter— each one, in some way, seemed simply to dissolve before our eyes certain conceptions which at one time would have been thought to be unsusceptible to challenge. The scientists of the seventeenth century went so far as to maintain that the crucial predicates in the language of science (as we would speak of it today) are in no sense observation predicates. Rather, they are terms which have reference to "primary qualities" of objects. These terms require no explanation, even if they could be explained (as they allegedly could not) in terms of observation predicates. The "secondary qualities," expressed in observational language, were stigmatized as "unreal" in contrast with the primary qualities of the world. So, as Nietzsche puts it, "The physicists believe in a 'true world' after their own manner."[62]

That some of our concepts should have collapsed in the light of science would hardly have dismayed Nietzsche: they all are false anyway, and essentially are subject to challenge on grounds of greater utility. Nothing is impervious to that. Nor is there anything sacrosanct about observational language, for the terms here are already structured in such a way that it would be pretense to suppose that we see what the world has to show: we have learnt to see comformably with our language. Nietzsche, however, could not be expected to tolerate the boast that science, in repudiating common sense, has discovered the "true" world. Rather, it would have developed some useful tools and read off them, so to speak, an ontology equally suspect with that of common sense. It is just here, as a precocious philosopher of science, that Nietzsche's difference from the Positivists of our time is perhaps plainest, however sympathetic he might otherwise have been to their antimetaphysical animus. Science is not a summary of sense observations but a creative organization of the world, an arrangement which stands to observation in complicated ways.

The Pole Boscovich has proved to be, along with the Pole Copernicus,* the greatest and most successful enemy of "what meets the eye" [die Augenschein]. Whereas Copernicus had to persuade us to believe, contrary to all our senses, that the earth did not stand still, Boscovich taught us to disavow the final "fixed" thing in regard to the earth— the belief in "substance," in "matter," in the little residual earthly clot—the atom. This was the greatest triumph overt he senses that was ever achieved on earth. One must go further and give up the need for atomism. . . .[63]

The physicist is not philosophically abreast of his own theories and discoveries. He is likely to suppose that the atomic structure of matter is just a statement (if not the statement) of how the world really is, having nothing whatever to do with us, with the way we think. But in fact the need to posit entities is wholly a matter of how we think:

The atom, which [the physicists] posit, is inferred in accordance with the logic of consciousness-perspectivism [Bewusstseins-Perspektivismus] —and is thus itself a subjective fiction. The world picture which they project is through and through indistinguishable in essential respects from the subjective world-picture. It is but construction by thinking through the senses, but they are our senses.[64]

The structure of physical thought is the structure of our ordinary thought. Because we take things to be real, and not mere con-

---

* It must be recalled that Nietzsche prided himself on being a Pole and thus in the natural line of succession to his illustrious fellow countrymen.

venient "arrangements," we naturally are going to credit scientific reference to *hidden* things as more than arrangements too. We will think of them as genuinely explanatory. "Physics has our eyes and ears on its side."[65] So it is in the end somewhat disingenuous for physicists to pretend to have erected a structure which displaces common sense. Essentially, structurally, the physical "real world" is our world too, with perhaps a different mythology. In contrast with the fictions of metaphysics, those of science are useful. They contribute to human vitality and increasingly make us masters over the world—again unlike metaphysics, which is hostile to life and this world, beckoning us on to another and better one. In this regard, Nietzsche endorses science, as long as it does not credit itself with having done more than it has actually achieved. For example, discovering the truth. It has not done that. For there is none to discover.

VI

Enough has been said to make clear what must be the general outlines of Nietzsche's Perspectivism. He did not work it out with any rigor, or in great detail, but he thought it through consistently in a number of areas and applications. We are left with a good many problems (indeed most of the problems of philosophy), and to certain of these I must direct my attention before turning to some of the more elaborate discussions of aspects of his teaching. Perhaps the best way of doing this is to discuss his notions of the concept of causality, of which he offers an analysis very much like Hume's.

Hume arrived at an analysis of causality which entails that causes do not occur in nature. Rather, nature, or our experience of nature, consists in isolated events (or, more strictly, in isolated perceptions of events); *causes* simply are relations between pairs of events. "Causes" is a two-place predicate which takes classes of events for its terms. These will be classes whose members have been found constantly conjoined; and the alleged necessity of the causal relationship was analyzed away, by Hume, as purely of psychological origin and consisting solely in a habit of mind. Nietzsche's discussion is much along these lines. Even though there are very few references to Hume in his writings, he may very well, for all I know, have derived his views from Hume. There are some differences, however.

Hume felt that we did not and could not have access to the "hidden springs" which genuinely move the world, because we are separated, as it were, by an impenetrable curtain of our own experiences from the world as it really is. It is not easy to see with what justification Hume, by his own criteria, could sensibly *talk* about objective causes. Like Nietzsche, he frequently expressed his skepticism in the language of the views he meant to attack; moreover, he seems to have taken some gloomy satisfaction in saying that we never shall penetrate to the truth of the world's causalities. Nietzsche believed, as Hume should have, that the concept of causality has no application outside our experience, so that the notion of "objective cause" must be strictly meaningless if it suggests something any different from what the word has been analyzed to mean in terms of experience. But, as so typically happened when Nietzsche wrote, he expressed his views in an objective mode by saying, simply, that there are no causes in the world.

A certain thing is each time followed by another. We, when we perceive it and wish to give it a name, call it cause and effect. What fools we are! We have but seen the image of cause and effect. And this makes it impossible for us to see a more fundamental connectedness [*Verbindung*] than constant conjunction.[66]

This is fairly straight Humean doctrine, but the following posthumous note deviates somewhat:

Causality is made by thinking *force* into sequential processes. A certain "understanding" emerges through this—we have anthropomorphized the process, made it "intelligible." [But] the intelligible is only the customary. . . .[67]

There is no great disagreement with Hume, except, first, that the building up of our causal conceptions (not our concept of causality) is more a social than an individual process: "Hume was right about habit, but it was not merely the individual's habit."[68]

Second, our notion of causality is rather more a projection of our own image than the quotations so far suggest; that is, we tend (he says) to think of the effect as the *purpose* of the cause. I shall take up his claim later when I discuss the perspective of psychology. Now it is important only to state Nietzsche's suggestion that with our concept of causality we are helplessly locked into our own perspective, since the causal tie is between *discrete things,* and it presupposes a generalization process he has characterized as mythopoetic.

A continuum stands before us from which we isolate a pair of fragments, just in the same way as we perceive a movement as isolated points and therefore do not properly see but infer it. . . . There is an infinite set of processes in that abrupt second which evades us.[69]

The concept of causality is therefore a fiction because it logically depends upon fictions. There are no separate things to be related, and hence no true relations between isolated things. Finally, in *Beyond Good and Evil*—which we may always take as representing his maturest philosophy—he writes:

One should not mistakenly objectify [*verdinglichen*] "cause" and "effect" in the manner of the natural scientist (and whoever, like him today, thinks naturalistically). . . . One should make use of "cause" and "effect" as pure concepts only, that is to say, as conventional fictions for the purposes of designation and communication, *not* for explanation. In the *an sich* there is nothing of "causal connection," of "necessity," or "psychological unfreedom." There is no following of effect after cause. No laws hold. It is *we alone* who have invented the causes, the after-one-anothers, the for-one-anothers, the relations, the constraint, the number, the law, the freedom, the ground, the purpose. And if this sign-world is thought into things, as though they were something in themselves, we conduct ourselves once again as we always have done: we think mythopoetically.[70]

This is an exceedingly radical view. We are familiar enough with a train of philosophical thinking which, since Kant at least, has maintained, in much the manner of Nietzsche here, that various structural features which we think are inherent in the world are instead only our ways of thinking about the world, having no objective residency. But Nietzsche has gone further along this path than have most philosophers. Kant, after all, had maintained, perhaps to the detriment of his system, that there are things-in-themselves, outside of space and time and causality. But the *Ding an sich* is precisely a notion Nietzsche wants to "freeze," for it leads to a debasement of the "apparent world." To make another comparison, he is, like Spinoza, thoroughly disposed to reject the view that there is any moral order in the world, or that the distinctions between good and evil, right and wrong, beautiful and ugly, have any location in the world—"order, structure, form, beauty, wisdom, all are absent: [there is] to all eternity chaos." But he goes beyond Spinoza, who understood nature to have levels and distinctions, attributes and modes, as well as to conform to an iron logic of law and necessity. Like the *Ding an sich*, the Spinozistic notion of *substance* is frozen, it is repeatedly exposed to Nietzsche's critical accusations of "fiction," of "invention," and, more interestingly, as a *Verdinglichung* of grammar, where the grammatical subject of our sentences is converted, through the mythopoetic working of the primitive mentality of man, into the substance of the world.[71]

Nevertheless, Nietzsche could not quite bring himself to the point of becoming an idealist, for whom there is no world outside the articulations of the mind. Nor could he quite become a phenomenalist, believing that whatever is finally meaningful can be expressed in terms of our own [sense] experience. He could not do this because he felt, and not so differently from either Kant or Spinoza, that there was a world which remained over, tossing blackly like the sea, chaotic relative to our distinctions and perhaps to all distinctions, but there nevertheless. To some extent he was seduced by his own arguments. Because he wanted to say that all our beliefs are false, he was constrained to introduce a world for them to be *false about*; and this *had* to be a world without distinctions, a blind, empty, structureless thereness. In fact he never surrendered this residual belief, and he came, in time, to speculate whether something after all might not be said about the real world.

If there is such a world, it should be possible, after all, to say something about it. But what language we might use to say it must tax the intellect. For the languages we have commit us spontaneously to a metaphysics of the world it is meant to describe which must be false. And we have no other language. Nor have we, finally, the security that a new language we might frame would not commit us to a metaphysics any less suspect than the one we had hoped to have overcome. Nietzsche never sought for a new language, although I believe sometimes that his frenzied employment of poetic diction, his intentionally paradoxical utterances, and his deliberately perverted use of terms might be taken in the spirit of the Zen *koan*, calculated to crack the shell which linguistic habit has erected between ourselves and reality and to expose us to open seas. The incapacity of ordinary language to express his own visions, without at the same time and through the very expression of them distorting his thoughts and locating them in a system of implications which it was (partly) the purpose of his thinking to *destroy*, explains, perhaps, why he thought his philosophy was hard to understand. Strictly, it should almost have been impossible to understand. How are we to understand a theory when the structure of our understanding is itself called into question by the theory we are asked to understand? Would it not follow from the fact that we had understood it at all that we had misunderstood it? Because the concepts by means of which we had achieved understanding were just the wrong ones? If we are asked to understand in a new way, how are we to understand this new request? There could be no lexical bridge between our language and any that Nietzsche might frame. For then ours would be a translation of his, having the same meanings, preserving the same truths. That language would have to be learned anew, just as we have learned ours. But how it would be learned is hard to say. The act of ostension—pointing to what a word stands for—would be ruled out if there were no separable things at which to point. At best or, if you wish, at worst, Nietzsche's view of the world verges on a mystical, ineffable vision of a primal, undifferentiated *Ur-Eine*, a Dionysiac depth.

Yet if he was a mystic, it must be said of him that the motives which drove him had nothing to do with a union of himself with the object of his insight, nor had he the mystic's, or the Dionysiast's, hunger for self-obliteration. He was less interested in characterizing the world as it might be in itself than he was in bringing repeatedly, harshly, and unceasingly to our attention that what we believe about the world is all wrong, a web and meshwork of our own spinning, which we have cast upon a faceless world and then read as the world's physiognomy. He was less interested in stating what was true than in telling what was false.

But this then explains, as I have suggested, why he thought his teaching must be a dangerous one. For just to get into a position for understanding it must expose one to a certain peril. We could hardly survive in terms of it as human beings, for *our* survival is keyed to the concepts repudiated by his philosophy. Yet could we not perhaps, in some extraordinary way, survive in some other form? Need we perdure merely as human, all-too-human? Are there no other possibilities open to us? Why not try to go beyond man? Why not try to work out a different range of concepts which might liberate us from what we are? We might become something better, even though our new beliefs were no truer. One set of instruments can, after all, replace another.

We perhaps will never achieve truth in the old correspondence sense of the term. We can hardly be expected to do so if we will always require some system of concepts, and if any such system is an Apollinian imposition upon chaos. We could not in the nature of *saying*, say what was true. But, as we have seen, there was a quite distinct and liberating sense of truth in which we could always say something truer than what we had said previously. Those sentences which are capable of carrying us conveniently over the chaos, even though they are absolutely erroneous, are true in virtue of their success. In this regard, whatever has so far worked is insofar true. But surely others can work too. There is room for system after system, for the most daring experimentations. Let us, then, experiment with truth, he would say, and see whether we are able to find a language and a philosophy better than the one we have. A new language and a new philosophy, indeed, for a whole new sort of being, because we *are* what our language has made us, serving as the instrument of survival for just the sort of creature it has made us. Truth in the *deep* sense, the sense of corresponding with reality, is perhaps not very important and possibly not at all useful: "Truth is the most impotent form of knowledge."[72] Truth in the instrumental sense is crucial and exhilarating. The deep sense of truth has only a negative importance, assuring us that whatever we might believe is false. The instrumental sense is important for life, and in its name we might impose ourselves in such a way as to be transformed into fantastically more vital creatures. This was a liberating view for Nietzsche, and it made philosophy a singular adventure for him. It must be said that even in its most presumptuous phases, philosophy hardly ever claimed for itself a greater role than this.

FOUR

Philosophical Psychology

I

I HAVE spent some time in laying out Nietzsche's thesis, endlessly elaborated in his many books, that what passes at any time for knowledge is but a confection of simplifications and falsifications, brought forth out of ourselves, by means of which we may house ourselves in the blank, indifferent universe. "Our cognitive apparatus is an abstracting and falsifying mechanism," he writes in the *Nachlass*, "directed not toward knowledge but rather toward mastery and possession."[1] We have managed to live, and even to enjoy life, at the price of persisting in ignorance, and this is so no less in what is taken to be human knowledge in its highest exemplifications, in the sciences, in mathematics, and in metaphysics, than in the simplest and most ordinary thinking. The architectural forms of our scientific theories

have heretofore been allowed to arise only upon the solid granite foundation of nescience [*Unwissenheit*], and the will to knowledge upon the basis of a far more powerful will—the will to not-know, to non-certitude, to un-truth. And not as its opposite but—as its refinement! . . . We understand, and laugh over the fact, that the best of science wants best of all to hold us fast in this through-and-through artificial, thought-arranged, falsely-arranged world. How it unfree-willingly-willingly loves error because, being alive—it loves life![2]

We know, accordingly, only what has been prearranged to count as knowledge, and we remain forever imprisoned within ramified structures which, like spiders, we have produced ourselves; we must seek cognitive nourishment only on what is sufficiently gross not to pass undetected through the interstices.[3]

There are surprisingly few arguments in Nietzsche's writings to sustain these conclusions with which, by now, the reader hardly can be unfamiliar. Even when support of one or another sort is offered, it often consists in an appeal to facts about which, outside the context of the argument, Nietzsche could, and sometimes does, raise at least as many doubts. He might, for example, quite savagely impale a given scientific theory through appealing to another which he considers utterly to demolish the first—though in perhaps the same book he will write off the whole of science as fictive, distorting, and irrelevant. One has the sense throughout these books of an irresponsible shifting of ground, and an infuriating skeptical jugglery in which the juggler is part of the whirl he manages to keep aloft through some miraculous feat of light-handedness. The serious reader wants to protest that an impossible trick is not a trick at all, and that irresponsible doubts are neutralized by their very hit-and-miss casualness. Something, one wants to say, must be kept constant, some place to stand must be retained, and it is then only *groundless* doubt to doubt everything. One might, with equal justification—since justification has been ruled out—*believe* everything, for there can be no distinction between groundless belief and groundless doubt; it would be as meaningful, perhaps, to say that everything is true as to dramatize everything as false. Nietzsche was in no sense the circumspect epistemologist, retreating, stage by stage, from class to class of propositions, each of which is immune to the doubts that rendered untenable the class before it until, finally, some impregnable position, some doubt-proof sanctuary, is achieved.

Nietzsche sought no such asylum, and he regarded the quest for certainty as a measure of our weakness:

Some still have need for metaphysics. But also that violent *longing for certainty* which expresses itself these days in the scientific-positivistic masses, the longing always to get at something fixed . . . this is still the longing for a handle and a support, an *instinct of weakness* which, if it does not create religions, metaphysics, persuasions of every sort, nevertheless conserves them.[4]

His views regarding truth might be taken as rendering impertinent the epistemological quest for foundations, for if language is to be assessed *only* instrumentally, the question of certitude and permanence is beside the point, because the criteria of adequacy lie elsewhere. His own skepticism is stated from within the enemy camp, so to speak, using the old notions of truth and falsehood to throw his own into relief. And doubtless he would be right in supposing that the quest for certitude in knowledge goes hand in hand with a belief in fixity in the universe.

Surely, none of the familiar stopping points would have served him. He had already characterized logical sentences either as empty or false when taken as descriptive, though he thought it absurd to construe logic so when in fact it is a tool for operating with assertions rather than a set of assertions in its own right. So too with mathematics, which, in case it is regarded as descriptive, would require the existence of utterly fabricated entities. Synthetic a priori judgments are immune to doubt only because they are the least expendable of our errors; but they are dubitable to the extent that our entire conceptual scheme is. Many of the kinds of propositions ordinarily contrasted with those that philosophers have found it "possible to doubt" thus turn out to count for very little, the fulcrum of the contrast lying elsewhere than in their alleged incorrigibility. Conventions are supported by conventions and not, as one might have hoped, by the nonconventional bedrock of epistemology.

There remain, among the candidates for propositions which have sometimes been advanced as impervious to doubt, certain propositions about ourselves: introspective reports, "protocol sentences," descriptions of immediate experience, and the like. I may, Descartes suggested, doubt whether any of the ideas I entertain correspond to anything whatever outside myself; and I may doubt whether there is anything outside myself to which they may correspond. Yet I can hardly doubt that I *have* these ideas; and the more such doubts as I find myself able to raise, the more I discover about myself; and propositions about myself, Descartes felt, cannot be queried or seriously denied. *That* he was and *what* he was appeared to Descartes to be two of the things he knew with certitude: that he existed and was a thinking being were matters apprehended with the utmost clarity and distinctness. Whatever reservations philosophers since may have had with points in Cartesian philosophy, they have often acquiesced in Descartes's conclusion that skeptical quiescence is at last achieved in our knowledge of ourselves and of the immediate contents of our own consciousnesses. Nietzsche permitted himself no such comfort. There is nothing, he insists, about which we are more and more frequently wrong than we are about ourselves. There might, we can imagine him as arguing, be some validity to the objection that unless something is taken as certain, nothing can be seriously doubted. "Taken" is indeed apt; "stealing" might be a more honest description. We have no guarantee that our theft has netted us an honest truth, however, and the grasping implication of the word "take" perhaps should be retained, for it connotes the way in which men fumble for a handhold in the shifting chaos in which they dwell. There is no soporific like a good fiction; and no fiction as good as that we have snatched an unassailable truth when we have only laid down a stipulation. But to take for true knowledge of *ourselves*! That passes all limits: *nothing* could be more dark! We have hardly begun to locate the surface, much less scratch it.

The human mind and its limits, the precincts heretofore reached of inner experience in men, the height and depth and breadth of this experience, the whole past history of the mind and its still uncharted possibilities—this is the hunting ground of the born psychologist and the companion of the Great Hunt. But how often must he say, desperately, to himself: "One man! Alas, only one, single man! And this great forest, this primeval wilderness!"[5]

Nietzsche esteemed himself a born psychologist—"a born, inevitable psychologist and soul diviner"[6]—and despite the relative sophistication we have attained in our post-Freudian era concerning the devious origins and uses of our mental furniture, we can be stunned at times by Nietzsche's sure diagnostic hits. Some of the things he says about sex, for example, that most canvassed of psychological topics, go beyond what many thinkers have come to believe. It is, however, his contribution to *philosophical* psychology—his analyses of the logical behavior (as it is nowadays fashionable to say) of mentalistic concepts—that I shall be mainly concerned with here. For these complement his Perspectivism, insofar as we can separate them from the perspectival analyses just discussed; and they serve, in part, to explain some of Nietzsche's moral and religious theses. There is, as must appear more patent as we advance, a cluster of circularities in Nietzsche's thought. Our psychological theories are part of our perspective; but our perspective is to be explained with reference to psychological phenomena which are part of it. Our moral attitudes are responsible (in part) for the perspectives we seek to impose, including our psychologies; but psychology is appealed to in explanation of our having the moral perspectives which we do. Nevertheless, psychology is fundamental in Nietzsche's outlook, and, however intertwined it is with other parts of his thinking, it must be given a treatment of its own.

II

Nietzsche much approved of the psychological researches of his friend Dr. Paul Rée (who was his rival at one time for Lou Salomé, and then the third corner in an ideal projected *ménage à trois* with Lou and Nietzsche); and sometimes he spoke punningly of his own theories as "Réelism." But for the most part he regarded psychology as a completely skewed domain of inquiry, chiefly because of moral prejudices and fears:

The spirit of moral prejudices has pressed deeply into the most spiritual, and, seemingly, the coldest and most unprejudiced domain—and, as goes without saying, has damaged, blinded, obstructed, and distorted. A proper physio-psychologist has to battle with unconscious resistances in the heart of the investigator himself.[7]

Descartes, as we shall see, was hardly immune to pressures which he was perhaps unable even to acknowledge as operative in himself; and the self which he claimed to have discovered as his essence was no less a shadow cast by moral attitudes than the atom was a (perhaps unwitting) posit set down by grammatical coercion. Indeed, the two concepts are reflections of each other. For the material atom was allegedly an indestructable, impenetrable quantum of matter, which did not (and logically could not be said to) change, though all changes were accounted for in terms of it. What is the self but a dematerialized atom? The belief in the permanence and indestructibility of the self (or soul) is simply "psychic atomism—that fateful atomism best and longest taught by Christianity."[8] If things are fictions, mental entities are no less so; if the belief in material substance is misguided, the belief in mental substance is no less erroneous. "Matter is exactly the same sort of error as the god of the Eleatics," Nietzsche writes in one place,[9] and in another, "If there is nothing material, there is nothing immaterial either."[10] We shall see that it is always more or less Nietzsche's predictable view that distinctions between inner and outer, between matter and mind, and comparable polarities, come to nothing; and that, being logically correlative with one another, any attempt to deny the reality of one pole at the expense of the other is meaningless. One must accept either both or neither of these antitheses; and Nietzsche always presses for neither, virtually as though it were his methodological directive to abolish distinctions whenever found. Whatever description he will finally give of reality as he sees it, it will at least have to be neutral to any of the distinctions we are accustomed to draw. So there is, so to speak, no psyche, as a substance, which it is the task of psychology to explore. Psychology, rather, has to do with the way in which we organize our lives—if we may construe this in the broadest possible terms—and hence it stands fair to "once again be recognized as the mistress of the sciences, all the others preparing the way and serving her. Psychology is once again on the way to the basic problems."[11] Thus did Nietzsche conceive of his task. But, by his own diagnostic pronouncement, in order to get on with it he had to disabuse himself of the moral prejudices which heretofore had disfigured and maimed psychological inquiries. He fought, thus, on two fronts at once. He hoped to attack morality (or moralities, rather) by exhibiting the illogicality of the psychology it (they) stood com-

mitted to, and to attack this psychology by attacking the moralities it presupposed. The attack upon the soul, or self—in which he
claimed to find the gist of modern philosophy—was at the same
time "an assassination attempt upon the fundamental presupposi-
tion of Christian doctrine."[12]

It is somewhat difficult to lay out Nietzsche's psychology in full
array without having before us his doctrine of Will-to-power,
which it would be inconvenient to present at this point. I shall
save that for the last, because it serves to integrate many of the
things we must discuss. Synoptically speaking, however, one mode
of the Will-to-power consists in an imposition of forms of thought
upon reality, and language is a form of thought. But language is
a falsifying structure, alien to whatever it is imposed upon,
although it serves to organize the latter for the purposes of the
speaker. Language interprets, in the sense of arranges, reality; and
interpretation is an instance of the Will-to-Power. One is always
tempted to say that someone *does* the interpreting, for it is difficult for us to think that interpreting is an activity which goes on
by itself, as it were, without someone doing it. To the extent that
it is difficult for us to see this, we show how far embroiled we are
in the metaphysics of our language and how difficult it is for us
to speak in a Nietzschean idiom. It is entirely a matter of our
perspective being as it is that we feel constrained to seek an agent,
an actor, for each activity, and a subject for each verb. We are
altogether dominated by this view that something must be responsible for whatever goes on; and we are wrong to be dominated by
it. "One must not ask 'Who then interprets?'—for interpreting
itself, as a form of the Will-to-Power, has being (but not as a
being . . .)."[13] This hints at the complexity of the Will-to-Power
doctrine. We need this much of it anyway if we are to find our
way through Nietzsche's involved discussion. We must always
bear in mind that he is thinking of active processes or powers as
having a certain reality, from which it does not follow (according
to him) that there are entities which act or exercise powers. The
concepts of agents and of active entities are *impositions* once
again. Let us document some of this as we proceed into the
psychology.

The idea of a *thing* has been rendered suspect, and therewith the idea of a *thinking* thing or subject:

The subject, too, is such a creation of imagining, thinking, sensing, and wishing, a "thing" like any other: a simplification for the purpose of designating the *power* which supposes, invents, and thinks, as distinct from all supposings, inventings, and thinkings.[14]

This is reflected in our language, or is a reflection of it, the psychological and the grammatical subjects being of a piece:

One believed in the soul as one believed in grammar and the grammatical subject. We used to say that "I" is the condition, "think" the predicate which conditions—thinking being an activity for which a subject, as cause, *must* be thought.[15]

Predictably enough, given the structure of Nietzsche's philosophy, a mythical interpretation of language hardens into a metaphysic of mind; we end by believing in our own invention, laying down a "self" which is distinct from and causally related to "its" own activities. Because the Ural-Altaic language group has a weakly-developed subject form, any philosophers brought up to speak those languages "in all probability look out upon the world differently from, and follow different directions than, Indo-Germanic or Arabic [thinkers]."[16] Regardless, because of the subject-predicate form of our sentences, *we* are metaphysically coerced into thinking that whenever something happens, there is an entity, separable from the happening, whose effect is the happening. Or better, that the happening is an activity [*Tun*] of an agent [*Täter*]:

Reason believes in the ego, in the ego as substance, as a being, and projects this belief in ego-substance onto all things. It first creates thereby the concept of a thing. . . . Being, which is construed as cause, is thought into things, and *shoved under* them: the concept of "being" follows and is derived from the concept of the ego.[17]

It is in this way that our physics and our psychologies are images of one another (which makes a logical space for the Unity of Science!) and in which our world conceptions are anthropomorphic projections. Indeed, our concept of man is an anthropomorphization, to speak perversely; for after all, the self, the ego, and the soul are inferred entities, based on our prejudice that something must underlie, as its agent, whatever happens—including thoughts. Physics and psychology have, then, a common etiology and a parallel, mythic structure.

Causal necessity "is not a fact but an interpretation."[18] It now turns out to be based on the distinction between subject and object, the subject acting upon the object and standing in alleged causal connection with whatever happens in the object as its *effect*. If we surrender the concept of "thing," hence of subject and object, we necessarily and at the same stroke surrender our conception of causality. A path is opened then for a whole new way of thinking (which will prove to be the Will-to-Power doctrine). "A great deal," Nietzsche hints, "follows from the recognition that the subject is not something which 'effects,' but is merely a fiction."

If we no longer believe in the effecting subject, the belief in the effecting thing collapses, as well as the reciprocal action of cause and effect between those phenomena that we call things. . . .

The *Ding an sich* also collapses: for this is basically the conception of the Subject-in-itself. Once we understand that the subject is an invention, the opposition between *Ding an sich* and appearance becomes untenable—so the concept of appearance collapses.

When the *subject* is given up, so is the *object* it works upon. . . . If we give up the belief in subject and object, then the concept of substance goes too—and, as a consequence, all those other modifications, e.g., material, "mental," hypothetical entities, the eternity and immutability of substance [*Stoff*], etc. We are free from *substantialism*.[19]

It would be remarkable to find that so vast a philosophical structure indeed rests upon so fragile a grammatical foundation, or that a mere shift in grammar could pay such immense philosophical dividends. The proper evaluation of these stupendous claims lies beyond the scope of this volume. If the history of philosophy had so turned out that Nietzsche, who anticipated so much of contemporary philosophical thought, had instead been a direct influence on it, one might say that the circumspect work being done from a linguistic point of view in philosophical psychology today is a collective and continuing evaluation of these seminal ideas. At any rate, if Nietzsche should be right, we would be obliged to concur with his wry, rhetorical query whether, after all, "the belief in the concept of subject and predicate is not a huge stupidity?"[20]

III

If I have correctly maintained that in his final description of the world in its reality, Nietzsche must employ an idiom neutral as to the common distinction between mental and material, then the Will-to-Power must seem an inconsistency. Will, after all, is a mentalistic term. In fact, however, this is not quite the case. For Nietzsche no more than for Schopenhauer are we to associate the ordinary mentalistic connotations with the term "will" in its metaphysical employment. The Will-to-Power is not mentalistic; unless this is emphasized from the start, a good many of Nietzsche's destructive remarks on the *psychological* concept of the will are going to pass as inconsistent or unintelligible. He wishes to attack a notion, subscribed to not only by philosophers, that there are such things as *acts of will*, performed by us (and by agents in general), with reference to which our various actions (bodily and mental) are to be explained. Acts of will (read: volitions) stand to actions as causes to effects. Thus, when I voluntarily raise my arm, this is to be understood as the effect of a causal act of will. "Reason generally believes that wills are causes . . . that the will *is* something that *effects*, that the will is a power. . . . Today we know that it is only a word."[21]

At one point in the *Enquiry Concerning Human Understanding,* Hume raised, and dismissed, the possibility that we do after all have an experience to which our idea of the causal nexus might correspond—the experience, namely, of the operation of our will upon bodily parts or upon our thoughts. We have, Hume countered, absolutely no idea of how the will operates, and, whether seriously or in irony, he speaks of the connection as utterly mysterious and dark. If only for purposes of polemic, Hume goes along with the supposition that there really are acts of will; in this respect Nietzsche's discussion is the more radical. It is not that the connection between will and whatever it acts upon is dark, but rather that there is nothing *between* which and our actions a connection is to be sought. In other respects his analysis resembles Hume's,* except that he dismisses the belief in volitions as an instance of the Error of False Causality. "We believed ourselves to be causal in the act of will: we thought that here, at least, we had caught causality in the act."[22] But presupposed in this bit of self-congratulating was not merely a mythical notion of explanation and a mythic entity (the will), but a belief (which is *the* Cartesian belief) that our own mental processes are immediately transparent to us, that we know how we think and which mental processes are taking place, that we know this directly and not inferentially, and that there is no room here for error. Nietzsche's destructive analysis here is to compass and "freeze" a number of interconnected ideas. I shall work my way back to the will through a number of intermediate steps.

Let us consider the celebrated intuitive certitude we credit ourselves with possessing, in regard to mental processes we are living through at a given moment. Descartes at the moment of doubting could not doubt that he was doubting—or at least could not doubt that he was thinking (doubt being a case of that), and so that something was thinking at the time; namely, himself. It follows that he thought and existed: *cogitabat ergo erat*. Already we must see in this celebrated argument a prime exemplification

* It is odd that Nietzsche, whose thought bears such singular resemblances to Hume, so seldom cites his skeptical predecessor. Of course he would have known of him through Kant, but the sparsity of reference suggests his acquaintance to have been at second hand. Salter, in *Nietzsche the Thinker*, finds only two references. There are more, but the fact that Salter, a careful scholar, should have remarked only two indicates that they are not plentiful. One might suggest that Nietzsche, concerned to emphasize his own originality, would have suppressed references. But this would have been silly; he was enough of a scholar to know better. Besides, he was always delighted to find a predecessor. He was overjoyed when he first read Spinoza. He wrote to Overbeck on July 30, 1881, that it made him feel less alone and perhaps on the right road. I incline to suppose that he did not know Hume directly. Writers whom he did know directly come up frequently, e.g., the Abbé Galiani, who was only a wit. Nietzsche's poor eyesight prohibited wide reading after his academic days.

of the impulse to assign an agent to any event, in this instance a subject that does the thinking, whose existence follows, through the courtesy of grammar, from the fact that thinking of some sort is taking place.* In fact, Nietzsche maintains, the correct analysis of "I think" is exceedingly complex; and Descartes carried with him so vast a set of unacknowledged presuppositions that it is difficult to begin to make explicit everything that would have to be true if *cogito* were to be true. It is neither so clear nor so distinct a matter as Descartes pretended. Yet "even today there are harmless self-observers who believe that there are 'immediate certainties,' e.g., that 'I think.' "[23] It may be all right for ordinary men to believe in immediate certitudes—or certitudes at all— but

The philosopher must say to himself: When I analyze the process which the sentence "I think" expresses, then I obtain a set of rash judgments, the establishment of which is difficult and perhaps impossible. For instance, that *I* am, which thinks; that thinking is an activity and the effect, on the part of a being which is thought of as its cause; that there is an ego; that it is already determined what "thinking" is to designate—that I know what thinking *is*. For, had I not already decided upon this, how should I be able to say whether what is going on might not be willing, or perhaps feeling?† Enough! Each "I think" presupposes that I compare my momentary situation with others, which I recognize, in order for me to determine what it is; and as a consequence of this referring back to other "knowledge," this situation has no "immediate certainty" for me.[24]

There are, indeed, answers to so many hard metaphysical questions assumed in such a statement that Nietzsche finds it difficult to see how anyone dare suppose they could be grounded merely upon "appeal to an intuition of knowledge"; this deserves from

---

* " 'It is thought, consequently there is a thinker.' Out of this originates the argument of Cartesius. But this means that our belief in the concept of substance is already taken as 'true a priori.' That when thought occurs, there must be something which *thinks*, is merely a formulation of our grammatical habit of supposing a Täter for every *Tun*."[25]

† In fairness to Descartes, these would have been instances of thinking, just as doubting was. Descartes leaves room for being wrong as to whether he is doubting, but not whether he is thinking. He may be mistaken in the instances, but not in the case.

the sophisticated philosopher "a smile and two question marks."[26] In the end, it is far from clear that "I"—supposing this designates something—does anything at all: "A thought comes when it will, not when 'I' will."[27]

As with the *cogito*, so with the alleged direct intuition I have, according to Schopenhauer and others, of "I will."[28] "The philosophers tend to talk of the will as though it were the best-known thing in the world: indeed Schopenhauer gives us to understand that only the will is really known, known from top to bottom, and without discount or surtax."[29] In fact, this is not the case. There is no simple, separately identifiable mental operation known and directly intuitable as an act of will: "There is no will: that is only a simplifying conception of the understanding."[30] Rather, what we take to be an act of willing is something which is "above all, complicated, and which has unity only as a word."[31] The "forever incautious philosopher" has been dominated by the unity of the word to infer the unity of the phenomenon, but the phenomenology here is exceedingly complex, and should we decide to be "unphilosophical" for a moment (as Nietzsche sardonically puts it), we find something like this:

In every willing there is first of all a multiplicity of feelings: the feeling of a condition from which we get *away*, a feeling of a condition *to* which we go, the feelings of this "away" and of this "to" themselves. Then again an accompanying muscle-feeling which, even if we do not set our arms or legs in motion, comes into play, through a sort of habit, the moment we "will."

Then there is a concomitant of ongoing thinking:

There is a commanding thought—and one had better not suppose he can subtract this thought from "willing" and have the will itself remain over!

Finally,

The will is not alone a complex of feelings and thoughts, but is above all a passion [*ein Affekte*]—the passion of the command. . . . A man who wills commands a something in himself which obeys, or which he believes will obey. [But] we are at the same time commander *and* commanded; and as commanded, we know the feelings of forcing, pushing, pressing, resisting, and moving which begin directly after the act of will.[32]

It is because all of this is conflated, designated by a single synthesizing name, and assigned the personal pronoun that "there arises a whole catena of erroneous inferences, and consequently a false estimation of the will."[33] Perhaps the chief such fallacy is the belief that "willing suffices for action."

One may disagree with the accuracy of this phenomenological analysis. There is, I think, very little of the sort of thing that Nietzsche here identifies as feelings of commanding and obeying, not at least in connection with voluntary actions, so-called. His description sounds more apposite to certain effortful pieces of behavior, for example, rising up from bed when one would languish, shouting inner encouragements and threats to one's resisting self. When one does something "unwillingly," one might suppose this to be done in consequence of an exercise of the will, and then transfer, from such grudging cases of behavior, the mechanism of "will power" and resistance to the normal case where in fact there is none of this resistance within oneself. Perhaps the reluctant riser is a paradigm of the alleged efficacy of the will, and Nietzsche is simply discussing the paradigm. Whatever the case, when the sleep-drugged man engages in that unedifying inner combat, he might in the end conclude that he springs finally to his disinclined feet as the result of a volitional shove, and so raises, by an act of will, the hulk of his somnolent carcass. This may be our myth.

What Nietzsche wants most to insist upon is that the so-called act of will is taken to be sufficient for the execution, say, of a bodily motion or a thought, only because the latter was an *expected* event on the part of the individual who credits himself with acting. We learn, in what I suppose Nietzsche would regard as an inductive manner, how our body is going to behave under standard conditions. We do not consider the will to have been operative in the case of unexpected bodily motions which take us by surprise. Or again, if my body begins to act strangely, in unexpected ways, and outside the normal repertoire, I should not suppose these were *my* acts. Nietzsche, indeed, is inclined to believe that just as a thought comes when it will and not when I will, so my body moves when it will and not when I will. Because we behave in reasonably predictable ways, and habits of expectation arise, and we refer our bodily behavior to ourselves as subjects (*Täter* to *Tun*), we claim credit for the action: *L'effet c'est moi*. Then, inasmuch as our concept of cause and effect requires every event to have a cause, the will is introduced in explanation of our behavior. Successful prediction gives us a sense of power "which all success produces." Nietzsche suggests that the same thing happens here as happens in any community: the ruling class identifies itself with the community.

This is a singular analysis, and a detailed explication would require more space and subtlety than would deserve to be given it in a book of this sort. There is, I think it fair to say, little in the preceding literature of philosophical psychology to match it, either in penetration or in refinement, and it is only since the epochal work of Wittgenstein that philosophers have come at all near to analyzing mental concepts with a comparable finesse. Whatever we may think of the details of the picture he has sketched, we can see plainly enough why Nietzsche felt justified in concluding that the will should not be credited either with existence or power. "The inner world is full of false pictures and spooks, and the will is one of these. [At best] it merely accompanies what goes on, and can even be absent."[34]

If there is no will, there is no free will (nor unfree will either).[35] This is too abrupt an inference: the doctrine of free will does not depend at all upon a psychological theory of the will as a mental phenomenon; "free" has application to actions, not to the will. Nevertheless, it sometimes is offered in support of a claim to having free will that we have an immediate datum of freedom. But Nietzsche argues that this in fact consists only in a pleasurable feeling one has when one's body is behaving in an integrated and effective manner. Had we no expectations of how we should be behaving from moment to moment, we would have no sense of freedom; and we would have no expectations if our body behaved randomly and sporadically. It is through the building up of habits and expectations that we achieve our feeling of being free; and this then depends on what one might term the lawlike behavior of the body. One might anticipate that Nietzsche would be saying what amounts to the current thesis that free will is compatible with determinism and inconceivable without it. He might acknowledge the attractiveness of such a position, but the logical interdependence of the two traditionally antithetical notions would be for him mainly an excuse to excise the entire problem. Both positions, in fact, stand or fall together, he felt, much as with the antitheses of the real and the apparent world; the free-will controversy could, accordingly, be "put on ice." Indeed this is his strategy for the most part. The notion of the free will owes itself, he claims, to a "logical rape." But he adds:

Suppose that someone gets somehow behind the peasantlike artlessness of the famous concept of the free will, and drives it out of his head. Then I bid him to carry his "enlightenment" one step further, and drive that counter nonconcept [*Unbegriff*] out of his head too: I mean the "unfree will," which derives from a misuse of cause and effect.[36]

He has, of course, long since abandoned cause and effect as a fictional pair of concepts, convenient but undesignative. So let us, he urges, put away "two popular concepts, necessity and law: the first imposes a false coercion, the second a false freedom, upon the world."[37] Finally, as far as autonomous or self-caused behavior is concerned, this is "the most contradictory notion ever thought up."[38] It tries to fuse two antitheses, which are bogus at any rate, into an impossible synthesis. The correct exit is not to *affirm* both sides in the controversy, as this idea seeks to do, but to deny each of them by showing how they depend completely on a sham physics and a false psychology.

It then remains only to explain why people are interested in taking one or the other side in the old feud. Nietzsche's answer is typically psychological. The one group wishes to avoid giving up, at any price, its own personality and faith in itself. The other side wishes "to get rid of the burden of themselves at any price."[39] In the philosophical controversy which has dominated Western discussion for centuries, we find, if I may make the inference these words suggest, behind new masks as it were, the old counter-posed antagonisms of the Apollinian and the Dionysiac person-alities: the Principle of Individuation opposed and interlocked with the Principle of Primal Unity!

IV

The inner and outer worlds are images of each other, projec-tions and reflections, each of each, and the reality of the world is captured in neither our mental nor our physical sciences. The per-spective which the latter imposes is only an exportation of false ideas concerning ourselves. We have not yet gotten to the heart of Nietzsche's psychology, and it would be mistaken to suppose that he worked it all out merely in polemic with philosophers. In part he was endeavoring to break the grip of a prejudice we are almost unaware that we are dominated by; namely, that we know what we are better than we know anything in the world. Each of us is convinced that however others may be mistaken about our feelings and sincerity, we ourselves cannot be in error, and that we exercise, in at least this one domain, an unimpeach-able authority. This prejudice is underwritten by the common philosophical teaching that we have immediate access to the workings of our own minds. But consciousness as such, or con-sciousness of ourselves (hereafter self-consciousness) has seldom been submitted to any refined philosophical analysis. Perhaps it is because the knowledge I am alleged to have of myself in self-consciousness is considered direct and intuitive that the phe-nomenon has been thought to be too simple for analysis. For what could analysis produce which would be any simpler or more readily comprehensible? And what can we know better than the manner in which we know ourselves, since nothing is more con-stantly within our scrutiny than consciousness itself? Be this as it may, Nietzsche offers a remarkable and, to my knowledge, utterly original theory of consciousness which I shall now try to describe. This will serve, I hope, to connect a good many loose strands and to conduct us to the core of his psychologizing.

Let us first distinguish between consciousness and *self*-consciousness. There is a connection, of course, but not everything that is conscious is self-conscious. A dog might be aware that someone is calling him, but he need not be aware that he is aware; his consciousness is not, presumably, something of which he is conscious. Here we are concerned with "knowing that we know" in contrast with merely knowing. Some philosophers have contended that there is no difference, that it is the same thing to know and to know that one knows. Whether this is so or not it is generally acknowledged that human beings (at least) are in possession of this reflexive knowledge of themselves celebrated in the introspective tradition of philosophy. Nietzsche wants to know *why* this should be the case: Why are we self-conscious?

"Consciousness first becomes a problem for us when we begin to appreciate the degree to which it is dispensable."[40] For the fact is that "we could think, feel, will, remember; we could likewise 'act' in every sense of the word; and yet none of this would need to 'come into consciousness' (to put it metaphorically)."[41] What Nietzsche is saying is plain enough: Much of my behavior is automatic, and much of what I do I am not "aware of" when I do it, or I can become aware of it only when I make a special effort of self-observation. I should, for instance, have to direct careful attention to my fingers, while typing, in order to know or to become aware of which keys they happen at the moment to be touching. Mainly, I type without looking at them, and without being conscious of where they are at the time they are there. Then, of course, a good deal of the activity of my mind goes on without my being aware of it. Remembering, for example, is seldom something I am conscious of doing, although I must be doing it all the time. Also, it very seldom happens, and then only in pathological moments, that "the interplay of bodily functions *ever* comes into consciousness."[42] Imagine what it would be like if we had to be aware of the breakdown of fats, or if digesting was something *we* had to do. Consciousness, in this regard, does not accompany much of what is most efficient in the working of the body; the question is why it is needed anywhere. Nietzsche acknowledges the phenomenon and supposes that it developed, fortunately, only late in the evolution of the human species.

Innumerable mistakes stem from consciousness, bringing it about that an animal or a man is destroyed before it is necessary. . . . Were it not that the conserving bond of instincts were so much more powerful, [consciousness] would not serve as a regulator: through its wrong judgments, and open-eyed dreaming, its superficiality and credulity, in short, through consciousness, man would otherwise have long since been destroyed.[43]

Consciousness is, and always has been, a "danger to the organism." Where the mind and the body (speaking with the vulgar) operate mechanically, there is mechanical efficiency. But where consciousness supervenes, there is suddenly room for clumsiness and error. This sounds like an authentically Nietzschiesque teaching, and out of context it would, or could, reassure the suspicious reader that Nietzsche was anticipating the horrendous Nazi injunctions to "Think with the blood!" or, more innocuously, the current fashionable and nostalgic admonitions, by novelists and self-appointed social critics, that we revert to the instinctual life which has been so bruised by civilization, and find self-fulfillment through aggression or sex. With this sort of atavism Nietzsche has scant sympathy, and he is stating only the beginning of a difficult philosophical idea. To be sure, in most of our vital functions we can and do get on without the operation of consciousness; and much the same also holds for many of our higher activities. It is, moreover, important to recognize that consciousness may indeed be a danger to its possessors. But this is so, Nietzsche urges, because it is only an insufficiently developed "organ" in our make-up. Because it has come into existence late in the evolutionary scale, its scope and function are not plain and its power not yet optimal. Until it develops further, we need the protective unconsciousness of our instincts, releasing us for attention to other things. Before repudiating consciousness, we had better determine its function. For (and the implicit methodological principle behind this is apparent), "Consciousness is there only insofar as it is useful."[44] Since, however, "the whole of life might be possible without its seeing itself, so to speak, in a mirror; and [since again] even now the largest part of life is actually played off without this mirroring—even thinking, feeling, volitional life, however painful this may sound to the older philos-opher"[45]—the question must be what extra function consciousness discharges. We cannot assume that it is wholly superfluous, for the question of its existence at all would then be intense.

The answer, which is certain to sound odd at first, is that consciousness has little to do with the individual himself, who might indeed get on in some instinctual and automatic fashion. It has rather to do with relations between individuals. Nietzsche offers what he calls "an extravagant hypothesis." The "funda-mental mistake" is to think of consciousness as an individual attribute, and the highest form of individual existence, rather than "understanding it as a tool in the collective life."[46] Con-sciousness is "only a means of communication; it is developed in [social] intercourse, and with regard to social interests."[47] The "strength and subtlety [of consciousness] stand in proportion to the capacity for communication of man (or animal); the capacity for communication in turn being proportional to the need for communication."[48] This *is* an extravagant hypothesis, but it is a philosophically fascinating one, which requires careful elucidation.

First, the formulation suggests, which it does not intend, that he who is the greatest master of communication is he who stands in greatest need of communicating and is hence in the greatest need of society. Nor is it intended to say that we are only con-scious when we have a need to communicate. It is rather that in social life, over a long period of time, both for the preservation of the group and for the individuals who are its members, there is a continuing need for "rapid and subtle communication"; what is termed consciousness "generally has developed only under the pressure of a need to communicate."[49] It does not follow, of course, that what one might call an act of consciousness *now* is always a response to such a need, but only that consciousness "as an organ" developed as the result of such need. Thus we our-selves are able to use idly what developed in response to necessity, just as, supposing that language itself emerged in response to a need to communicate, it would not follow that language, once developed, could not be used in a number of ways, including just to babble. The critical point in Nietzsche's theory, which is intimately bound up with his theories of language, is that "consciousness is only a connecting network between man and man" and that it "developed only in proportion to its utility."[50] Reflection, which philosophers have often taken as essentially a *private* performance, is *social* in its origin; it rose in answer to a social need or, if you wish, the individual's need for society: "As the most threatened of animals, man needed aid and protection."[51]

Should men then have developed in relative isolation, as "wild beast sorts of humans," they would not have become conscious of themselves, for there would have been nothing for them to communicate with. Such persons, supposing they could survive, would get along on a purely instinctual basis. But in fact it is unlikely that men could have survived so: the nonsocial human is more a *Gedanken Experiment* than a real possibility. The human infant is almost totally dependent on ministrations of others. He has to make known his needs and "for this he required consciousness: he had to know what he lacked, to know what he felt, and to know what he thought."[52] He has to express his needs with accuracy or else perish; accordingly, "the development of language goes hand in hand with the development of consciousness." It is "only as a social animal that man becomes conscious of himself."[53]

Thinking as such need not be conscious. There is no contradiction in the concept of unconscious thought. "Man, like every living creature, thinks continuously without knowing that he does: the thinking which becomes *conscious* is the smallest part, according to us the most superficial and the worst part." But then, "only what is conscious comes into language, that is to say, in communication-signs, wherein the origins of consciousness reveal themselves."[54] Paradoxically enough, it will follow that allegedly private words—words which have reference to our own inner states—form the basis and the original part of our common and *public* language. According to Nietzsche's analysis, the structure and the content of our inner world, as that of the outer world, are constituted out of distinctions we have found it useful to make. These, in turn, are reflected in our language. In this connection, one cannot but think of the views of J. L. Austin—

a philosopher as remote from Nietzsche as it seems possible for someone to be and still remain a philosopher. Austin wrote: "Our common stock of words embodies all the distinctions men have found worth drawing, and the connections they have found worth marking, in the lifetimes of many generations."* For Nietzsche, there is nothing in consciousness which is not essentially public; and the words we employ to describe our interior lives are precisely the words we use to express the needs that must be serviced if we are to continue to exist, and these words must be understood by others if the needs are to be taken care of:

> My motion is that consciousness does not belong to the individual existence of men, but to what is the community- and herd-nature . . . and consequently that each of us, with the best will in the world of understanding himself as individually as possible, of "knowing himself," will always bring into consciousness the nonindividual and the average. . . . Our thought is always translated back into the perspective of the herd.[55]

Consciousness, accordingly, expresses the "genius of the species," and "even if our actions are, at bottom, to an incomparable degree personal, unique, and absolutely individual," still, "as soon as we translate them into consciousness, they no longer appear so."

Of all Nietzsche's theses, this one is perhaps in closest harmony with contemporary views. It is traditional to philosophy to suggest that in trying hopefully to describe the world I never am doing more than describing my own experiences, that I have no grounds for knowing whether anyone else's experiences are remotely like my own or even whether others have any experiences at all. If they have, they must always be understanding me in terms of their experiences, and so we never understand the same things at all, or at least cannot know that we do. Nietzsche's point is that unless I am understood, I could not survive, and if I survive, I do so on the same terms as others, for my words will have had to be understood by them. This is logically little different from the account given of the possibility of private languages in Wittgen-

---

* J. L. Austin, "A Plea for Excuses," in *Philosophical Papers* (Oxford: Oxford University Press, 1962), p. 130.

stein's *Philosophical Investigations,* which has been the basis for so much contemporary discussion. It strikingly resembles the conclusions reached by P. F. Strawson, so much so that I must cite the following passage from Strawson's book on descriptive metaphysics:

There would be no question of ascribing one's own states of consciousness, or experiences, to anything, unless one also ascribed, or were ready and able to ascribe, states of consciousness, or experiences, to others of the same logical type as that thing to which one ascribes one's own states of consciousness. The condition of reckoning oneself as a subject of such predicates is that one should also reckon others as subjects of such predicates. . . . If *only* mine, then *not* mine at all.*

It is, as Nietzsche puts it, "our relationship with the outer world which has developed our consciousness." It is philosophically disingenuous to raise doubts about the external world on the basis of consciousness and our purported intimate relationship with, and epistemologically superior access to, our own states of mind. Yet Nietzsche draws some consequences from this analysis which later philosophers would disagree with in all likelihood.

V

Nietzsche would hardly have endorsed the slightly sacrosanct attitude toward ordinary language that has at times been adhered to by linguistic philosophers. Ordinary language is called correct language, and deviations from it and the rules governing its employment are what lead us into waywardness and nonsense and, as Wittgenstein has suggested, into philosophy. Philosophy, Nietzsche has told us, has been not so much a deviation from ordinary usage as a projection of the grammatical structure of ordinary language onto the neutral screen of reality. Philosophy has been not so much an independent user of language as a supine accepter of the crusted categories of daily speech, flattering, rather than rectifying or purifying the entrenched erroneous-

---

* P. F. Strawson, *Individuals: An Essay in Descriptive Metaphysics* (London: Methuen, 1959), pp. 104, 109.

ness of the human mind so far. "Everything that becomes conscious," and hence everything that succeeds in being formulated in ordinary language, "thereby becomes shallow, small, relatively stupid, general signs—*herd* signs."[56] Just in the nature of the case, assuming as correct his analysis of the origins of both language and consciousness, "it was fundamentally the experiencing of only the most average and *common* experiences which must have been, of all the forces that have shaped mankind, the most powerful."[57] Just as men with finer sensibilities than ours might have reasoned differently (and more accurately) and perished through their excellence, so here "the run-of-the-mill sorts of men were and always are at an advantage. The extraordinary, the sensitive, the strange and difficult to understand sort of men easily remain alone, or, through their apartness, meet with mishap, and seldom propagate themselves."[58]

There is, then, an extraordinary pressure upon each of us to think like all the rest, and to fit to the common pattern. How then should we set about describing or expressing any *different* sort of experience? What language could or should we use? Suppose one is that kind of exceptional person not shaped by the common mold? "Words dilute and stupidize; words depersonalize; words make the uncommon common."[59] Man has not the language with which to express his uniqueness nor the individuality of his thought. Literally, he cannot, if he is in the least degree out of the ordinary, *say* what he thinks or feels. Nietzsche must then himself have felt constrained, through the logic of his position, to develop new terms to give odd and special twists of meaning to old terms, to warp common speech or to hammer out a whole new tongue. Any attempt to translate it all back into the mother idiom, into the language of the ordinary person, would be to cheapen and make banal his eccentric ideas. He felt, therefore, that he must be understood poorly or not at all by the men of his own time, and that he was writing for a new and different generation, perhaps for a new race of beings, as yet unevolved, to whom his message might come home. Perhaps no philosopher before or since him has felt so inhibited and crippled by language. Zarathustra is made to sing, "I go new ways, a new speech comes to me; like all creators I grow weary of the old tongues. My spirit will not wander any longer on worn-out soles."[60] He felt he had frightening and unfamiliar things to say, but that their frightfulness was in some measure due to their unfamiliarity and virtual inexpressibility. But how, he wanted to know, are we ever to extend ourselves unless we expose ourselves to the unfamiliar? And how shall we do this unless we can break loose from the language in which we have grown stale? The old theory of his youth, in which art breaks language loose with metaphor, and induces, perhaps, conceptual tensions calling for philosophical reconstruction, is later echoed in this characteristic idea.

To speak of extending our knowledge does not do justice to his views, however, for we are apt to be taking "knowledge" in the honorific mode in which it is used in our language, whereby ascribing knowledge to a person commits us logically to say that what that person knows is *in fact* the case. It customarily follows from "*a* knows that *p*" that "*p* is true"; and if *p* is false, then it is false that *a* knows that *p*. For Nietzsche, by contrast, knowledge— *das Bekannte*—is only "that to which we are accustomed, so that we no longer wonder at it: the commonplace, any kind of rule which is fixed, whatever we are at home with."[61] Knowledge is bound up with utility, as was truth in his novel theory. Yet it was precisely in this logical feature of the ordinary use of the term that he would say that knowledge is *false*, that the familiar is made up of those entrenched and deeply sunk errors which he was seeking to identify. These errors are so close to us, so much taken for granted, that it is difficult indeed to realize what they are. "The known [*das Bekannte*] is the familiar, and the familiar is what is most difficult to 'know,' that is, to see as a problem, as alien, and 'outside us.' "[62] Thus his task was to *doubt* knowledge, to put our perspective in perspective, to ask whether there were not other and better possibilities open to us. But then this exposes us precisely to the chaos which our conceptual scheme has shielded us against; and awakens once again the feelings of fear which the unstructured, uncaring universe stimulates in us. So his philosophy was frightening, he thought, if liberating. And it was the one because it was the other.

VI

Nothing has seemed more familiar to us, and hence more a paradigm of knowledge, than we ourselves. But the analysis we have been tracing through will have shown, if it has any cogency or merit, that what we take ourselves to be is a falsification of the fact, that we have an idea of ourselves which is not at all what we are, and that what we are is perhaps beyond the power of thought and speech to capture.

When we only observe the inner phenomena, we are to be compared with those deaf mutes, who guess at the words they do not hear from the movements of the lips. We infer from the appearances of our inner senses to other, imperceptible phenomena which we might perceive if our means of observation were more adequate.

For this inner world we lack all finer organs, so that we experience a *thousandfold complexity* as still a unity; and fictively insert a causality wherever a ground of movement and alteration remain invisible to us. The following upon one another of thoughts and feelings is only certain processes having become visible to consciousness. But that these sequences have anything to do with any [genuine] causal connections is altogether unworthy of belief. Consciousness presents us only with the *illustration* of cause and effect.[63]

Let us consider in this connection one further piece of Nietzsche's psychology, his analysis of dreams. He reflected on this topic often in his intellectual career—we encountered it in his earliest work—and it serves perhaps better than any other to illustrate his notion of "imaginary causes." During sleep, he suggests, "our nervous system is, through manifold inner causes, in a state of excitation. . . . There are thus a hundred occasions for the mind to be surprised by, and to seek the causes of, this or that excitation. The dream is the *search for* and the *representation of* the causes of each stimulated sensation, that is, the apparent causes."[64] Dreams are "interpretations of our nervous excitations during sleep, very free, very arbitrary interpretations of the movement of blood and bowels, of the pressure of the arms or the bedclothes, of the sound of the bell tower, the weathercock, night-flying things, and so forth."[65] Consider, to use his own example, that a man's feet were bound during sleep. Because of this stimulus he dreams that snakes are coiled around his ankles. There is a mental image of this and, at the same time, the interpretation that "these snakes must be the cause of the sensations which I, the sleeper, have."[66]

It is a common enough experience, known to each of us, to weave some external stimulus—an alarm clock, say,—into the fabric of one's dream. We create, so to speak, an image to account for the noise,—for example, a person in the dream screams, and the screams turn out to have been the alarm clock. This means, in effect, that the dreamer "explains it from afterwards, so that he thinks he first experiences the conditions responsible for the noise and then the noise."[67] This is to reverse things completely: it was the noise which caused the image that was then used to explain the noise. "I maintain," Nietzsche says, "that as man still reasons in dreams, so also he reasoned when awake, for many millennia. The first cause which entered his mind as explaining something which required explanation, satisfied him, and passed for truth."[68] In a later passage, he makes the stronger claim that in this regard there is no difference between dreaming and waking, and that perhaps our entire conscious life is "a more or less fantastic commentary upon an unknown, and perhaps unknowable, but merely felt, text."[69]

This analysis remained a permanent element in his philosophy; in his late work, the *Twilight of the Idols*, he took it up again under the heading of "The Error of Imaginary Causes." This was one of the "Four Great Errors."* An *imaginary* cause is an

---

* The other three are "The Error of Confusing Cause and Effect," "The Error of False Causes," and "The Error of Free Will." Professor Walter Kaufmann, in the introductory remarks to his translation of the *Götzendammerung* in *The Portable Nietzsche* (New York: Viking, 1954), pp. 463–464, makes the extremely important point that the word "idols" in the title of the book is to be taken in the sense in which Bacon used it, where idols are merely pernicious habits of belief which hold men in thrall to error. Nietzsche's four errors, save in number and in philosophical import, do not correspond at all to Bacon's four idols. It is worth noting that the subtitle of the book—"How One Philosophizes with a Hammer"—sounds a good deal less forbidding when we realize the hammer is to be used to strike graven images in the spirit of the iconoclast. It sounds even less forbidding when Nietzsche writes, somewhat humorously, "eternal idols here touched as with

erroneous reversal of sequence: "The representation which a certain state *produces* is taken to be the cause of that state."[71] It is this which the phenomenon of dreaming helps to illustrate, but in fact it has a wider application than merely to dreams. It indeed is exemplified by the whole of our vaunted introspective powers, which do not give us access to the causes of the contents of our mind, but permit us only to relate these contents to one another. "To what an extent our ideas of ideas, of the will, and of feelings are totally superficial! Even the 'inner world' is 'appearance.' "[72]

In the end, the conceptions we have formed of our interior existences are made up of the same concordances of fragmentary experiences and false explanations—or "arrangements" taken as explanatory—which characterize our conception of the outer world. We know ourselves no better and no differently than we know other things, and the distinction between two kinds of knowledge collapses on scrutiny:

I also maintain the phenomenality of the *inner* world: everything of which we become *conscious* is, through and through, merely arranged [*zurechtgemacht*], simplified, schematized, interpreted. The actual situation behind inner perception, the causal uniting between thoughts, feelings, desires, and between subject and object, is absolutely concealed from us, and is perhaps a pure fancy. This "apparent inner world" is manipulated with just the same forms and procedures as "the external world." We never hit upon "facts."[73]

It is not to be wondered that this should be so. If Nietzsche's analysis has been correct, it cannot but be so. For the structure of the outer world is nothing but a projection of the structure of our minds, and in the one case as in the other, we are dealing with fictions and the obverses of fiction.

---

a tuning fork—there are in general no idols which are older, more convinced, more inflated—and none more hollow . . . to hear, as an answer, than that famous hollow sound which testifies to bloated entrails."[70] Of course, all knowledge is a matter of habits, on his analysis. The errors, then, are pernicious habits. Habits are neither good nor bad as such, but there are good habits and bad ones. Without habits of some kind, we should not be able to live.

The following after one another of thoughts, feelings, and ideas in our consciousness does not mean that these are causal sequences. They are so only in appearance. Upon this appearance we have built our entire notion of mind, of reason, of logic, etc. (none of which exists: they all are fabricated syntheses and unities), and these then are projected back into things and *behind* things.[74]

Inner and outer, then, are strictly correlative. As he said somewhat obscurely in *Daybreak*, "things are but the boundaries of man."[75] We can now perhaps see what that oracular utterance meant. Nietzsche's psychology and his perspectivism are internally related.

VII

The world has no rational structure other than what we have given to it, recapturing with a philosophical left hand what we have given with a psychological right one. But then no more are we rational beings than is the world a rational place. This does not mean that we are irrational, but only that the distinction between rationality and irrationality fails to apply. We have, once more, hardly the words to express ourselves. Nietzsche often lapses from his critical insight to use terms which it was (or should have been) his philosophical triumph to have superseded. It is sheer dramatization, sheer verbal perversity, to say that whatever is true is false, that knowledge is ignorance, and the like. These are tiresome philosophical jokes which we can understand only if we are prepared to work through his analysis. It is similar when he speaks of the irrationality of reason, or states that we are not really rational after all. He means only that reason has application to the surface of things, of ourselves and of reality, and that the highest paradigms of reason are only fantastic edifices sprung forth, insubstantial and unanchored, from the forming imaginations of men. This does not mean that we are to abandon these airy structures, for we have no others, and we need some sort of shelter; and we at any rate could not find any that we did not make for ourselves. But we are to recognize it all for what it is, to be made at once modest by acknowledging our limitations and bold by recognizing that the only achievements there are, are ours. It would be difficult to suppose that we could ever have planned what we have done. It was always just our sheer great luck to have made these unspeakably precious mistakes.

So much, then, for self-knowledge. Here we are as ignorant as we are anywhere:

Those thinkers in whom the stars move in circular paths are not the deepest thinkers. Whoever looks within himself, as into an immense space, and carries galaxies within himself, *he* knows how irregular all galaxies are. They lead him into the labyrinth and chaos of existence.[76]

That the heavenly bodies move in circular orbits was, as we know, a moral prejudice of the ancients, carried over to the very threshold of modern scientific astronomy. Circular motion was a "superior" sort of motion, it being only proper that planets, as noble and celestial fires, should move in the noblest of ways. It is more noble not to move at all, however, and Kepler, who was a *great* scientist, believed it was appropriate that the noblest body of them all, our sun, should stand forever immobile in the center of the turning world. We may smile in condescension at such ideas. What we do not realize, Nietzsche would tell us, is that our way of looking at the universe still is *durch und durch* interwoven with the colored strands of moral prejudice, so close to us, perhaps, that we do not see them for what they are. There was nothing he wished us to be conscious of more than the grip in which our moral attitudes hold us fixed. The blows against morality, which make up so substantial a portion of his writing, are attempts to dislodge us from our unthinking obeisance to these dominating habits of judgment and thought, to get us to see these attitudes from without, to appreciate, as he puts it, "morality as a problem." Once loose from this, we might make a new philosophy and a new life. I turn thus to his moral criticisms.

FIVE

Moralities

I

I⊤ is not a criticism of the beliefs we hold regarding the world when one says that all of them are false. It is not the fact that they are false to which Nietzsche objects when he considers these beliefs critically. "It is here that our new language sounds perhaps strangest."[1] What he is concerned with is a belief *about* these beliefs, a second-order belief, in accordance with which they *should* be true, that they *should* correspond with facts as they are. It is not our language, as we might say today, but our metalanguage which goes astray, insofar as it makes demands on our language which it cannot and need not subserve. The fact that our beliefs are false relative to that theory of truth (the Correspondence Theory) in accordance with which we demanded that they be true is perfectly irrelevant as to whether we should hold these beliefs. Propositions which were true, in terms of corresponding with reality, would do us little good indeed, since there is nothing about reality to be said (or, about reality, there is only *that* to be said); and to say of our beliefs that they are false is not per se to recommend their abandonment. We are being asked only to abandon an expectation concerning these beliefs which we were ill-advised to hold from the beginning. "The real question," Nietzsche goes on to say, "is how far a belief [*ein Urteil*] furthers and supports life, maintains and disciplines a species."[2] To renounce our beliefs merely because they were (absolutely) false would in effect be to renounce life, for these beliefs are conditions for life and "the falsest beliefs—to which belong the synthetic a priori judgments—

are the least dispensable of all."[3] It is, then, not the ordinary beliefs of ordinary men which are under attack, but the philosophical justification of these beliefs by philosophers who may have begun as critics, but ended as apologists of the systems of thought they pretended so fiercely to expose to their purifying scepsis. Nietzsche's polemic has been with philosophers.

It has often been the avowed enterprise of philosophers to reconstitute human knowledge upon permanent, hopefully immutable foundations. Criticisms and construction have typically gone hand in hand: one rejects only to replace, discarding (one thinks) only what is nonsense or beyond justification. So far as the plain man goes, "the greater part of his conscious thoughts must be reckoned as instinctive activities."[4] By contrast, the philosopher was to have been cautious and self-conscious, controlling rather than being carried along by his thoughts, eliminating what did not strike him as clear and distinct, or as self-certifiably true, or as satisfying some other, stringent criterion of admissibility. But in fact, Nietzsche seems to have felt, earlier philosophers were slack: they never really succeeded in calling into question, or even recognizing for what they were, the deep falsehoods and unexpendable fictions which were worked out in the predawn of the human mind. Consequently, philosophers were locating their foundations upon foundations already there, so to speak, their edifices conforming to a conceptual geography laid down by the primitive mentality, and so familiar as not to have been detected as even present. "The most self-conscious thoughts of a philosopher are guided by his hidden instincts, and forced into determined paths."[5] Whatever they finally bring forth out of the depths with their purportedly critical soundings, and exhibit as *basic* truth, "is at bottom a preconceived dogma, a fancy, an inspiration, or, at most, a heart's desire made abstract and refined, and defended with reasons sought after the fact."[6] Indeed, "every great philosophy has so far been . . . the self-confession of its originator, and a kind of unintentional, unaware *mémoires*."[7]

Nowhere Nietzsche thought, is this more the case than in moral philosophy, where much the same ambition has prevailed as in epistemology or in metaphysics; only in this instance it is to put our *moral* beliefs on unshakable moorings, to make a *science* of morals. But what each such philosophy has been *au fond* is a piece of special pleading on behalf of a moral perspective misconstrued as inherent in the order of the world. Nor could it have been easy for philosophers to have believed otherwise. For it is not easy to isolate moral from factual claims or to distinguish the moral factors in our perspective from the rest. Our very sense perceptions "are altogether permeated with valuations (useful or harmful, hence acceptable or unacceptable)":

The individual colors even express a value for us (though we seldom, or only after a long exclusion from these colors confess it, like those imprisoned in error, or in jail). Even insects react differently to different colors, one preferring this, another that. . . .[8]

The precise terms we use in our analyses of perception, or in the philosophical discussion of cognitive claims, are interpenetrated with normative attitudes and moral preferences. In a striking discussion in the *Nachlass*, "Moral Values in the Theory of Knowledge Itself," Nietzsche lists some examples:

The trusting of reason—why not mistrust?
The "real world" must be the good one—why?
Appearance, change, contradiction, and strife are morally disvalued. [This is] desiring a world which lacks them.
Inventing the "Transcendent world," therewith a place remains for "moralistic freedom" (with Kant).
Dialectic as the road to virtue (with Plato and Socrates: evidently because sophistry was judged the path to immortality).
Time and space ideal: consequently "unity" in the essence of things, consequently no "sin," no evil, no imperfection—a justification of God.
Epicurus denied the existence of knowledge: in order to maintain moral (specifically hedonistic) values as the highest. Augustine the same, later Pascal ("the corrupted reason") on behalf of Christian values.
The contempt of Descartes for everything mutable; similarly that of Spinoza.[9]

The remarkable first part of *Beyond Good and Evil* is devoted to this subject. Nietzsche identifies, and impales with perspicuity and wit, the moral casuistry with which the great philosophers have imposed on us their own moral preferences. Not, of course, that this can easily be helped. Philosophy "always creates a world after its own image,"[10] because the imposition of moralities is a form of the Will-to-Power and "Philosophy is this tyrannizing drive itself, the most spiritualized Will-to-Power."[11] Again, it is only the beliefs about their beliefs which Nietzsche stigmatizes. Philosophers might acknowledge that they are lobbying and not reporting.

The making of choices and the holding of preferences is hardly a thing man (or any creature) can avoid. For life itself simply means "valuing and preferring":[12]

In evaluation are expressed the conditions of [one's] preservation and growth. All our sense organs and our senses are developed only in relation to these conditions. The trust in reason and its categories, in dialectic, and hence the *valuing* of logic, proves only that through experience these have been shown useful, and not that they are true.[13]

Schemes and tables of valuation, schedules of preference and rank, are ingredients in our ocnceptual structure, and as such internally related to our language. Just as philosophers have miscredited themselves with discovering facts about the world which were facts only about their language, so their *moral* discoveries have reference to nothing in the world itself, but only to themselves. The alleged description of moral facts is merely an expression of moral atti-tudes. But these moral attitudes are involved with the terms of our survival. "There are no moral phenomena," he says (and says fre-quently), "but only moralistic interpretations of phenomena."[14] "There are altogether no moral facts."[15] This follows as a speciali-zation of his general thesis that there are no facts, no order, and hence no *moral* order in the world. But it is as though his entire general philosophy was a preparation for this application.

We are not being asked to abandon, or at least not to abandon merely as a consequence of this analysis, the moral beliefs we hold. We are being asked only to abandon our meta-ethical beliefs (to use contemporary terms) as to the possibility of justifying whatever moral beliefs we have. Just as we are not required to jettison a single scientific belief (but only a belief about science) when told that scientific theories all are conventions, so here we may advocate and bring up our children to accept the same moral code, even if this code depends on us alone, and is itself neither true nor false. There is no constraint to the abandonment of beliefs. But there is no telling what changes in our moral attitudes might not come about in consequence of our changed meta-ethical beliefs; for once divorced from the idea that moral ideas, if they are to be accepted, must be supported by some external authority or some reigning moral order in the universe at large, there opens up to us the possibility that an entirely different *kind* of justification might allow us a choice among moralities far wider than we had imagined. We may see which moral outlook suits us best, and conduces most effectively to our prevailing over obstacles. It may well be that the one we now subscribe to will do best. Yet, should it now chafe, or be found inhibiting, or be felt in any way destructive of ourselves, we must opt and, if required, fight for its modification or replacement. Hence the critique of moral systems, which Nietzsche sustained during his productive period, was *not* incompatible with his fierce and militant advocacy of the overthrow of one morality and the acceptance of another.

Nietzsche played the roles of moral critic and moralist at the same time, often in the very same aphorism, commenting in a general way about the logic of moral concepts and enjoining a specific moral reform at once. When he spoke of himself, as he often did, as an *Immoralist*, he was sometimes implying simply that he was speaking as a philosophical critic of moral systems generally, concerned with morality as a problem and not with the endorsement or condemnation of any specific moral system. At times, however, he meant that he was taking a particular stand against the moral attitudes of his own place and time and tradition, and speaking out in behalf of another and more liberating way. Again, when he exhorts philosophers to follow his lead, "to take a stand beyond good and evil [and] to put beneath one the illusion of moral judgments,"[16] he is asking that they appreciate, with him, the moral neutrality of the world and the subjective coloring of every moral judgment. Sometimes he is certainly also seeking to enlist them in a moral cause, to now take stands against that specific moral system in which the terms "good" and "evil" contrast, a moral code which, he thought, might cause irreparable human damage if it had not already done so.

Nietzsche's two roles vis-à-vis morality must be kept distinct, because Nietzsche has been understood, discussed, and condemned in just one of these capacities. This condemnation, of course, is not difficult to understand, in view of his strident accusations, his incendiary language, and his seemingly uncontrolled denouncements of Christian morality. This phase of his writing we must assess in time, but he meant to keep the two roles apart and be primarily a moral philosopher rather than a preacher or evangelist:

Moralists must now accept the fact that they are to be regarded as immoral because they dissect morals. . . . Men confuse the moralist with the moral preacher. The older moralists dissected too little and preached too much, and this is the basis for that confusion, and its unpleasant consequences for the moralists of today.[17]

There can be little doubt about the aptness of this comment, even if Nietzsche later obscured, even for himself, the extramoral with the contramoral positions he came simultaneously to occupy. The extramoral position has the most interest but the lesser influence, and I shall now seek to identify some of Nietzsche's characteristic theories in moral philosophy.

II

There is a celebrated and influential argument ascribed to Hume, to the effect that we cannot logically derive an "ought" from an "is," and hence no amount of knowledge regarding what is *in fact* the case will entail a single conclusion about what *ought to be* the case. Unless our premises contain some expression of value able to be stated as an imperative, in addition to factual information expressed in indicative sentences, no expression of value and no imperative may legitimately be deduced. It must in fairness be said of the philosophers who have sought a factual or objective basis for their moral views that they were not always victimized by exactly the logical error which Hume identified. They did not suppose they were basing moral judgments upon *non*moral facts, but rather upon *moral* facts, for it never occurred to them to doubt that there were any. The Humean attack is telling only in case the one it is aimed against actually does draw a distinction between the two orders of judgment and then seeks the logical connection between them. It is a gratuitous attack, however, if no such distinction was drawn, or if moral facts were regarded as part of what the world contains. Nietzsche's attack is against this view. He holds that indeed there is no distinction to be drawn, not because there are no moral facts, but because there are no facts at all, only interpretations. If Hume were to say that at least there is a logical gap between factual and moral interpretations, Nietzsche would be ready with a challenge to show how the distinction is to be made, for, as we have seen, he contends that our factual claims are fused and amalgamated with our moral ones, the distinction being (at best, and in present idiom) metalinguistic.

Nevertheless, there remains a question of how we are to explain the phenomenon of moral interpretations. Given Nietzschean methodology, we must suppose that these interpretations have a use and answer to a need if they are practiced at all. If we found this to be so, it would not be deriving an *ought* from an *is* but, rather, explaining the nonmoral provenance of moral interpreting[18] and its function in life. Just what, he asks, "is the value of value?"[19] Merely to be in a position to ask this question is to have located onself "beyond good and evil."[20] He was posing a question in what we today would perhaps call social psychology. To some degree his answers are not really unfamiliar; at times they are almost clichés of the social sciences. I shall mention them only to the extent that they serve to clarify the philosophical points they illustrate.

To begin, we might say that morality consists just in obedience to customs, whatever these might be.[21] Customs are traditional practices, and wherever there is no traditional way, there is no morality, for there is nothing with which to conform. It is not in the least required of these customs to have intrinsically served any use whatever. There are innumerable customs whose obvious utility is doubtful. However, just to *be* a custom, independent of content, is already to have a certain utility. There may be no rhyme or reason to the customs one obeys, but there is some rhyme and reason to the obedience of customs per se. "Any rule is better than none. [This] is the principle which stands at the beginning of civilization."[22] It is in this respect that Nietzsche seeks to explain the seeming irrationality and arbitrariness of the traditions adhered to, at times with the most horrendous sanctions for their abrogation, by societies the world over. Accordingly, the question has to do with conformity in general to custom, and customs are plainly indispensable if there is to be any society at all, whatever specific anthropological content they may have. But deviating from a set of customs is immoral relative to that set, and insofar a challenge to the society these customs make possible.

A morality does not consist merely in a set of customs. It often, and typically, offers some reasons why *these* are the rules to be obeyed. In actual practice, as Nietzsche saw the matter, the imposition of custom is simply the imposition upon an individual of the Will-to-Power of the group, or "herd." But a morality is hardly recognized as the naked exercise of power on the part of the group, exclusively for its own perdurance and advantage, irrespective of the price in suffering to be paid by the individual who obeys. Morality demands such sacrifices. This means, among other things, that any number of impulses which the individual might have must be ruthlessly repressed if they or their expression in any way conflict with the authority of the group. The natural and the effectively desired consequence is that each shall be like each, and all think and feel and talk alike. This means, finally, the unremitting pruning of the deviant or exceptional individual (whose individuality is in some measure a function of exactly those prohibited impulses). This idea, which we have touched on already in connection with consciousness and language, will be taken up again. I am concerned here with the reasons and justifications given by the group for the traditions it upholds.

These reasons, which of course reinforce the practices they sanction, basically are "imaginary causalities," once again, "believed in as the basis of morality."[23] Custom becomes accredited by "some falsely explained accident."[24] It is for this reason that science, and especially the scientific examination of moralities, is regarded as immoral, for science is often required to be incompatible with the irrational *phantastischer Kausalitäten* upon which our moral code rests, so that any intellectual challenge by science is a threat to the way of life it supposedly supports. It is then in the interest of the group as a whole, or so it seems, to keep its beliefs quarantined in order to protect its practical demands. So morality stupefies: "it works against our acquiring new experiences and of correcting morality accordingly, which means that morality works against a better, newer morality."[25] However useful a morality might be in preserving the life of the group, any morality, reinforcing beliefs as well as attitudes and making it impossible for the members of the group to distinguish one from another, becomes at last a shell which inhibits further moral growth. Instead of becoming a means for the successful conduct of life, it becomes a brake against the furtherance of life and fulfillment for the living. Again, the critic of moralities exposes the irrationalities of the beliefs which are drawn protectively over moralities, and the critic cannot but be counted as their enemy. Nietzsche wants emphatically to claim that

The moral judgment has this in common with religious judgments, that each believes in a reality which does not exist. Morality, which is only an interpretation, or better a misinterpretation of certain phenomena . . . belongs to a stage of ignorance at which the concept of reality, of any distinction between imaginary and real, is lacking.[26]

In such comments one feels a tension in Nietzsche's thought. How, after all, can *he* distinguish real from imaginary? What sense can he give to the notion of "reality" at all except a negative and unspecifying one? But this general reservation apart, it is not easy to connect his views on morality into a coherent account, in part because he goes back and forth between sociological and psychological considerations which should at times be kept distinct, particularly because the connection is not always plain. Sociologically, societies enforce certain rules and demand the extirpation of impulses and actions which might, through disconformity, be

destructive of the order defined by these rules. Any deviating impulse is potentially dangerous. Consequently, the same sets of
mind are reinforced everywhere within the group, and these, consisting of feelings, impulses, and the like, become virtually instinctual: "Morality becomes the herd instinct within the individual."[27]
Once this interiorization occurs—what today is sometimes called
the superego—there not only would be little room for independent
thinking and evaluating but also the very idea of being on one's
own would be terrifying rather than liberating. "All sorts of terrors
and miseries were associated with being alone."[28] So far there is a
reasonable connection between the sociological and the psychological thesis. Now, suppose a man began to sense impulses to do
or to think differently from the rest of society. Naturally he would
feel threatened by these impulses and he would seek an explanation of their occurrence. Some typical explanations might be that
he had sinned, or he was guilty of something, or his ancestors were
guilty and he was discharging their debts. These are of course
imaginary causes, but it does not take long for imaginary causes
to stabilize into mythologies and mythologies into systems of
belief, and then for these beliefs to come to reinforce men into
the accepted ways of behavior. Our moral codes are curiously
strengthened by our own pathology and our propensities for seeking out imaginary causes. A man feels, for whatever reason, life at
some ebb in him, and he seeks to explain it in terms perhaps of his
guilt when it is the sense of guilt which, the other way round, is
to be explained in terms of the ebbing vitality. It is thus that
moral beliefs, or those beliefs which imprison us within the cast
of custom, "belong in whole and in part to the psychology of
error. In every single case we find cause and effect interchanged."[29]

Such seems to have been Nietzsche's account. The gist of it is
plain enough. The proclaimed causes for our practices are never
the correct but only the imaginary ones. These cannot be taken
seriously as explanations, but one can profitably take them as
"symptoms and sign language."[30] Then one might have some
remarkable insight into the internal working of primitive menta-
tion. In a similar way, perhaps, one can hardly countenance references to astral influences in the explanation of behavior. But one

may *use* such references as some index to the working of those intellects which believe astral influences to count. Nietzsche's program in moral psychology is:

The moral judgment is never to be taken literally. As such, it contains but nonsense. But moral judgments remain invaluable as semiotic. They exhibit, at least to the knowledgeable, the most valuable realities of the cultures . . . which did not *know* enough to know themselves. Morals merely are sign language, purely symptomatologies. One must first know what it is connected with in order to make the least use of it.[31]

One is to go from the moral philosophy to the biography of the moral philosopher, just as one must go from the moral code to the social psychology of the culture which enforces it. None of this, however, will be altogether clear until we have worked through the doctrine of the Will-to-Power.

III

The differences between Nietzsche's mature philosophy and the views he expressed in the period of *The Birth of Tragedy* are nowhere more evident than in his discussions concerning the relationship of group and individual member. In that early volume one has the sense that he was much occupied with the problem of solidarity. He hoped to find in art, and especially in the Wagnerian avatar of tragic art, the instrument through which individuals might, if but for a time, be melded into some sort of communion, their differences effectively obliterated for that time. Certainly, he believed that this was the power of the old Dionysiac rites. In the ideal presentation of tragedy, as in the frenzied crises of the Dionysiac ritual, differences and boundaries were washed away; each shared, as it were, a common dream or vision. He was concerned, in brief, with the sort of problem which Marx (far more realistically, I should think) pursued in connection with class consciousness, or which the syndicalist Georges Sorel, many years later, sought the solution to in social myths. In the later philosophy, there is little of this. Or rather, Nietzsche came to feel that there was a sufficiency of solidarity and not *enough* individuality in life—

an emphasis which has especially attracted to his writings those of an anarchistic bent.

The more interesting point philosophically, however, is his suggestion that the concept of individuality, indeed of individuals *as such*, is a late concept, a suggestion which finds its polemic context within the speculative anthropologies of Hobbes or Locke. It has always been a temptation (it was so already for Glaucon in the *Republic*) to think of men as primordially individuals, with societies then formed out of these as perhaps compounds are formed of elements or, better, molecules of atoms. As the latter can be resolved into their atomic parts, so societies can be dissolved into their individual constituents. Social relations are then purely external, or, in Hobbes's terms, "artificial": we have always the option of turning back into that natural state whence we derived, retrieving our aboriginal individuality. This would have been the analogue, in social philosophy, of the epistemological theory that ideas are simple or compound, and that the latter are built up out of the former. This implies that an individual, with all his required senses and no external aid, might, after all, compound all the non-simple ideas he should require. On such a view it is a problem, all our simple ideas being essentially our own, how we should ever communicate. Perhaps the analogue to this in (empiricist) social philosophy would be the problem of how individuals could inter-relate with one another, each having a sufficient endowment to survive on his own with no true need for others except for protection.

We have already seen that Nietzsche rejected such a theory; his view was that consciousness, as language, has a social origin and function, so that individuals achieve consciousness only of the ideas which everyone has in common with everybody else. As an individual could scarcely survive without a society, so he hardly could achieve a sense of himself as an independent unit. It would therefore only be late in the evolution of things that (however it takes place) individuals may begin to think of themselves as such, and even wonder, as philosophers, whether others have feelings and interiors at all. It indeed becomes logically tenable to defend a solipsism which could hardly have been so much as expressed earlier.

Nietzsche seems somehow to see an individual emerging from the herd in something like the manner in which the individuated, Apollinian hero emerged from the homogeneous chorus of the ancient tragedies. On his theory of that evolution, there was for a prolonged period *only* the chorus, just as, according to his anthropology, there was for a long period *only* the herd. The herd would have been made up of individuals, but they could not have been aware of themselves as such, and deviations from the norm would simply have perished, cast out like alien bodies, through inability to express their wants. Within each herd there would be a profound and virtually irresistible force making for homogeneity. Perhaps, indeed, explanations and justifications would come only when this prolonged communion had begun to give way, and men had to be kept in line. Regardless, there could have been differences between *herds*, because each would have worked out its language against the conditions that made for its survival; and as these vary, so do herds. We get, then, moral homogeneity within the herd and moral heterogeneity *between* herds. Nietzsche emphasized moral relativity, not least of all because it provided plain evidence of the possibility of other moralities, which implied that, practically speaking, there was nothing universally compelling about the moral perspective of one's own herd. This is especially taken up in *Thus Spake Zarathustra*:

> A people which did not evaluate could not live; but if it is to preserve itself, then it dare not evaluate the way its neighbor evaluates.
> Much that one people calls "good," another calls "shame" and "disgrace." So I found. I found much that was here named evil and there decked in purple honors. . . .
> A table of values hangs over each people.[32]

These oracular verses distill what Nietzsche said on this (not unobvious) topic in his sprawling corpus. Zarathustra speaks of the varieties of good and evil to be found throughout the world, and of the power—"no greater power is to be found on earth"—of evaluation. Men, or more correctly, social groups, "gave themselves good and evil." They did not discover it in nature, for it is not there to be found. Nor did they receive it from on high (whatever they may offer in explanation of their codes and decalogues). Men "laid values into things, in order to preserve themselves" and so created themselves at the same time as they created the world. Hence "evaluation is creation" [*Schätzen ist Schaffen*].[33] These are familiar teachings. More pertinent to our topic is Zarathustra's claim that "People were creative first, and only later individuals. Indeed, the individual himself is only the most recent creation." And "Pleasure in the herd is older than pleasure in the self; and so long as good conscience is called 'herd,' bad conscience is called 'I.'" He who so much as thinks of himself, in the primal unity of herdhood, as someone apart feels guilt for his apartness. Such a person would wish for nothing so much as reunion with the group. As Nietzsche suggested, there is terror in aloneness, and as long as the singleness of individuals is explained with *reference* to concepts like sin, deviations are apt to be internally as well as externally sensed as punishments rather than opportunities. And *that*, Nietzsche wants to say as a reformer, *is* a sin.

A problem which must vex us is: How could the individual have attained to a consciousness of himself as distinct? For, on Nietzsche's analysis, whatever he did become conscious of would be translated directly into the common idiom. Nietzsche nowhere answers this with any definiteness, any more than Plato tells us how it happens that someone gets loose from those chains that bind the rest of his fellows in the cave. Plato's liberated philosopher, however, is able to return to the cave and liberate those still enchained amid shadows. But Nietzsche has given an account which makes it, one would think, quite impossible that anyone so detached should be understood: his fellow herdsmen must look upon him amazed and uncomprehending. Nietzsche did think (not excitingly, it must be admitted), that we may dangerously weaken the bonds which hold the group together by analyzing dispassionately, through the techniques of the "science of the origin of ideas," the stupidity of the beliefs which support the group's morality. This is slow work at best, and the weight of language and tradition must press heavily upon the free spirit struggling to get loose. It requires, indeed, almost superhuman abilities and "immense counterpowers" to "thwart this natural, all-too-natural *progressus in simile,* this continuing forming of men into the similar, the average, the ordinary, the herdlike—into the common!"[34]

It is edifying, of course, and scarcely deniable, that one way of easing the pressure of custom is to replace the old monsters of tradition with scientifically sound knowledge. The neurotic must be told repeatedly that his fancied explanations are false, and that the true reason for his obsession or compulsion is found elsewhere and must be carefully identified and illuminated if he is to get beyond that domination of the derangement of imagination. Nietzsche has another, and perhaps less obvious, prescription to offer than merely additional scientific research. Let us assume, for the sake of exposition, his not unreasonable idea that we are born into a scheme of concepts, at once evaluative and descriptive, and that we spontaneously ingest a morality and a metaphysics through simply learning our language. Let us (more dubiously) suppose along with him that what we know of ourselves is that, and that only, which our language permits us to know; also we are conscious only of what words permit us to say. Language and morality function repressively in two ways, excluding from survival anyone who is different to any dangerous degree from the rest of the herd, and throttling within a given individual any feelings or thoughts or ideas which might fail to pass dully into the group idiom. Now let us suppose that into our model community are born some individuals more sensitive than others, or open to a greater range of experiences, or subject to some different order of passion. It is not likely these persons will perdure or be understood, at least not with regard to their deviation. Yet, one might urge, it would only be through the existence of such individuals that new ideas could come to refresh and modify the group's repository of concepts, inasmuch as there could be no natural alternative source. All of this, whether correct or not, should be at least readily identified as something that Nietzsche believed. But let us draw from all of this some (loose) inferences. The first is that it is at least possible that a great deal is always going on within each of us which we never become conscious of and never, accordingly, talk about. Because groups differ, it is possible again that interior processes which are unconscious and inexpressible within one group may be articulable and conscious in another. This might very much depend on differences in the conditions under which these groups find it possible to survive. Of the total set of interior conditions, then, some are conscious in one group and unconscious in another; this, in turn, might serve to explain the differences in perspective and morality from group to group. But this finally means that we all have within us what it would take to modify the conceptual structure. We all have what Nietzsche calls *affects* or *passions*: "the life-conditioning affects" [*Lebensbedingende Affekte*]. Some but not necessarily all of these are represented in consciousness; some but not all are repressed by social pressure; some but not all are permitted expression. There is the possibility that with a difference in the form and degree of pressure, different affects come into consciousness; perhaps through the release of some of these the moral system itself could be changed. This is a strange and devious theory, but it seems in one or another form to have been held by Nietzsche, who tells us, of these passions or affects, that they "must be further developed if life is to be further developed."[35]

It is not necessary here to query the truth or falsity of this theory, but only to assess its importance in the structure of Nietzsche's system. It is important because it is his view that what the herd and the morality of the herd are repressive of is the passions which must be antisocial in nature. "All the old moralistic monsters are unanimous in this," he wrote in an essay called "Morality As Anti-nature" (which is in the *Twilight of the Idols*), "that one must kill the passions [*il faut tuer les passions.*]"[36] It is just at this point, however, that Nietzsche falters badly. Given his theory, he is entitled, I suppose, to say that whatever passions are contrary to the interests of the group must be antisocial. This is virtually a definition. Then, as a moral revisionist, Nietzsche becomes an advocate of antisocial passions and that again is permitted him. However, he found himself specifically endorsing a set of passions and passionate actions which are *specifically* recognized as antisocial within *our* morality. But it hardly follows that every antisocial (meaning merely "out of the ordinary and not to be tolerated") impulse is going to give rise to fresh moral horizons. Nevertheless, Nietzsche found himself writing what seem to be bald apologies for and exhortations to lust, cruelty, violence, hatred, and brutality of every sort. Thus he had no one but himself to blame for his wicked reputation. Still, before completely harmonizing with this condemnation, we must say a few words regarding what were his beliefs in contrast with what I shall call the *rhetoric* he lapsed into when expressing them. His rhetoric must be conceded as inflammatory; so must his beliefs. But there was a considerable difference between them.

IV

When Nietzsche speaks of morality as antinature, he has in mind the way in which morality is repressive relative to what we might regard as the unrestrained expression of wants and needs and appetites. This expression is "natural" in perhaps the way it is natural for bushes to grow in whatever random shapes they take without the external modeling given them by gardeners with shears. We might then think of a "natural" person as one who simply satisfies his needs and freely pursues the stilling of his desires, without care or concern or guilt, without submission to any external and certainly no internal regimen. He would act as does an infant, or perhaps an animal, or perhaps, more exactly, a late Roman emperor. Obviously, part of the socialization of an individual consists in his being disciplined to a point where he internalizes his group's taboos and applies them to himself. When this happens, as we all know from the most personal experience, there often are conflicts. Philosophers since Plato have been impressed with the conflict between appetite and "reason," and the reader browsing through Nietzsche is almost certain to find him singular in this tradition, as one who openly advocated, or so it seemed, the primacy of the appetites and impulses which operate at the subrational level of the human psyche. Nietzsche has been both admired and admonished for this, but the truth is that we shall find him to be far more conventional than either his language or his notoriety suggests.

In the very passage in which he inveighs against the sworn enemies of the passions, he writes that "all passions have a stage in which they are merely fatal, dragging their victim down with the weight of their stupidity."[37] Let us again recall the crucial distinction, so often overlooked, between barbaric and hellenized Dionysianism, and remember that Nietzsche primarily advocated the latter. He was never an enthusiast for mere moral or emotional *laisser aller*. Admitting that "Every morality is, in opposition to *laisser aller*, a bit of tyranny against 'nature,' even against 'reason,' " he goes on to remark, "but that is no objection against it."[38] Finally, in fact, the value of systems of value is precisely the "enduring restraint" which they impose. Moral systems are relative and arbitrary, but it must be emphasized repeatedly that conformity to rule—to any rule rather than none, as he put it[39]—is the beginning of civilization, and that which makes life meaningful and worth living:

The remarkable fact is that whatever is of freedom, subtlety, daring, dance, and masterly firmness, that is or ever was in the world, be it in thinking, or ruling, or in speaking or persuading, in art as in moral conduct, is made possible primarily by this "tyranny of arbitrary laws." Indeed, in all seriousness, the probability is not slight that this is "Nature" and "natural"—and not any *laisser aller*.[40]

This teaching runs through his writings from first to last. In *The Wanderer and His Shadow* he writes, "The man who has conquered his passions enters into the possession of the most fecund region, like the colonist who has become master of woodland and marsh."[41] And again, in *Beyond Good and Evil*:

The essential thing "in heaven and on earth" is that there be long, continued obedience in a specific direction. Something always comes of this in the end, on account of which it repays one to live in this world—virtue, or art, or music, dance, reason, or spirituality—something glorifying, purifying, of divinity or madness.[42]

It cannot be said that Nietzsche stood for the "natural" discharge of emotional energy and a ruthless pushing back of emotional restraint. What he did stand for is plain enough, if less exciting. He is, as usual, employing language whose power is so in excess of the point he wishes to make that it drives him past his message into bordering conceptual territory. Yet he seems to have felt that unless he used excessive language, he could not reach his point at all. He is urging a qualification on our attitudes toward the emotional and passionate side of men. He is attacking what he takes to be a tendency to *extirpate* rather than to spiritualize or discipline the passions. Philosophers, he felt, were frightened of the passions, which indeed have their dangerous aspects. But like any force in nature, their danger is compensated for by their utter necessity, and the problem is essentially how to give them form and purpose. Nietzsche saw it as his specific task "to divest the passions of their fearful reputation and [at the same time] to prevent them from becoming dominating torrents, to convert passions [*Leidenschafften*] into joys" [*Freudenschafften*].[43]*

There are at least two kinds of stupidity in regard to the passions. There is the stupidity of a man who supposes he can become master in anything if he has not first become master of his own lusts, hates, and resentments.[44] There is also the stupidity of the belief that the passions are *as such* horrendous, and must, in the name and hope of virtue, be annihilated. But: "To annihilate passions and desires, merely in order to forestall their stupidity and the unpleasant consequences of their stupidity . . . is merely an acute form of stupidity."[45] This Nietzsche identifies as the attitude of the Christian religion, and it goes *some* distance (but I dare say only some) toward explaining his vitriolic, sustained, and famous invective against the Christian Church. "The Church attacked passion with excision in every sense,"[46] he wrote in the *Twilight of the Idols*. In the same passage, however, he *also* points out that the Church was far more an enemy of *intelligence* than it was of passion, that it was hostile always, and suspicious, wherever intellect was concerned, favoring the "poor in spirit" and expecting revelation from the mouths of babes. Because it addressed itself essentially to a community not

* The German here will not pass into English, but in part this is so because *Freudenschafften* is a word made up for the symmetry it gives with *Leidenschafften*. The latter has *Leid*=suffering as a component as the former has *Freud*=joy. If we remember the etymology of the word "passion," the contrast is roughly between passions and actions, as it is here between sorrow and joy. Unfortunately, "passion" is no longer used in the sense of "passivity."

especially open to suasion or analysis, it employed ruthless rather than intelligent methods, castrating, so to speak, rather than coping in some less radical manner. Rather than asking the reasonable question, "How are the passions to be made spiritual, beautified, and divine?" the moralists of the early church laid stress on plucking out the offending organ: "But to attack the passions at their root is to attack life at its root. The practice of the church is inimical to life."[47]

It is, accordingly, a much qualified paganism that we must attribute to Nietzsche. Celebrating, as he did, the Mediterranean values, if we may speak of them as such (for he had the northerner's romanticized view of the sunny Mediterranean life), he held the basically sane if perhaps dull view that the passions and drives of men be disciplined and guided by reason, that our lives be Apollinian and Dionysiac at once, in that balance of force and form which, after all, had been recommended from the beginning of moral philosophy. Language aside, then, Nietzsche hardly deviated from the tradition which goes back at least to Socrates.

He perhaps would have justified his language by saying that the ancients did not have the puritans to attack. His psychology, too, was distinctive. And it must be remembered that, in distinction to the ancient moralists, he was not seeking a "formula" for leading a happy life, with reason in the ascendant over the passions (as Plato did), and will supporting reason in an auxiliary role. Rather, Nietzsche was interested in breaking through to a new metaphysics and a new morality, and he believed that this could be effected only through modifications in our emotional life and release within us of the "life-conditioning affects." Self-mastery remained a preliminary requirement, and even here he felt that not everyone is capable of achieving it. For most people, the external restrictions of society are essential. For this reason, too, he was somewhat afraid that Pandora's box might be opened by his philosophy if it was heeded without sufficient subtlety. He cannot, of course, be completely exonerated from the misinterpretations that have been given of him. He might have said what he meant more plainly and with less conflagrating a language. He was too self-indulgent and too self-dramatizing in representing to himself the difficulty of his thought. It is, at this point at least, less difficult than it is dubious.

V

If we are to find our way safely through the heartland of popular Nietzschean philosophy—his doctrine of master and slave morality, his references to cruelty, suffering, blond beasts, supermen, and the like—we must go equipped with some clear understanding of his theory of passions, however unclear in itself that theory may be.

We must first state the way in which Nietzsche sees us, even though this is familiar enough by now. Each of us is a cluster of drives and appetites and passions, and whatever we do or think is to be explained with reference to these drives. They give us our momentum and direction. Of these, however, few are identified in language or come to consciousness at all. We are likely to give false accounts of those that do, connecting them up with one another (as the prisoners did with the shadows in Plato's famous cave) rather than relating them to the seething undersurface of the mind. Conscious of little, and often wrong about that of which we are conscious, we have scant understanding of what we are or why we act. Insofar as we may speak of our reality, or what we really are, this will be the bundle of passions of which we consist. To some extent this becomes systematically clear only in connection with the Will-to-Power theory; but Nietzsche is making the assumption that "Nothing is 'given' as real other than the world of our passions and drives; and that we can ascend or descend to no different 'reality' than the reality of these drives."[48] The extent to which Nietzsche quite *literally* means this—that *nothing else* is real—will, I hope, become plain by the end of this study.

Two further assumptions must now be made. The first is that each individual is endowed with more or less the same set of drives, but the drives will vary in intensity from individual to individual. In some they may be weak to the point of inappetency; and in others they may be strong to the point of obsessiveness.

The second is that nothing, short of killing or maiming an individual, may be done to increase or decrease the strength of these passions. We must understand this assumption, however poorly characterized, as some sort of conservational principle. A given drive D of a given strength S will manifest itself in different ways depending upon the different social circumstances in which the individual, whose drive it is, happens to have been raised, and relative to the morality which prevails in that society. Consider a man who has a strong sexual drive. In certain circumstances he will be able to exercise this drive almost as freely as he might wish; for example, if he owns a harem, or is a member of a conquering army with free access to the women of the vanquished force, or lives in a Bohemian society with relaxed standards of sexual conduct. Now imagine this person in an extremely puritanical situation, where extreme sanctions are attached to sexual action. He might defy this, resorting to violence where blandishment fails. But short of emasculation, the drive will (by the conservational principle) remain strong and indeed tormenting without any of the natural outlets. Between emasculation and pure *laisser aller*, there is a range of possible "spiritualizations" or, to employ a well-known concept from psychoanalytic theory, "sublimations," which offer more socially acceptable substitute outlets for a drive that could damage society if it were allowed its "natural" course, and damage the individual if it were eliminated from his make-up. Now, we may regard a morality—a set of customs which individuals are required to obey—as offering a way of disciplining the passions and drives while permitting their discharge "as a condition of life and growth."[49] Roughly, then, we may think of moralities as forms imposed on passions, harnessing, as it were, certain native powers (and hence meeting power with power) for the benefit of the society. Individuals, then, may feel happy or not depending on whether they are provided avenues of outlet for drives sufficiently strong to require discharge. In some societies, moralities are creative, permitting a genuinely productive use of natural energy; in others, they are repressive, forcing these drives underground, as it were, where they issue forth as crimes, or mental disorders, or are in some manner destructive to the individual or to society. Without ever having been made explicit, this seems to have been Nietzsche's theory of the passions, or the main assumptions concerning such a theory.

Let us suppose there is in each of us a drive, stronger by far in some than in others, which we shall call "aggression." This is sufficiently close to the Will-to-Power to do temporary service and sufficiently close to a word in our vocabulary to take on a partial meaning. Even though aggression essentially has to do with dominating, or exercising one's power over, or giving one's form to some external thing, it also must be understood in a wider sense. Each thing, or for our purposes, each person, is directed by this drive, and we might even regard most of his actions as explicable with reference to it—whether he is an artist, a businessman, a preacher, or a soldier. Let us now indulge in a piece of speculative anthropology. Imagine a model (not in the sense of ideal but only of idealized) society where each member is brought up in conformity with a moral code, which both disciplines the group's members and functions as an integrative instrument, holding all the individuals to roughly the same patterns of behavior, thought, and expression. Each feels himself in solidarity with the rest. Suppose that among the individuals the drive to *aggress* is markedly higher in strength than elsewhere in the group. It is extremely useful, under certain conditions, for there to be individuals with this degree of the drive, for instance, if the group is threatened from without. Then this aggression is discharged outward, in opposing the enemies of the group. "Strong and dangerous drives such as love of adventure, foolhardiness, vengefulness, guile, rapacity, and power seeking"[50] turn out to be, here at least, as socially useful a set of drives (we may count them as modes of aggression) as any. Because of their utility, they will be counted as *virtues* and their possessors will be honored within the group— "decked in purple honors," as Zarathustra said. Only naturally, then, the warriors within a group, and the better warriors (those more highly aggressive) within this class, are the honored ones in the group when, as has perhaps nearly always been the case, the group is surrounded by a pool of hostile tribes (and indeed we may think of aggression as a group drive as well).

Let peace now prevail. By our psychological assumptions, the same amount of aggression will be present as before, only now there is no external avenue for its discharge. The warriors, unused to keeping themselves in check, find their aggression turned, despite themselves, against the precise individuals in whose defense it formerly was exercised. Their fields are trodden upon, their women are stolen, and so on. By the precise criterion—utility to the group—according to which their drives were termed virtues and esteemed, they now are disesteemed, regarded as immoral and as a danger to the group. They will, in effect, have become criminals.

Now, as the roads for their discharge are closed, [these drives] gradually become branded as immoral and abandoned to slander. Now the opposite drives and inclinations come to moral honor. The instinct of the herd draws its conclusions bit by bit. How much or how little danger to the common good . . . lies in a situation, an affect, a talent, or a will: this is now the moral perspective. Fear, once more, is the mother of morality.[51]

Now the tribe begins to make demands upon its erstwhile heroes. They must either become like everyone else, law-abiding citizens, or be hounded as criminals. But to be like everyone else is impossible for these individuals, given their drive and its unremitting intensity, invariantly as to external condition. From this circumstance Nietzsche will draw some fascinating psychological consequences, but here it is simply required that these individuals, who happen to be outstanding in relation to their group, are always, actually or potentially, a danger to the group.

When these highest and strongest drives break out passionately, taking the individual far beyond the lowlands of the consciousness of the herd, the latter's self-confidence, its belief in itself, its backbone, so to speak, breaks. So it is best to brand and vilify these drives.[52]

We must remind ourselves, as Nietzsche did not always do, that we are dealing with speculative anthropology, with an idealized model that illustrates the working of certain forces and shows how the same thing will be evaluated differently in terms of variations in circumstance—itself hardly a novelty in moral theory. We must remind ourselves, again as Nietzsche did not always do, that the drive we have termed aggression is not and need not always be manifested or expressed in antisocial ways and exhibited in the *personae* of soldier and outlaw. Indeed, aggression—or Will-to-Power, which is its near analogue—must be understood as a general phenomenon, widely and variously exemplified. In Nietzsche's own philosophy, art, religion, science, philosophy, and morality itself are among its instances. Nevertheless, Nietzsche favored, as an unfortunate idiosyncrasy of his writing, a *dramatis personae* in which the hero, more frequently than not, was a military type (he liked to refer to himself, with the slimmest justification, as "the old artilleryman")—though, in the very passage from which I have been quoting, he goes on to say: "A high, independent intellect, a will to stand alone, even a great understanding, are experienced as dangers; everything that elevates the individual above the herd and frightens one's neighbors is called by them "evil" [*Böse*]. Nietzsche sometimes identifies intelligence and rationality as *Böse*, forgetting that he has said that "good" and "evil" are traits which men impose and do not find in an absolute sense in the world, just as he forgets, or permits his readers to forget at times, that "herd" is a descriptive word and not a mere pejorative. There could be a herd of Einsteins, after all.

It is not difficult to see how readers who feel themselves to be superior persons should have found Nietzsche to be *their* philosopher, especially if they also felt that their superiority was unrecognized or without appreciation. Finally, this was Nietzsche's own situation, accounting perhaps as much as anything else for the ascending violence of his prose, for the increasing nastiness of his imagery and illustrations. He could have retained the same analysis with a far less Guignolesque rhetoric (after all, we find it already in his early books) and with a far wider and more humane application, for, as I have suggested and hope to show, it belongs to a broad and general theory indeed. But his isolation and vanity conspired, I believe, to confirm him in a style of writing and a pitch of shrill invective which seems, often, to be a despairing threat. In a way he declared war on society, as though he were misled by his own imagery into believing that only in time of war is the superior person—whom in violation of his own theory he narrowly identified as the soldier—honored and recognized as such. But this is a digression.

VI

The relativity of morality, of which Nietzsche and his Zarathustrian *porte-parole* make so much, is only perfunctorily illustrated in his writings. One finds, here and there, a comment on the differing tables of value adhered to by the Greeks, the Persians, and the Jews. He was not concerned, however, to compile an anthology but rather to construct a typology of moral practices; strictly speaking, it impressed him that there were only two main types of morality.

In wandering through the many gross and subtle moralities which have reigned heretofore, or which still reign in this world, I found certain manifestations regularly connected with one another, and regularly recurring, until I hit upon two fundamental types, and a basic distinction appeared. There is *master* morality and there is *slave* morality. . . .[53]

Nietzsche clearly stressed that these were *types*, that they seldom were found in any pure state, either in a given group or in the value attitudes of a single individual. But he sometimes speaks as though there are, or should be, perfectly pure exemplifications. The distinction is a basic and an important one for him, although the designations are perhaps unfortunate. As usual, we must look to context rather than connotation to see what Nietzsche means by these two moralities.

They are connected, in some respects, with the differences in evaluation assigned by members of a tribe or herd to their superiors. This depends on the utility of the superiors to the tribe, itself a matter of external circumstance to some degree. Nothing need be different about these superiors for them now to be honored and now to be slandered: it depends on the outlets available to them for the release of the passions that define their character and determine their superiority. These individuals, in whom aggression is strong, and who would throughout millennia have been warriors, are specifically designated "masters" or "aristocrats" by Nietzsche. The average members of the tribe, for whom the others fight, and whom in peace they threaten, are called "slaves." This term is not used in either a social or an economic sense; perhaps Nietzsche had in mind an ancient Aristotelian thesis that some men are natural slaves, whatever their economic or social condition may be, and that not every slave in the legal sense is a slave in the metaphysical sense. I am certain that Nietzsche revived this ancient horror of an idea and he regarded the bulk of mankind as made up of slaves in this regard—though there is also a conflicting *statistical* sense in which the bulk of mankind is made up of just those who are statistically average, no matter what *absolute* characteristics they may have. This confusion is responsible for considerable mischief in Nietzsche's writing. Notice that we remain here within our little anthropological model; for if we never take it as more than a model, it is a convenient tool for working out these distinctions. The two moralities we are concerned with originate from the two main groups; it does not follow from the fact that the "aristocrats" are honored that they should be regarded as "good." This brings us to the crux.

Both moralities employ the word "good," but, apart from the supervenient force of commendation which this word has, they use it in distinct ways and by means of it point quite distinct contrasts. The two moralities, in other words, are representable in language; and Nietzsche charts their main articulations by examining the moral idioms which express them. He had a remarkable ear for moral nuance; in a note he appended to Part One of the *Genealogy of Morals,* he urged that some university establish a prize for the best essay on the light which linguistics, and especially etymology, throws upon the history and evolvement of moral ideas. His writings are filled with suggestions as to how the same moral term can be variously used by persons with different situations, so that they have distinct moral perspectives without being aware that they have: to one man "virtue" might connote absence of pleasure, for example, whereas to another it might mean simple freedom from a goading appetite, so that neither understands the other.[54] The different meanings of "good," through its contrasts with "bad" [*schlecht*] and "evil" [*böse*], indicate the different moral perspectives of those who use them so. Naturally, if you can influence someone to use a moral predicate in *your* way, you can also get him to modify, if not himself, then at least his conception of himself. Nietzsche has been insistent on saying how moralities influence our conception of the world and of ourselves. His thinking this through in some detail entitles him, whatever one might think of his specific analyses, to the status of a moral philosopher and not the mere crank he is sometimes taken to be.

I begin by considering master morality. The individual, whose morality this is, feels there is a genuine distinction of value between himself and his peers and whoever in point of fact is different from them; and that *he* and his like are, in an absolute sense, superior to whoever does not resemble them in that in which their excellence consists. Indeed, he feels the distance between his group and *les autres* to be immense; whereas his group is, in the nature of the case, far more sparsely populated than the other. He sees the world divided into two distinct classes of being: the word "good" is applied to one class because the members possess absolutely certain qualities; whereas the members of the other class, by virtue of either lacking these qualities or possessing them only to an inferior degree, are "bad." "Good" is *not* used prescriptively. For prescriptions are directives as to how someone, even someone who is not of a certain kind, *ought* to be. It is Nietzsche's view that he who is not good *cannot* be good, goodness being simply a matter of what one is, not what one might, through dint of effort, become. The good are *natural* aristocrats, and it is the prerogative of aristocracy to impose its own values on the world. He who is good in this sense

feels himself to be value determining. He does not need to be justified, he judges that "whatever is offensive [*schädlich*] to *me* is *intrinsically* offensive. He knows himself to be that which generally gives honor to things, he *creates values*: his morality is self-glorification.[55]

Such a person may be useful to the group of which he is a member, and so may be valued for this. But he does not see himself in such terms.

What is essential to the good and healthy aristocrat is that he does *not* see himself as a function (be it of king or commonwealth) but rather as its meaning and highest justification. . . . His fundamental belief is that society does not exist for society's sake, but only as a support and scaffolding by means of which a select sort of being might rise to a higher sort of task and a higher sort of *existence*.[56]

Toward those unlike (and by definition inferior to) him, his attitude is merely contempt. Unlike him, they are (and Nietzsche does not say "for example," though he should) "cowardly, anxious, petty, and think in terms of narrow utility."[57] He is content to see any number of such individuals sacrificed so that he, and others like him, might be. He might aid and nurture the weak and defenseless, not out of pity but because *noblesse oblige*, or, if through compassion, it is not the compassion of the weak; it "counts for something"[58] and is an extension of his power. It would of course be readily understood were he to exploit the masses under him for his own purposes. He does not do so because he is necessarily cruel, but because his perspective prevents him from thinking his behavior in the least reprehensible. Nietzsche is utterly dispassionate (and, unfortunately, frighteningly accurate) in his discussion. Suppose a rich man, a prince, takes from a poor man something he treasures. Or some Don Juan steals the sweetheart from a man to whom women do not come easily. The victim is certain to regard his tormentor as a wicked person because he took from the victim the little that he has, which means to him so much. But he is in error:

The other does not at all esteem so deeply the value of a single possession. He is accustomed to many. So he cannot imagine himself in the poor person's place, and does not act nearly so unjustly as the other believes. Each has a false idea of the other.[59]

We never, Nietzsche elaborates, feel great qualms about creatures we might hurt when the distances between them and us is vast; no one feels guilty over crushing a bug, especially when the bug has been a nuisance. Xerxes, for example, felt another individual to be annoying in much the same way, and it was not cruelty on his part which motivated him similarly to crush that individual.[60] The same action, viewed from different perspectives, is differently appreciated and assessed.

From the masters' perspective, those unlike themselves are merely *bad humans*; that is to say, humans who do not come up to the mark. This is similar to the way bad eggs are low in the scales of egghood. There is nothing *morally* bad in being a bad egg or, in this usage, a bad human. It is just the way one is. Too bad, then, for the bad. They hardly can be blamed for what they are; but they *are* bad.

The slave morality derives from what is in effect the Lilliputian view of Gulliver. Precisely the qualities which the masters prize are called *evil* by their inferiors. In compensation, it is the *bad*— the lame, the halt, the blind, the meek, the poor in spirit—who really are good:

The slave's eye looks unfavorably upon the virtues of the mighty. He is skeptical toward, and mistrusts, whatever is honored as "good." He might persuade himself that not even happiness is there. Conversely, those qualities are underlined and spotlighted which serve to ease the existence of the sufferer: pity, the kindly helping hand, a warm heart, patience, diligence, humility, friendship—these now are honored—for they are the useful traits and almost the only means for enduring the crush of existence. Slave morality is the morality of utility.[61]

In effect, the slaves are "good" (in their sense) because they cannot, as inferiors, be "evil"—not because they would not be if they could. They want the evil masters to come around, mend their ways, and be like the others. In fact, however, those who are *evil* cannot become *bad*. Life courses through them too strongly for that. Nevertheless, the slave cannot see this, and his use of "good" *is* prescriptive: it says how everyone *ought* to be.

Details of Nietzsche's exposition aside, the two moralities reduce to a fairly simple and, since Kant, a fairly routine distinction between an absolute and unconditional value, and a hypothetical or contingent value. Some things are categorically good, others are so only conditionally. The master could be anyone who gives unconditional values. The slave, concerned with utility and consequences, has no absolute values at all. But we could hardly see the justification for using *master* and *slave* as sobriquets for these two types of evaluation, and Nietzsche does not discuss the matter in sufficient abstractness for us to take them up on that level.

VII

Morality, Nietzsche says repeatedly, is all a lie, if a necessary one—a *Notlüge*. It is necessary because "without the errors which lie in the presuppositions of morality, man would have remained an animal."[62] As it is, man is an *Übertier*, an ambiguous expression (as *Übermensch* will prove to be) meaning a higher animal, something which is higher than an animal, or an animal which has got beyond its animality. However it is to be interpreted, it is to be *explained* in terms of morality; and morality is, beyond doubt, often repressive of the animalities it lifts us beyond. Because it does this, Nietzsche, as an "immoralist" in the specific sense of opposing Christian morality, finds himself speaking at times in favor of this animality, forgetting that by his own analysis every morality is opposed to animality, not this one alone. We must be more careful in interpreting him than he was cautious in expressing himself.

His primal horde, or herd, which serves admirably as a model, has scant application to contemporary society, and it is hardly a satisfactory guide, much less ideal, for the resolution of society's moral problems. It must be remembered that when we abandon the strict compass of the primal herd the master morality is not to be identified as those practices carried out by lords and heroes, for these are only illustrations of it, and at any rate the master was to have been a giver of values. In the wider context of Nietzsche's discussion, masters simply are distinguished individuals of whatever sort who impose values on the world. They can be artists, they can be philosophers, they can be whom you will. Nietzsche filled the pages of his notebooks with criteria for answering the question "What is it to be distinguished?" [*Was ist vornehm?*]—and his lists come out to be strikingly autobiographical.

Finally, as though forgetting completely his main perspectivistic message, he goes on to speak of aristocrats and slaves as natural kinds. The aristocrat rises up over the masses, to use his revealing metaphor, as the Javanese ivy creeps up and finally overtops the trees that support it.[63] In what sense is the Javanese ivy superior to the oaks it climbs? Nietzsche often falls into the stupidest errors of the social Darwinian, identifying survival with excellence, although for some perplexing reason not seeing through to Huxley's devastating point that a slight shift in the chemistry of the atmosphere and perhaps only some lichens might survive, lords of the universe.

Now that we have said all this, there is something important and interesting in the theory that there are these moralities, and we should have a distorted view of Nietzsche's moral theories if we dropped the matter here. Indeed, we should have failed to see what happens when the masters apply to themselves the slaves' evaluation. This cannot be explained save with reference to religion and religious psychology, a topic on which Nietzsche was original and deep.

SIX

Religious Psychology

I

The Genealogy of Morals, as a title, nicely conveys the intentions of the book it names. It perhaps would have been a shocking title to the nineteenth century, at least more so than to our own. For it suggests that moralities have a genealogy, which is to say that they descended and evolved and were not, as it were, handed down from on high by some supreme and superhuman giver of laws. It is an old and well-entrenched idea that the bases of our morality are commandments, transmitted to us, which we *must* obey. People have often felt that the idea of a supreme lawgiver—a god—must be seriously defended, for if it disappears, they have feared, morality must go with it. If it proves to be a myth that there is, or ever was, a commander, a moral dictator, then what reason would men have any longer for being moral? It would, indeed, no longer make any sense to speak of acting in *obedience.* Thus the fear of moral anarchy has sustained the belief in gods down the ages.

Nietzsche wants to point out, by using this title, that the force of morality is not a function of its divine or semidivine origin, and that crediting a god with our moral code is but a myth, the assignment of a false imaginary cause for what can be explained, both genetically and functionally, in purely naturalistic terms. Moralities are evolved, as natural phenomena, in answer to a need to hold societies together, to insure their perpetuation, and to help contain the drives and impulses which could, without some check or sublimation, threaten or destroy the fabric of the group. A combination of circumstances determines the character of a morality, and, as Zarathustra somewhat heavily puts the point, "If one first knows the need, the land, the sky, and the neighbors of a people, one can readily make out the law of its overcoming, and why it climbs toward its hope upon this ladder."[1] A similar enough point has often been made with regard to individuals: if one knew their character and circumstances, their behavior could easily be predicted. This version of determinism has its analogue in Nietzsche's views on the emergence of a morality: it is traceable to plain circumstance, and the morality of a people "did not descend to them as a voice from heaven."[2]

A morality has a use and function. Yet there is always the possibility that a morality can outlast its utility, can, now as *mere* custom, go on being protected by sanction and by law, be taught and transmitted from generation to generation, when the conditions under which it possessed its utility have altered. Should this happen, a morality might serve to stunt the growth of that civilization for which it provides the basis. We, then, growing up in this morality, shall find ourselves to be victims of rules worked out in different conditions than we live under, by persons—our ancestors —different from us, portending ideals irrelevant if not harmful to our own condition. What then? Should this happen—as he indeed believed it had—a new morality is needed. As a contribution to its emergence, he hoped at least to show the natural conditions under which our morality had developed, or at least to show that moralities in general come about in this way. If we then persist in endorsing our present moral practices, we shall do so without any mistaken notions of what we are doing or what is the correct belief. He *hoped* we would create new values, or that the superior men among us would do so. It is this hope, in conjunction with his diagnostic aim, which perhaps helps to explain why his diagnoses are interlaced with diatribes and why an analysis shifts tone midway, ending in a denunciation or a plea.

The discussion of the two idealized moralities, the master and the slave morality, together with the linguistic expressions in the value-opposition of "good" with "evil" and with "bad," was deepened and sharpened in *The Genealogy of Morals* and complemented with a more refined psychological analysis of the mentalities of the two *human* types whose moralities these were. Nietzsche felt that linguistics, if it is to be an adequate instrument in his sort of inquiry, must be supplemented with psychology (of which he believed himself a master) and even with physiology and medicine.[3] This must be the case if we decide to treat not just morality as such, but any given morality, as a "problem," asking what is the value of *its* values. We must decide, for example, whether a certain table of values favors this or that human type, or this or that form of life; whether it encourages the appearance of a "more powerful sort of individual," or merely the longest possible survival of a given group. These ends are neither interdependent nor, for that matter, even compatible.[4] Here, however, we are interested in the psychological innovations Nietzsche made in this connection. Two of the psychological concepts which played a prominent role, clarifying a good deal in his philosophy, were *resentment* and *bad consciousness*.

The slave (if we may acquiesce in Nietzsche's unhappy nomenclature for purposes of keeping clear the connections with his idea) does not merely fear and magnify the *Bosheit* of the master; he *resents* the master's strength as well as his own relative impotency. To be sure, he must recognize in this that he is *schlecht*, a less than perfect specimen. Yet he is not able to accept the idea that he is to be treated any differently from anyone else, however high or low; or that he is to be treated as a means to the master's purposes or pleasures. As a human being, he feels that he has been treated with insufficient dignity, or with none. And so his consequent feeling of resentment. Yet what is he to do? He can discharge none of his hostilities in the manner open to the aristocrats, and this, indeed, is the source of his difficulty. If it *is* to be discharged—and Nietzsche's psychology contains an assumption that feelings will somehow find a way to expression—then this must be done in some devious, unobvious way. If he strikes the master an ordinary blow, he will be floored, worse off than before. So he must use guile, achieving revenge obliquely.

The particular revenge which slaves historically took (according to Nietzsche) was the basis for our own code of moral conduct. It consisted in getting the master to accept the value table of the slave himself, and to evaluate himself from the *slave's* perspective.

Through this odd strabismus in moral optics, the master becomes *evil* in his own eyes and reprehensible for exactly those values in which his erstwhile goodness as aristocrat once lay. He also has adopted the slave's notion of goodness and regards it as a prescription for himself. He feels morally obliged to be as "they." But this he cannot do. Now that he is unable to discharge those superabounding aggressive high spirits outward, dominating all before him, he turns them *inward, against himself*. His power reflected back in self-aggression, the slave has harnessed a force harmful to himself and rendered it inoperative.

How was this fantastic transvaluation of values effected? Nietzsche's answer is that it was the work of religion. Through religion the strong were yoked into a straitened set of imperatives under which they could not but suffer cruelly. Religion was the instrument of revenge which the resentful lowly discovered. The aristocrat had always, in the time of his license, given value to "a powerful physicality, a blooming, rich, overfoaming healthiness, together with whatever conditions the preservation of these—war, adventure, hunting, dancing, jousting, and in general everything that embraces strong, free, and joyful action."[5] This would have been in the contempt of the [Christian] religious outlook and the object of priestly rancor. Here we must not expect historical accuracy, and we shall come to terms with the nature of this strange account when we have more of it before us. Nietzsche claims that priests (whom one might think of as the tacticians in the triumph of the slave morality, if this was due to religion) happened to be at the opposite end of a scale of vitality whose top calibration was occupied by aristocrats: "priests are the most impotent of men," and they sustain the maximal degree of *ressentiment*. "Due to their impotency, their hatred waxes monstrous and gloomy, poisonous and clever. . . ." And the transvaluation of values, in the end, is their "act of the most spiritual revenge."[6]

II

One would think that if there were just the two basic types of morality, the foregoing would be a schematized account of what takes place more or less everywhere. The premises are psychological, after all, and it would not be just one specific group of slaves who would feel *ressentiment*: anyone anywhere might, if the analysis is sound. Nevertheless, Nietzsche has plainly in mind his own civilization and tradition, and he is making some implicit historical claims—although the degree to which these claims, should they prove false, are required by the theories he will base upon them is not quite clear. The religion he has in mind is Christianity, and possibly Judaism, for he blames (or credits) the Jews with having given form to the moral revolution which separates, in the West, modern from ancient times, and under which we now live.

Nietzsche's attitude toward the Jews has been a sore and moot point. He was himself not an anti-Semite. There were periods, or a period, when he was under Wagner's influence and a cocky young professor on his way up, in which he voiced the anti-Semitic views of Wagner and of Cosima—who was *plus wagnerienne que Wagner même*. His sister was married to a professional anti-Semite, Bernhard Förster. She was constantly trying to enlist Nietzsche in their cause; her unlicensed use of his writings during the time she was in South America infuriated him. He never allowed his philosophy to be so used, and if he was not a pro-Semite, he was anti-anti-Semitic. Any reader who wishes to determine his personal attitude, which was one of disdain and derision toward anti-Semitism (and toward the concomitant racist theories), need only consult the correspondence. One can find in his writings exceedingly complimentary things said about the Jews. Yet if we take such claims as: "The meaning of the Jewish people was the transvaluation of values . . . with them began the slave revolt in morality,"[7] it is hard not to suppose that he meant to imply that the Jews were really natural inferiors and enemies of life if the slave morality itself is life-contrary—which he often enough says it is. It would have exacted a measure of subtlety utterly unreasonable to demand from his readers that they see in this anything but ascription of blame to the Jews for the evils of the modern world. If he was not an anti-Semite, his language is misleading to a point of irresponsibility. I have no doubt but one can show that he is saying the Jews are to be credited with whatever is *best* in modern civilization, and indeed I dare say he would have acknowledged this. Nevertheless, it would require casuistry to show that the message is *not* the obvious one (and part of this book is such an exercise in casuistry). It must be conceded that a Nazi propagandist, with a far more straightforward reading, could find, in at least certain passages, justification for his most bigoted ideologies. Of course, the subsequent disaster of Nazism, and the semiofficial adoption of Nietzsche as the philosopher of that ghastly movement, have given to this negligible aspect of his thought an importance quite out of proportion to its systematic relevance. If some insane dictator had come into power on a program of misogyny, and consequently been responsible for the death of six million women, we should be disinclined, supposing this man had read and been inspired by Schopenhauer, to regard that philosopher's antipathy toward women with the indulgence we now assign it. At any rate, I am grateful not to have to disentangle the unedifying story of Nietzsche's influence upon the history of anti-Semitism in the world.

Nietzsche holds *ressentiment* historically and psychologically responsible for the development of the concept of Christian love. For it was an original fear of one's neighbor that led man to demand love from that neighbor. This could not happen unless he could disarm that neighbor in some way, and emotionally reorient him to honor, at his own expense, the weak, the humble, and the *schlecht*. But this requires further elucidation.

Nietzsche contends that slave morality could not *but* have arisen out of hatred. This is, oddly enough, less a historical than a logical claim; at least, it is based upon what seem to be the logical features of the system of morality under scrutiny. It is so in the sense in which it is logical to Hobbes that in the state of nature there is no injustice, because injustice logically presupposes a sociolegal structure by definition absent in the state of nature. Or in the sense in which it would be illogical to speak of an isolated individual acting *selfishly*, since one can act selfishly only with regard to the wants and needs and interests of *others*. Slave morality logically requires that there be evil persons, or at least something relative to which "good" may be *negatively* characterized.

Slave morality begins in saying "no" to an outside and an other, to a "nonself." This "no" is its creative act. . . . Slave morality requires for its origin a world external and opposed to itself, it needs, generally speaking, external stimuli in order for it to act: its action is through and through *reaction*.[8]

Nietzsche makes much of this point. His descriptions yield a picture of men who are constantly looking outward, each adjusting himself to the next person, who, it happens, is also looking for guidance outside himself as to what he should do. The slave, in this regard, is effectively demanding that each be like each, externally adjusted one to another. His morality is the morality of the group to which he belongs. The master morality, by contrast, is specified independent of external criterion, and the aristocrat does not seek to adjust himself to others: "all noble morality grows out of a triumphant self-affirmation":

The "well-born" feel themselves to be happy, they have no need to construct their happiness artificially through glancing at their enemies and hence, as all men of resentment are obliged to do, to *persuade* themselves, to *lie* to themselves. As healthy men, surcharged with power, they cannot separate action from happiness. . . . All of which contrasts with the "happiness" of the impotent and oppressed, obsessed with poisonous, malevolent feelings.[9]

Hatred, negation, the desire for others to conform, are essential features of the morality of slaves. The noble, to be sure, may at times hate, but it is not essential to their character to do so, and part of the reason for this is psychological. When the powerful person hates, he may discharge his hatred through direct action, and get it out of his system. The weak, however, cannot do this. They must *contain* their hatred, which acts as a psychological toxin, poisoning the spirit. This is the cause of rancor and resentment.

There is implicit here a peculiar physio-psychological theory which, if it were false, would severely challenge Nietzsche's entire analysis. A drive that is not discharged tends to remain at a level of strength which has a toxic effect upon the one who contains it. This does not mean, of course, that a drive must be discharged in its "natural" mode, but only discharged somehow. The slave in fact would be no better as an artist than as a soldier; his aggression, if bottled up within him, would be insufficient to do much except cause resentment. There is currently a theory, popular among social workers and progressive educationists, that it is good for children to let out aggression, as though there were a certain amount of this stuff and that it will, like the product of some unextruded suppuration, corrupt the psyche if not allowed expression. This is a dubious view at best, and complicated, in Nietzsche's case, by a characterization of the slave as one who cannot expel the accumulated burden of his spite. "The resentment of the distinguished man is consummated and exhausted in an immediate reaction: and so it does not poison [whereas] it is inevitable with the impotent and weak."

This is not simply a strange and vagrant theory. Nietzsche is nowhere more human, all-too-human, than in his admiring descriptions of the antics of the distinguished men of what I have been calling his model community. There can be scant doubt that he admires these creatures, more the product of his fantasy, one thinks, than anything else, having reference rather to his pathology than to his philosophy. In partial mitigation, one must recognize in these passages a strain of *épater le bourgeois*, something akin to the excesses we find in some of our contemporary writers on sex, who are apt to dramatize matters in proportion to the inertia they feel they must overcome as erotic reformers. Nietzsche particularly dwells upon the barbaric elements in the make-up of his aristocrats:

There is at bottom a beast of prey in all these distinguished races, an unmistakable *blond beast*, roving and magnificent, lusting for victory and booty. This hidden disposition must be discharged from time to time, the beast must emerge, and revert to the wilderness.[10]

One must shudder at the expression "blond beast." It is important to recognize that it has not any specific reference to Germans or to Aryans. He refers in this passage to "Roman, Arabic, Germanic nobles, Homeric heroes, Vikings." "*Blonde Bestie*" is almost certainly a literary cliché for "lion," the so-called king of beasts. Had lions, through genetic accident, been black rather than tawny, the expression would then be Black Beast and, leaving Nietzsche's point unaltered, provide support for African instead of German nationalists.

But more important than this by far is that he was not an enthusiastic commender of barbarism *because* of its excesses. He would have regarded this only as an accessory concomitant of their essential vitality, and a consequence of the fact that under Viking social conditions, for instance, relatively few spiritualizing structures were available for the sublimation of these drives. He has much the same attitude toward such individuals as he had toward the passions: they should not be brought down *simply* because of their excesses or (in his words) their "stupidity."

One has every right to fear that the blond beast, which lurks in the depths of every noble people, will get loose: but who would not a hundred times over prefer fear, together with admiration, than *lack* of fear together with the disgusting sight of the aborted, bedwarfed, embittered, and poisoned?[11]

This is doubtless a rhetorical query, and the contrasts it daubs for us are garishly overcolored. Suppose we were to answer the question naïvely by saying that we *would* prefer lack of fear, that fear of violence is not at all a good thing, and that the privilege of having these distinguished types among us is scarcely worth the price. If the last four adjectives in his passage are to characterize us, we might say that we do not look so bad to one another. Regarding the beasts among us, let them remain as ornaments to society, unless they cannot repress their bestial instinctualities. In that case, we shall have to take what measures we must.

Nietzsche has a *riposte* to this expression of preference, which brings us back to philosophical terrain at last: We are victim here of one of the Four Great Errors. Men, he will continue, have no choice, in the required sense, to be other than they are. To "demand that strength not express itself as strength is as absurd as to demand that weakness express itself as strength."[12] Here indeed is evidence that we have been traduced by the logic of our language. We are constrained by grammar into supposing that strength is, as it were, an activity of an agent, that showing strength is something which *he* does. In a similar way, perhaps, people might think of lightning as an entity which *does* something—namely, flash—but is distinct from the activity for which it is responsible. But lightning just *is* the flashing, not something distinct from it which may flash or not as it chooses. Because we are compelled to search out a subject for every verb, we fail to see that we have made a factual error based upon a logical requirement of our tongue. This then has moral repercussions.

The strong simply *are* acts of strength, not individuals who may or may not behave in a manner of strength. Because they are what they do, they have no option to do something else, for that would require that they *be* something else. It is not within the discretion of a flash not to flash, the strong not to "strength," or for "the bird of prey to be a lamb."[13] Nor, for that matter, can the *weak* be distinguished from the weakness: they *are* humility and patience, in the sense of identity and not predication. Yet they presume to call "the bird of prey to account for being a bird of prey!" The illusion dissipates when we see humility not as their achievement but as their essence, as brutality is not a lapse but the nature of the strong.

This is a logically invulnerable contention. But it is so on a thoroughly trivializing interpretation. A bird of prey is indeed a bird of prey, and logically he cannot be any other thing. This is a truth of logic, which perhaps explains the triumph of certainty with which Nietzsche presents his argument (misguided, one must think, in one who rejects the principle of identity as part only of *our* perspective). An analogous thesis was advanced once by Thrasymachus, in the *Republic*. He trivialized his definition of justice as acting in the interests of the stronger party by refusing to call strong anyone who failed to so act. A mathematician, analogously, is not a mathematician when he makes a mistake. This sounds astoundingly as though mathematicians are never in error, but this only allows us to infer, in fact, that whoever is in error, as men frequently are, is not to be called a mathematician at such points. In order to account for mistakes being made at all, we need the notion of an individual who is distinct from his office as mathematician, and who is sometimes wrong (but not *as a* mathematician). Thrasymachus, and Nietzsche, have elevated a triviality in logic into a metaphysics of morals. One must almost say that if anyone has been tripped up by a grammatical feature, it is they.

In fact, however, we cannot end the matter by this simple trump. Nietzsche's claim was subtler than that of Thrasymachus and less directly connected with mere stipulation. He was grappling with a difficult and dynamic conception of the world, a new and complicated metaphysics, in which the ontological category of *entity* was to be replaced with an ontological category of *power*. The world, he wanted to say, is in some sense composed of pulsations rather than things which pulse. A pulsation, being distinct from something which pulses, cannot, so to speak, *not* pulse; only a thing could do that, and pulsations are not things. This, it turns out, is the Will-to-Power doctrine (in part). If we were to allow it to be correct, we would find it very hard indeed to go on talking as we do, and we would feel, almost as certainly as Nietzsche felt, that our language was misleading from the start, never saying what was the case. This would have meant little to him, of course, for he was convinced that language muddles. He knew it would be difficult to work out a language for all of this—a language composed of verbs and adverbs, I suppose, but no nouns or adjectives. It would give even a special sense to his Nihilism, suggesting now that there are no facts, no things, only, as it were, pulsations—and a pulse *is* not any *thing*. Something like that. He then could argue that our moral ideas are based upon an inadequate metaphysics, expressed in a wayward language. It is this complex interconnection of Nietzsche's moral and metaphysical theories which makes him rather a more difficult philosopher to pin down than either his friends or his detractors have supposed.

It remains something of a puzzle, then, supposing the theory concealed behind all this were correct, how the weak should have prevailed over the strong, disarming them in some manner as to get them to behave like the weak. If, on that theory, a hawk acts like a lamb, a hawk *is* a lamb, since a lamb is what a lamb does, and the doing is the whole of its reality. How are the strong not to *act* strongly, this being, on the theory here assumed, an impossible and indeed a logically impossible situation? The answer is that the strong continue to act strongly no matter what. It is just that their strength is exhibited in acts different from the jolly mayhem of the Viking aristocracy. Nietzsche may be correct in saying that the strong cannot be weak, and that they are just their acts of strength and nothing else. It is irrelevant to his philosophy, and a quirk in his thinking, that he should have continued to harp on a certain *set* of acts of strength—the barbaric acts—of which he so relished to write. There are many modes of acting with strength, many forms for the discharge of power. One can be both strong and un-barbaric, for barbaric modes of discharge are only one such kind. There is nothing inherent in the theory which should lead us *not* to disapprove of barbarism. So rhetoric and analysis have to be distinguished once again.

We have not yet gotten to the source of Nietzsche's indictment of slave morality. If *we* disapprove of the discharges of vital energy which the barbarians and blond beasts exhibit, *Nietzsche* dis-approves of those acts of strength *now* engaged in by men who would, under another dispensation, have been happy warriors. But he need not approve of warriors as such. There are other ways of discharge, preferable to either, and many ways to felicity heretofore unexplored.

III

Let us think of the world, at least of the human world, as a contest of wills with wills. Simply by being alive, we are constantly involved in exercising our power over other persons and other things, and they over us. This is the way the world is. There is always suffering, if only objectively, in that sense of suffering which simply means being acted upon rather than being active in one's own behalf. In this sense, then, we always are either suffering or causing to suffer, and this, again, is the way the world is. For those with some awareness, to witness the suffering of others enhances, if but for a moment, their own sense of power. It is thus always an intoxicating sight to observe suffering, and an even more intoxicat-ing experience to cause it in another. The wood must suffer if the table is to be built, the deer must suffer if the tiger is to live, but

men, more subtle always, take an increment of pleasure—a malicious joy [*Schadenfreude*]—in the sheer spectacle of suffering: in
fights, executions, humiliations, bullbaiting, cockfights, and the
like. This is human, all-too-human. That life is suffering, in this
extended sense, is perhaps merely a dramatic way of epitomizing
metabolic interchange. That men should enjoy the show of suffering, and find in it an affirmation of their own power, is an independent psychological thesis. The former thesis entails that if we
are to live, we must impose and put up with the imposition of
suffering. To wish to eliminate suffering is to wish to eliminate life.
That suffering thus construed cannot be abolished has nothing to
do with the second and psychological thesis. The causing of gratuitous suffering, not that we may live but that we may enjoy our
sense of power, is hardly licensed by the fact of metabolism. Nietzsche often speaks as though it is. But, with his characteristic
elasticity, he also condemns the human, all-too-human delectation
of pain. As always, we must distinguish among his attitudes.

The imposition of form and order may be broadly construed as a
cause of suffering. We must push and pull and rearrange, and in so
doing we interfere with the natural thrust of whatever is so modified. Where there is form, there is, in this special sense, suffering
as well. Where there is form brought into human affairs, there is
subjective suffering, or *pain*. Pain is a good part of what holds
societies together, and historically it has a singular importance. On
this point Nietzsche speaks with originality. He characterizes man
as the animal that makes promises (that, even more remarkably,
keeps promises), and so possesses a "memory of the will."[14] A
contract is an interchange of promises; our legal systems are based
in part on the assumption that individuals will live up to their
agreements. If not, our systems also enforce their being honored.
He who makes and then breaks a promise is thereby exposed to
sanctions sufficiently powerful that, discounting intrinsic sentiments of honor, it is the exception rather than the rule that men
give in to the temptation simply to forget the obligation under
which they have placed themselves. Even the sense of honor can be
explained as the internalization of these promise-sustaining mechanisms which society has evolved.

Forgetting is not something that *happens* to us. It is something we do. Nietzsche speaks, in prefiguration of the psychoanalytic notion of the "censor," of a certain "concierge" at the threshold of consciousness, permitting certain thoughts simply to lapse, *putting* things out of mind. Man is a "naturally forgetful animal." In this way of thinking, remembering is just *not*-forgetting, *not* putting out of one's mind a will to do something; and this is the "memory of the will" he invokes in describing promising. If one thinks about it, it is extraordinary that individuals count themselves the *same* persons who made the promise which *still* continues to be binding on them. Only through some such conception could there have been any society at all, at least as we know it. For in achieving the memory of the will, men think of themselves as continuant in time, as self-identical through an interval and, as Nietzsche puts it, they begin to appreciate themselves in causal terms. This is of course "a bit of tyranny against nature." It is achieved by getting men to conform to rules, to behave in a predictable manner, instead of discharging their energies spontaneously:

The problem of raising an animal that dares to make promises requires . . . as a condition and preparation, the prior problem of making men, to at least a certain degree, regular, uniform, and calculable.[15]

And *this* was done through the mechanism of inflicting *pain*.

Nietzsche is excessive in his discussion of this topic, but it need not be taken as diminishing the force of his insight:

When man deems it necessary to make a memory for himself, it is never done without blood, torture, and sacrifice. . . . The harder it is for men to remember, the more fearful is this aspect of their custom; and the harshness of their penal codes furnishes us some indication of how hard it must have been to achieve victory over forgetfulness, and to keep those slaves of momentary desire aware of a couple of basic requirements for social and communal living. . . . How dearly we have paid for reason, seriousness, and control over the passions. . . . How much blood and suffering is at the basis of all "good" things.[16]

Within proportions, we doubtless do think in somewhat this way. Inflicting pain is often enough spoken of as "teaching a lesson" to someone: a punitive person will accompany a cuff with "That will teach you!" Here our language betrays our educational theories. It may well be that the more primitive the person, the harder it is to "teach" him something, and greater is the amount of pain required to get a lesson to "stick." This may or may not be the case. Certainly with the advance of civilization there has been an unquestioned humanization in this area. Capital punishment, one hopes, is becoming increasingly antiquated, but one can hardly read the history of punition without disgust.

Pain is thus a social tool. But the matter does not end here. Nietzsche is impressed with the fact (which is independent) that social justice, as well as being a reinforcing mechanism in learning and a deterrent to "forgetting," has often consisted in exacting, on the creditor's behalf, a most peculiar compensation from the delinquent debtor. The creditor is entitled, by law, to what amounts to a quantum of pain from the defecting debtor. That a debt may in effect be *repaid* by a compensatory measure of pain suggests to Nietzsche that people must derive a certain pleasure from the suffering of others, or it would be a bad bargain indeed. Is the loss of a cow really to be canceled out with a hundred strokes on someone's back?

This is human, all-too human, to relish "the pleasure of being able to use one's power freely against someone who is powerless, doing harm for the joy of it; the delectability of the rape."[17] One has the exalting feeling of "treating another individual as lower than oneself." That *you* make *him* suffer establishes your *de facto* superiority. It is *not*, of course, suffering *as such* which we enjoy, and which is the aim of malice. It is rather our own pleasure we aim at; otherwise, there would be no point. We become conscious of our own strength by breaking twigs, dislodging stones, pitting ourselves against wild creatures;[18] and inflicting pain comes to the same thing. Philosophers have wondered, in the so-called Other Mind problem, whether we really have any grounds for supposing that other people do have pains. We do not infer that we do, I think Nietzsche would say, but we presume they do by the elevation of feeling their "pain-behavior" seems to cause in us. The following is written tongue in cheek:

To witness suffering is pleasant, to inflict it even more so. This is a hard saying, but it expresses a powerful old human, all-too-human axiom. . . . There is no festivity without cruelty: so teaches the longest, oldest history of humankind. Even in punishment there is something so very *festive*![19]

People, he says wryly, do not object to suffering, they object to meaningless suffering. "Meaningless suffering" is that from which nobody profits, which goes unenjoyed by witnesses. In an almost cruel paraphrase of a Berkeleian argument, Nietzsche claims that men invented the concept of an omniscient god so that there could be a witness to all the scraps of pain, just so they would not go to waste. This is an odd, sardonic footnote to the problem of evil. The gods did not cause it, *it* created the gods. This, incidentally, is not a mere obiter dictum in Nietzsche; we shall encounter it again, when we gather up the threads of the argument we are developing.

Whatever the case, the "beast of prey" is not housed solely in the bosom of the "strong." It is ubiquitous, a generic human trait. Civilization may have spiritualized it to a degree, but its presence is everywhere discernible. To be distinguished or to wish to be distinguished in any way above one's fellows is already a sign of this dark and universal drive:

A man will so behave that his appearance grieves his neighbor, awakening his envy, his sense of impotency and degradation. One will give him a taste of the bitterness of his fate by letting fall a drop of one's own honey upon his tongue—gazing sharply and triumphantly into his eyes while bestowing this purported benefit.[20]

Men will go to any extreme. One will use his humility as a torment for another. An artist relishes in advance the envy of his rivals whom he expects to outstrip through his great works. A nun uses her chastity as a way to punish women who live the natural female life—"With what punishing eyes she looks into the faces of other women!"[21] These are refined cruelties [*verfeinerte Grausamkeit*], but cruelties nonetheless. "The theme is brief, the variations numberless, and not in the least bit boring."[22]

It is the universality of cruelty which Nietzsche has in mind when he speaks of the wish that there were no suffering, that everyone were kind and good, as futile. For life is this way, and man is this way. But there are refinements, as we have seen, and modes. The barbaric war lord, whom Nietzsche sometimes perversely applauds, is described elsewhere as on the bottom rung of a "long ladder."[23] On the top rung of this ladder—which symbolizes the stages in civilization and in the spiritualization of cruelty—stands not the blond beast at all but the *ascetic*. He is the self-disciplined man, who is distinguished from others through his exercise of power not over others but *over himself*. So much, then, one wants to say, for Nietzsche's thesis that power must be exerted over others as the price of life. The ascetic, who dominates himself, is an avatar, a *persona*, of the beast at the bottom of the scale. Religion accounts now for the shift upward, for the ascetic is the aristocrat, whom the slaves so feared domesticated. He is what they have managed to bring about as the consequence of their resentment.

IV

Let us reintroduce some features of Nietzsche's theory of instinctual drives. Recall, here, that these are invariant as to social and moral structure, although certain social and moral structures may demand that this or that drive be checked. Even when this is so, however, the drive persists in intensity within the individual, even if the one it motivates should disapprove of himself for housing it: "The old instincts did not all at once stop making their demands—it only became difficult and rare to satisfy them [directly]."[24] The "strong," in whom by definition these drives worked to a high degree of intensity, would, like the "weak," be obliged to contain them or effect their discharge covertly (illegally or immorally) or indirectly. The indirect discharge, which involves a displacement of the "natural" object of the drive, gives rise to a remarkable phenomenon:

Suppose that aggression is a drive which is reduced in a natural manner only through discharge against some external object, and that countervailing moral forces exist which prevent drive-reduction in this natural manner. If we assume that a drive simply *is* discharge (as Nietzsche's theory seems to require), and not something which is the subject of the verb *discharge*, then there will be discharging during the time the prohibition holds; if the prohibition is obeyed, the discharge will not be against an *external* object. This leaves only the possibility of an *internal* object, the person himself, as it were, who turns his aggressive discharges inward. Intensity remains constant, only direction changes. "All instincts, which are not discharged outwardly, turn themselves inward."[25]

This phenomenon, which Nietzsche terms "internalization" [*Verinnerlichung*], plays a role in the further development of *consciousness*. It is through *Verinnerlichung* that "there first appears what one later calls the 'soul.' "[26] As the external avenues available for the discharge of instinctual energy are progressively blocked off, "the whole inner world, originally small, as though confined between two membranes, receives depth, width, and height":

Hostility, cruelty, the joy in pursuit, in ambush, in change and in destruction—all of this turns itself upon the possessor of these instincts. . . . Man, lacking external enemies and resistances, forced into a restricted narrowness and regularity of ethics, tore impatiently at himself, persecuted, gnawed, molested himself, as a wounded beast, wanting to rend someone, dashes against the bars of his cage. . . . Man makes himself an adventure, a torture chamber, an uncharted and dangerous wilderness.[27]

This inward hostility had complicated consequences. There was an unprecedented struggle of the will with itself, the Will-to-Power of a man reflected against itself. The Will-to-Power is in effect a will to *overcome*, to defeat, to subdue whatever it is the drive is directed against; here it is used to *overcome itself*, in which the imposer of order imposes an order upon itself. It was the triumph of morality to cause this self-overcoming in men who had before been as beasts; it is in this sense primarily that Nietzsche wants to say that it is morality above all things which puts us the other side of animality. But awakened thus to the possibility of *domi-*

nating himself, "mankind aroused an interest, a tension, a hope, nearly a conviction that with him something was being announced and prepared, as though man was not an end, but a way, an incident, a bridge, a great promise. . . ."[28] This is what Zarathustra is made to say about men, and in many ways it is Nietzsche's own prophetic vision and injunction. It must be perfectly plain that Nietzsche was *not* asking for a release from its cage of the beast which morality hemmed in; he was not, in the name of some specious theory of happy savagehood, urging reversion to barbarity, or to an infantile immediacy in the reduction of drives. Nietzsche was asking that we go *beyond* what we are, not *back* to what we were.

But the reflection of the will upon itself, although an indispensable *first step* toward a higher form of life, a means to some end, is *not* an end in itself; and Nietzsche felt that it had become so. There is a derivative product of moral restraint of instinct, which is self-aggression carried to an extreme and made a point of honor, so that, in effect, a man may become ill through an overdose of the instrument of therapy and cure. Men may become *arrested* at the stage of mere self-aggressions, or self-hatred. This Nietzsche calls *bad consciousness* [*Schlechtes Gewissen*]. It arises through the imagery and outlook of religion, for religions are repressive and venomous, inhibiting what we might call this-worldly salvation, to which inner discipline might lead, by promoting an impossible hope for salvation in another world. Religion teaches (so Nietzsche insists) a hatred of the world and of the flesh, and bad consciousness is the psychological reflection of this, being a virulence of self-detestation. By preaching a hatred of the instincts— which is what the flesh is—religion employs the instincts against their owners. The stronger the instincts in an individual, the greater his capacity for self-punition, and his magnified hatred of himself is the final form of revenge religion achieves for the weak.

V

The ascetic is a barbarian *en masque* and self-chastising, the blond beast crushed in his own jaws, the ravager ravaged in a career of self-bestialization. Nietzsche held the ascetic in great respect, as is consistent with his admiration for the old warring heroes of whom the ascetic is only a *persona*. His scorn is only for the weak who have triumphed over their enemies by making them enemies of themselves. The ascetic is no less strong, no less distinguished in his unedifying self-abasing, which is no less an act of power than if it were directed outward:

The triumph of the ascetic over himself, his thereby inwardly directed gaze which beholds a man split asunder into a sufferer and a spectator, looking outward into the external world only to gather wood for his own pyre: this final tragedy of the drive toward distinction, in which one single person stands in self-consumption, is an end worthy of its beginning.[29]

Nor is the old human *Schadenfreude*, the wicked pleasure in the beholding of suffering, any the less absent because one happens to be martyr and executioner at once. Indeed, one might increase the pleasure by increasing the suffering—anyone who has taken pride in his "will power" will know what this means. Religion abets this immensely: "The man of bad consciousness seized upon religion's presuppositions in order to push his self-torture to its most horrifying limits."[30]

Religion contributes to this painful vagariousness in rather a special way. Many religions claim that we stand to a god in the relationship of offspring to a father, and that whatever we have or are, we owe to the divine begetter. So we are, each of us, *in the god's debt*. But it is a debt which cannot be repaid, nor have we really any way of paying it except the way our human, all-too-human equation of value with suffering suggests: we pay through our suffering. Because the sight of suffering provides a sense of ones ascendancy, we project upon our god an anthropomorphic pleasure in *our* suffering as a mark of his ascendancy and plenitude. Then, the greater the debt, the more we owe; and the more powerful we conceive our god to be, the greater the suffering demanded on our part. This means, in effect, that we must constantly increase the distance between ourselves and our god, rendering the god more powerful and ourselves proportionately more impotent and valueless. The higher our regard for god, the lower our esteem for ourselves until, when we make god out to be all-perfect, we must logically make ourselves out to be maximally contemptible. Religions then teach the goodness of god and the baseness of man (that sinner and ingrate) and it is, finally, through this sense of his own cosmic inferiority that the ascetic finds his most exquisite instrument for self-torment. And this is a form of insanity:

Here is a sort of madness of the will, a spiritual insanity the like of which surely has never been seen: man's will to find himself guilty and worthless, and inexpiably so. . . . Man's will to erect an ideal— that of the "Holy God"—in the light of which he could be assured of his own unworthiness absolutely. What a mad, sorrowful animal man is! . . . So much in man is terrible . . . the earth has been a madhouse for so long a time![31]

Belief in gods need not have this consequence. It did not in Greece. The Greek Olympus, according to *The Birth of Tragedy* was invented in response to suffering, in its mitigation, and not (he thought) a contribution, as was the Christian conception of God, to the increase of human anguish.[32] And so we have Nietzsche's railing denunciation of Christianity, as a cause of suffering (and what, one wants to know, has happened to the bold declaration that there is no life without suffering?) and, more significantly, as an ideology of dishumanization, teaching, as he thought it did, the low estate of man. Christianity prevented ascent to a higher form of existence.

This invective appears more frequently in the later writings, which lack the psychological brilliance of the early and middle books, and which *The Genealogy of Morals* superbly exhibited. It is almost as though the work of diagnosis were over, the time having now come to combat. The *Antichrist* is unrelievedly vituperative, and would indeed sound insane were it not informed in its polemic by a structure of analysis and a theory of morality and religion worked out elsewhere and accessible even here to the informed reader. He who has followed this volume through will easily enough detect the thoughts behind the screen of insult which makes up the following sample passage from *Antichrist*:

Man ought not to ornament and embellish Christianity. It has waged a *war to the death* against these *higher* human types, it has placed under ban all the basic instincts of this type, it has distilled evil and the Evil One out of these instincts—the strong man as the typically unworthy man, as "refuse." Christianity is the partisan of all that is weak and degraded; it has constructed an ideal out of the negation of the survival-instinct of the strenuous life; it has corrupted the reason of those spiritually strongest through teaching them to interpret the highest values of the spirit as sinful, misguiding, seductive. . . . It is a sad, awful spectacle which breaks upon me: I draw the curtain back from the *corruption* of manhood. . . . All the values that now define what man must find most desirable are *decadence-values*.[33]

In the final, nearly apocalyptic tirade in *Ecce Homo*, Christian morality is called a catastrophe, the Christian conception of God is denounced as poisonous and inimical to life; one by one each element of the Christian teaching and faith becomes bathed and coated with the spume of rage and intemperance, the inventory capped with *"Ecrasez l'infame!"* and epitomized as "Dionysus against the Crucified"—*Dionysos gegen den Gekreuztigten*.[34]

These may be seen merely as the words of incipient madness or as blows struck in the name of humanity. Or as both. The matter is sane if the style is beyond the permissible limits of manic utterance. He was, however, speaking as a prophet, and, as he tells us at the end of one discussion in the *Genealogy*, the raising of an altar demands the breaking of an altar. He was offering what he regarded as a new and liberating faith in place of an old and truncating one. This will bring us, in a short time, to Zarathustra.

VI

We must not quit the topic of religion without touching, if but briefly, on two further aspects of Nietzsche's theories which belong with his discussion of religion. One belongs to the dark, cruel *illustrative* side of Nietzsche, the other exhibits his singular gift for discerning resemblances between seemingly diverse phenomena, discovering, as he would have liked to put it, that they are only different masks behind which stands the same force. The latter has to do with various forms of activity which are essentially religious, even though to someone unaware of the connections they may be regarded as antireligious. This will involve a broadening of the concept of religion. The former aspect has to do with the destiny of the weak under the influence of religion when the latter is *narrowly* construed. I shall discuss this first, as the least philosophical.

Nietzsche is notorious for having taken a deprecative and indeed a hateful view of altruism. As always, one must introduce caveats in describing Nietzsche's views, and we have already noted that compassion, which comes from strength and not weakness, counts for a great deal, especially when it involves the protection, by an aristocrat, of others weaker than himself.[35] Fellow-feeling— *Mitgefuhl*—is even listed as one of the four virtues he would enjoin. When Nietzsche speaks of the proper conduct for a distinguished person, his recommendations often resemble those of Confucius, offered by the Chinese sage as normative for the gentleman, or *chün tsu*: his behavior should be dignified, circumspect, courteous, and discerning, as, indeed, was Nietzsche's personal behavior. Yet it is almost as though certain words release in him a spring of covert hostility, and when this happens, we get an illustration which blackly accompanies his text, almost as a verbal equivalent of a German woodcut, giving a particularity to his thought it neither demands nor requires. His "philosophy" has often been thought to consist in these illustrations rather than the text which they usurp. "Altruism" was apparently one such word.

"For what," he demands, "does the compassion of those who suffer count? Or the compassion of those who *preach* compassion?"[36] He doubtless held an eccentric view in his conception of compassion, sympathy, pity, and the like, and to a degree he was taken in by the German word for "pity," *Mitlied*—to "suffer with." But only to a degree, I think, for it is ingenuous to suppose a trained philologist could not see through this primitive etymology. In fact, he warns explicitly against being taken in by "the crudeness with which language covers so polyphonous a thing with only one word."[37] He is engaged in a polemic with a specific philosophical tradition, identified especially with Schopenhauer, who believed that pity—"which he knew so superficially and observed so badly"—was the source of every moral action. Schopenhauer himself was but a representation of a school of moral sympathy theorists. Against pity, Nietzsche has (at least) two objections. The first is that he who feels pity suffers with, and hence is brought down to the level of, the one whose object is the pity—making him "melancholy and ill."[38] It is along these lines that Zarathustra said God dies of pity, having been, I suppose, made ill through the suffering with which he empathized. To demand pity of the strong is, in this (peculiar) regard, to demand that they become weak. Nietzsche also objects that pity conduces to the attempt to meliorate the sufferings of the weak out of feeling sorry for them. When compassion is elevated to "the basic principle of society," as he thought it was in Christian ethics, then the injunction shows itself in "its true colors: as the will to deny life."

Life itself is *essentially* appropriation, injury, overpowering of the alien and weak, oppression, hardness, imposition of form, incorporation and, at the very least—gain. . . . Appropriation does not simply belong to a perverse or imperfect or primitive society: it belongs in essence to *living things*, as an organic basic function. It is a consequence of the actual Will-to-Power, which is just the Will-to-Life.[39]

This passage brings out a central confusion in Nietzsche's thought. By definition, the distinguished man stands out above his fellows. The distinguished man, moreover, is healthy, animal, powerful. The opposite of distinguished is undistinguished. Those who are undistinguished are, in opposition to the distinguished person, sick, effete, and weak. Hence the herd consists of the sick, the weak, and the impotents. This is as nakedly a fallacious inference as could be drawn, but it is fairly clear that Nietzsche drew it:

Mankind, like every other type of animal, produces a surplus of the abortive, diseased, degenerate, feeble, and necessarily suffering. The successful instances are the exceptions among men.[40]

The exceptional man, accordingly, is not regarded merely as a statistical deviant but as a splendid instance in its kind, surrounded by a mass of miscasts and culls. Only by taking the mean as the standard would we be led to believe otherwise. But in fact, Nietzsche might argue, it would be wrong to believe so. The average manuscript submitted to the average publisher is likely to be a reject, not worth printing. The printable manuscript is the exceptional one. In seeking a candidate for a job, the *average* person who applies will be rejected; we always think of the job as filled by not the average but by the best person we can find. The man who seeks a perfect specimen, whether of women or sea shells, is certain to find that *most* of what he finds fall away from perfection by a considerable degree. All of this may be granted out of hand. Yet to say that most men are misfits makes no logical sense. To say that most men are unhealthy is simply false. There are epidemics, to be sure, but strong and weak alike are felled: if more peasants than nobility die of the plague, it is because there are more peasants to die, or they are less able to escape. Of those exposed, the immune survive, and this has to do not with strength or fairness but with inoculation. A vaccinated churl will survive where the pride of the nation perishes. Perhaps we should vaccinate only the strong and the beautiful and let the others perish. If we were motivated by purely eugenic considerations, we should do this, I suppose, as we might with the animals we breed. That we do not Nietzsche attributes to the Christian morality. It serves to maintain "too much that should have perished"[41] (and the converse, too, I suppose). Consequently: "The species does not grow in perfection: the weak are forever prevailing over the strong."[42]*

One would think that strong is as strong does, and that it is

* In part, this triumph of the weak over the strong is due to their greater cleverness—a thesis of Nietzsche's which makes one pause to wonder whether he is paying a compliment to the Jews when he says, as he often does, how clever and intelligent they are. If the strong really *is* exceptional, of course, by *one* of Nietzsche's characterizations of exceptionality, it is easy to see how he might not be very clever. He would be outside, or at the edge of comprehension of the language of the herd, and thus not able to express himself very well. Hence his "dumbness." This, of course, is only a joke. But it serves to bring out that the word "exceptional" has no absolute sense in Nietzsche's philosophy. Dolt and poet alike are exceptional.

Nietzsche writes that "the weak have more spirit."[43] But this once more is hardly a compliment when we look to the context from which it comes. It is always a problem, when citing Nietzsche, to make sure one includes enough virtually inconsistent to say of x and y that x is weaker than y, but y succumbs to x. But the truly incoherent element in Nietzsche's thought is his speaking as though an objectively better type of being can be talked of, whereas it is wrong to take normative criteria as having the least bearing on the way things are to be judged in reality. This is an unpleasantly tangled pocket in his system, and an aberration from the overwhelmingly dominant direction of his thought. But I see no way of explaining it away.

VII

Were the reader to select only the parts of Nietzsche's books which bear upon his eugenic despairs, his seeming nostalgia for the neolithic freedom of the happy brute living in unaware animal felicity, he might be surprised and shocked to find Nietzsche saying that had it not been for religion, after all, human history would have been a dull business. Of course it would have been dull. There was, as Hobbes recognized, no civilization to be found in the state of nature, and the story of life would be a

---

of the context so that the meaning of what he says is sufficiently plain and consonant with his intentions. Even so able an expositor as Professor Kaufmann, who has been a devastating critic of those who have quoted Nietzsche to their own purposes by lifting passages out of context, cannot always avoid this himself. Thus, in his *Nietzsche: Philosopher, Psychologist, Antichrist* (Princeton: Princeton University Press, 1950), p. 258, he cites Nietzsche as saying that "Darwin forgot the spirit." Nietzsche does say this, in exactly the passage from which *I* have been quoting in the *Twilight of the Idols*. But now Kaufmann goes on to make the claim that Nietzsche is implying that you cannot explain human behavior in purely material terms, without reference to man's "spiritual life," and that this was what Darwin overlooked. Nietzsche of course was not a materialist, regarding "matter" as a fiction. But his point against Darwin is *not at all* what Kaufmann says it is. The passage continues: "One must need spirit in order to acquire spirit—one loses it when one no longer needs it. The strong dispense with spirit." He defines "spirit"—which by itself sounds very exalted—as follows: "By spirit I understand caution, patience, cunning, dissembling, great self-control, and whatever is mimicry. To the latter belongs a good bit of so-called virtue." This has almost nothing to do with Darwin not thinking about mental factors. Rather, it is used to make the point that "spirit" is something the herd has, but which the strong do not need, although through spirit the herd is able to triumph over the strong. Thus spirit leads to the debasement of the species. Darwin is implicitly criticized for having thought that the "better"—or the "fit"—survive when it is the "unfit" who do instead. If Darwin had not forgotten about spirit, then,

monotonous iteration of bashings and rapes. If there has been a history, it is due to religion, and hence to "the intelligence furnished by the impotent [priests]."[45] This brings us to what must be said on behalf of religion: "Man, *the animal*, heretofore had no meaning. His life on earth had no purpose. 'What is man for?' was a question without an answer. . . . Man did not know how to justify, explain, or affirm himself."[46]

Here we get an echo of a note sounded in *The Birth of Tragedy*. Religion, art, and philosophy were said to be ways of responding to and overcoming suffering. They provide for men an architecture of significance in the bare, unmeaning world. By virtue of being conscious at all, men are lifted out of the unwitting oneness with which animals and other beings are at one with the world. "Man is sicker, less secure, more changeable, less stable than any other animal," Nietzsche writes. "Man is the *sick* animal." But then he adds,

Certainly he has risked more, defied more, invented more than all the other animals put together. He, the great experimenter with him-

---

he would have seen that there is no progress but a deterioration through evolution. The species gets worse and worse. This, I think it plain, is Nietzsche's point.

It is not a very compelling point. Darwin rather less than the Darwinists of the nineteenth century thought in terms of upward evolution, identifying the "fit" with some higher type of being. So it is rather unfair to Darwin as such. Nevertheless, it was a common enough idea, and one based, just as Nietzsche's own criticism of it was, upon an unwarranted insertion of a normative component into the notion of fitness or unfitness. Blond beasts would drop like flies were the oxygen to disappear for ten minutes from the earth's atmosphere. But clams might survive that nicely.

We get an inconsistency, and a dominant one, in Nietzsche, if we read "spirit" as consciousness or self-awareness:

No differently from the way that happened with those aquatic animals who were forced either to become land animals or be destroyed, these half-animals, adapted to wilderness, war, wandering, and adventure, had their instincts all at once devalued and unhung. They must now go on foot and bear themselves up where water had heretofore supported them: a frightful heaviness weighed them down. They felt inept for the simplest performances; and in this unknown world they could not count upon their old guides, the unconscious, regulating instincts. They were obliged to think, infer, reckon, combine causes with effects, reduced, these unfortunates, to their "consciousness"—their weakest, most fallible organ.[44]

self, the unsatisfied and unslaked . . . how should such a brave, rich animal not also be the most threatened, the most deeply sick among the animals?[47]

Many philosophical writers speak, as it has become fashionable to do, of the sickness of mankind and the hopeless alienation, but it is never terribly clear in what this metaphysical pathology consists. We might suppose it consists, in part, in the fact that men have self-awareness, and so recognize that they are different from the objects of their consciousness. In this regard, perhaps, starfish are healthy and metaphysically *chez soi*. Nietzsche speaks of the primeval condition in which men lived a completely instinctual existence, consciousness coming only late and ineffectively as a supernumerary organ. Man, then, thrown on his higher but hardly adequate mental resources, finds life fraught with dangers undreamed-of in the somnolent deeps of preconscious subsistence. Or the sickness, if we may continue to call it that, is not merely the fact of our apartness from the rest of nature but our disharmony with ourselves, as though, once beyond the level of instinctual comportment, we must displace and spiritualize the entirety of our battery of instincts, blocking them off from their natural objectives and forcing them to find new and artificial outlets. We tend to distrust the uncontrolled and unspiritualized instincts, intensively so in religion perhaps, and then to wish for a purely rational, uninstinctual, totally spiritual life. But, remaining animals *quand même*, we suffer from the disparity between what we are and what we hope. Yet, if in either instance there is suffering, it is suffering with a point. Religions give a sense and meaning to the fact of suffering, even if they cause suffering as well. And "any kind of meaning is better than no meaning at all."[48] There is pain all along the struggle out of the uterine oneness of primitive naturality, but

In spite of this, man was saved. He had a meaning. He was no longer a leaf in the wind, a plaything of unmeaning. [Here was], of course, a counterwill, a will against life, an opposition to the fundamental presuppositions of life. But it was and remains a *will*. . . . Man would rather will *nothingness* than not will at all![49]

So in bad consciousness and asceticism, the same instincts remain at the same intensity as always. The Will-to-Power is unextinguished, only deflected. The degree of our sense of unworthiness before an impossibly perfect deity becomes the measure of our own power. The more we cause ourselves to suffer, the stronger must we be.

Now we must begin to see this in a more general way, and this brings us to the second topic I mentioned. The ascetic ideals are only *exemplified* in religious life; and religion itself, as Nietzsche wishes to see it now, is only *exemplified* through what would in common speech be called religions. There are forms of religion, in this *broad* sense, which are antireligious in the *narrow* sense. We have already seen this shifting from a narrow to a wide sense of a term.

A man may be religious in the wide sense and antireligious in the narrow sense when he calls religions into question in the name of something else, such as reason, or science, or historical criticism, or truth. In contrast with each of these, men have found religions to be irrational, obscurantist, mythical, and false. It is these other things which should command our allegiances. But in committing themselves to reason, truth, history, science, or whatever else it is they believe to be higher and greater than themselves, men are but ascetics in disguise, *personae* of the religious impulses which only incidentally are expressed in actual religious forms.

Does one see these, perhaps, as the sought-for enemies of the ascetic ideal? As *counter-idealists?* . . . They believe themselves to be as unattached as possible to ascetic ideals, these "free, oh so free spirits." So I reveal to them what they cannot see, since they stand too close to it. This ideal is also exactly *their* ideal. They themselves represent it today, they themselves are its spiritual heirs, its spearhead warriors and spies. . . . These are not *free* spirits by a long shot: *for they still believe in truth.*[50]

This will hardly be a puzzling statement to anyone who has kept in mind the Nihilistic theories, which we have hardly touched upon for many pages. Let us now take this statement in conjunction with a section he added to the *Gay Science* in 1886. He there poses the question: "To what extent are we still pious?"[51] He answers this by saying that we are so insofar as we continue to believe in *truth*.

One sees that even science rests upon a belief. There is no science without preconceptions. The question whether truth is needed must not merely be affirmatively answered, but be affirmed to such a degree that the proposition, the belief, the persuasion that "nothing is needed *more* than truth and in relation to this everything else has a secondary value" demands expression. . . .[52]

But this is to say that science feels it necessary that there be an order and a reality which it must try to discover and with which it must seek to bring its judgments into conformity. Nietzsche continues:

And insofar as one affirms this other world—well? Must one not therewith deny its opposite, namely *this* world? *Our* world? Thus it may be grasped what I mean when I claim that our belief in science rests upon a *metaphysical belief*. And that even we knowing ones of today, we godless and antimetaphysical ones, even *we* take *our* fire from a torch which a belief a thousand years old has kindled, that belief of Christ's which was also Plato's belief, that God is truth, that truth is divine. . . .[53]

Let us pause to draw an inference. Zarathustra says that God is dead. If he is right, and God is identified with truth, then *truth* must be dead. Is this not another way of stating that there is perhaps no truth, no objective order, *nothing* which we must acknowledge as higher than ourselves, as fixed, eternal, and unchanging? Which is *nihilism*? Nietzsche indeed means this inference to be drawn, and the passage I have been citing at such length ends with this crucial question to which his entire philosophy is an answer:

But what if this were increasingly unworthy of belief, what if nothing any long proves itself divine? What if God turns out to be our most enduring lie?[54]*

* Here I must take strong exception to Professor Kaufmann's thesis. He makes a great deal of the passage I have just quoted from *Die Fröhliche Wissenschafft*. He cites it in his own book to support his thesis that belief in the truth is Nietzsche's faith, and that in this sense he remained a "pious" man. See Kaufmann, *op. cit.*, p. 314. He does *not*, however, cite the last

Nietzsche credited himself, thus, with raising the ultimate question concerning truth:

> From the moment we deny the God of the ascetic ideal, *another problem presents itself*: that of the value of truth. The Will-to-Truth demands a critique. . . . The Will-to-Truth is experimentally *put in question.*[55]

Because the scientist (and the scholar) is committed to truth, the matter cannot be decided scientifically: "Let no one bring up science when I seek after the natural antagonists of the ascetic ideal."[56]

Since Copernicus, man has seemed to be on an inclined plane. He rolls faster and faster from the center—whither? To become nothing? To the "sharp awareness of his own nothingness"? But is this not exactly the straight road to—his *old* ideal? *All* science, natural as well

---

sentence, which I have just quoted, in which Nietzsche precisely rejects this interpretation, making it plain that he is not *fromm.* Nor does Kaufmann reprint this sentence in his anthology, though he does reprint the rest of the lengthy aphorism. Here is a plain example of how much mischief suspended dots can do, and how even the best-intentioned of writers about Nietzsche will often ascribe to him their *own* views, and, by ample citation, give the appearance of documenting them. This, I am afraid, is Professor Kaufmann's admirable enough faith, but hardly Nietzsche's. For I find the claim that it is Nietzsche's quite inconsistent with the theory of knowledge he elaborated and with the antimetaphysical bias which drove him to attack the Correspondence Theory of Truth. It could perhaps be countered that Nietzsche really did not work out his epistemology in any detail. But I would then insist that Kaufmann's claim is inconsistent with the attack against truth in *Zur Genealogy der Moral*, III, 24, where a fragment of this passage from *Die Fröhliche Wissenschafft* is actually quoted. (Nietzsche grew increasingly fond of self-citation.) This fragment includes the last sentence which Kaufmann omits in two places. Perhaps he did so because he could not see the point of including it, which is quite possible when one is convinced that one has a correct interpretation. I dare say I may have done the same thing at times.

I fear we must take seriously Nietzsche's claim that everything is false. It is an unsettling idea, until we have given some philosophical explication of it, as I have sought to do. The motto of Book Five of *Die Fröhliche Wissenschafft* is: "*Carcasse, tu trembles: tu tremblerais bien davantage, si tu savais ou je te mène.*" It is hard to suppose that he then had in mind something so comforting as truth exists and God is truth. The *destruction* of this idea was what was frightening and intoxicating. Much of his philosophy is by way of emotional response to things which, like the Pragmatic Theory of Truth, are taken in without demur by freshmen in philosophy.

as *un*natural . . . is today concerned to talk man out of his self-respect.[57]

Science, like religion, is an interpretation and a perspective. But it is taken as truth, as though there were something outside of man to which he must attune himself and from which he derives his meaning extrinsically, as it were, and derivatively. Science then proves that we are meaningless. How pointless and how false Nietzsche regards this. Let us realize that we have made these things, and that they are only fictions to be used by us. Those who take science *literally* are "a long way from being *free* spirits because they still believe in the truth. . . ."[58]

Dostoevski wrote, "If God does not exist, everything is permitted." Zarathustra says that God is dead. And Nietzsche wrote, in what must surely be a paraphrase of the Russian novelist he so admired, "Nothing is true, everything is permitted." [*Nichts ist wahr, alles ist erlaubt.*]

This is freedom of the spirit. The belief in truth has given notice. Has ever a European or Christian free spirit wandered in the labyrinthine consequences of this proposition?[59]

This was the Nihilism to which I referred in Chapter One. What to make of it is of course not altogether clear. If one has a taste for the detection of the self-stultifying thesis, one might find in it a further instance of what Nietzsche contested against elsewhere—making of a feature of our thought a resident, in this case a negative, feature of the universe. He had hit upon the idea that for a statement to be true, nothing need correspond to it. Then he made a metaphysical principle of this "not" by saying that *nothing* corresponded to our proposition, so that—since they meant to say *something*—all propositions were false.

However this may be, Nietzsche felt himself utterly liberated, as well he might, by the idea that the world is ours to make, not discover, and that we are the center and the lawgiver of it all:

We philosophers and "free spirits" feel ourselves to be shone upon by a new dawn with the news that God is dead. Our heart flows over with thankfulness, amazement, presentiment, expectation. Finally! Our ships can embark again, and go forth to every danger. Every hazard is again permitted the inquirer. Perhaps there never was so open a sea.[60]

This *cannot be read* as an appeal to return to the instinctual swamplands of the primitive psyche. It is a call to creativity, to new structures and to fresh ideals, in the light of which we might make ourselves over in an image of our own. God being dead, there is no reason to cringe in the corner of an unreal guilt. And let not something else take the place of this superannuated god, to make us feel humble and insignificant. The guilt is unreal, but so is everything. Let us will our way.

These are Nietzsche's general messages. The rest of this book is an elaboration upon them.

SEVEN

Übermensch and Eternal Recurrence

I

NIETZSCHE's Nihilism—his idea that there is no order or structure objectively present in the world and antecedent to the form we ourselves give it—has, he believed, the consequence that the men who accept it will have no temptation to disesteem human life by contrasting it with something eternal, inalterable, or intrinsically good. As a metaphysician, he sought to provide a picture of the world as it actually is—a blank picture, as it happens, since the world has neither structure nor order—so that men might have no illusions either about it or about themselves, and, unimpeded by mistaken views, might set about their proper task, which was to make of humankind something more than it had been. It was his view that men had failed to fulfill their lives because they accepted what he regarded as wholly false philosophies; as a result, he attached a high value to philosophical criticism. He felt an urgency remarkable among philosophers, who are not generally inclined to suppose their achievements will have much direct bearing upon the way men are to act, for it seemed to him that only through an adequate philosophical understanding could men break loose from an acceptance of their unsatisfactory condition in which custom and bad thinking reinforced them. *His* philosophy must not, he felt, provide an instrument for the impoverishment, debasement, or stagnation of life. He felt it was his great good luck "after whole millennia of aberration and bewilderment, to have once again found the way which leads to a Yes and a No."[1] I hope we have a fair idea of that to which he was saying No. His affirmations must concern us now.

At least two of his affirmative ideas, each of them puzzling and both, it will turn out, connected, are presented in what he regarded as his masterpiece, *Thus Spake Zarathustra*. The historical Zarathustra (Zoroaster) believed the world to be the scene of a vast conflict between two cosmic forces, one of good and the other of evil. In this warfare it is our duty, Zarathustra taught, to side with the forces of light. Because Nietzsche was "beyond good and evil," he did not believe in the cosmology of the Zend-Avesta. But since Zarathustra was the first to have made the error of supposing moral values to be objective features of the universe, he should be the first to rectify the mistake and speak for the new philosophy.[2] Thus Nietzsche chose him as his "son," and as the literary *persona* through which his philosophy was to be spoken.

Nietzsche's Zarathustra announced the relativity of all values and moralities, saying, in various ways, that each people heretofore had adhered to a different schedule of values, worked out for them in connection with the local conditions of their perdurance. There have been, he says, a thousand goals. But so far mankind *as such* has had no single goal or universal morality: "Till now there were a thousand goals, for there were a thousand peoples. Only a yoke for a thousand necks is lacking, the *one* goal is lacking. Humankind as yet has no goal."[3] Zarathustra is to redeem this moral lacuna and to provide this unitary human goal. This is to be the *Übermensch*. "Look!" he intones, "I teach you the *Übermensch*! The *Übermensch* is the meaning of the earth!"[4] This is the first of Nietzsche's affirmations which we must consider.

I have employed the German *Übermensch* in preference to its familiar translate "Superman," not so much because the latter has been pre-empted by playwrights and cartoonists—readers of philosophical books might be supposed capable of disregarding such incidental connotations—but because the prefix *super-* cannot but be somewhat misleading. It connotes, in connection with *man*, that the *Übermensch* is superhuman. And so he might be, but in what way? There is superhuman strength, intelligence, appetite, endurance—Nietzsche could, without contextual specification, be taken as enjoining upon us a rather more athletic ideal than he intended. Some of Nietzsche's commentators have used the prissy "Overman," but this, to me at least, sounds too domineering, with its suggestion of overlord and overseer, and it cannot truly escape the particularizing unfortunateness that "Superman" has proved to have. If it is *over-* it is so in the sense of "over the hills and far away" and not "I take my orders from the man *over* me": it connotes *beyondness* as well as *superiority*, and neither of these is present in the *super-* prefix. If I wanted to be eccentric, I would use the available English prefix *preter-* as in "preternatural" or "preterhuman." But this might sound too ghostly, and "preterman" too confusing, so I have opted to leave untranslated the German word. This way, as with a primitive term embedded in a set of axioms, we can let it be specified by the contexts in which it appears, and rest content with implicit definition.

The *Übermensch* idea, for all its notoriety, hardly appears in Nietzsche except in *Zarathustra*, and it differs from most of the characteristic views he held which are found much reiterated throughout the sprawling corpus. Even in *Zarathustra* itself, no specific characterization is really furnished. As the ideal we are to pursue in our capacity as humans, it is a goal of singular indefiniteness and unspecificity. The *Übermensch* is contrasted with what Nietzsche calls the "Last man"—*der Letzte Mensch*—who is and wishes to be as much like everyone else as possible, and who would be happy just to be happy: " 'We have invented happiness,' says the last man, and blinks."[5] This is the herd-man of contemporary life, and Nietzsche–Zarathustra holds him in contempt. It would not do to particularize the target, however, because he has in mind men, no matter where or whom, who are complacent or resigned and prepared to let well enough alone, taking the world as they find it. They are, I suppose, the men who feel that human beings are what they are, that human nature cannot be changed. Against these, Zarathustra says:

Man is something that shall be overcome. What have you done to overcome him?

All beings have created something higher than themselves. And would you be the ebb of this great flood, and return to the animals rather than overcome man?

Man is a rope, tied between beast and *Übermensch*—a rope across
an abyss.

What is great in man is that he is a bridge and not a goal. What can
be loved in man is that he is an overgoing and an undergoing.[6]

Man is at once an overgoing and an undergoing. We go beyond
ourselves by overcoming something in ourselves, and it is that
which goes under, and is put beneath us. We perish as *merely*
human beings in order to become something higher. Human life
is a sacrifice, or should be, not to something trans- and extrahuman,
but to something attainable by *us*, providing we are able to overcome (parts of) ourselves. Unlike ideals of the ascetic, this ideal
does not demoralize. It does not render us worthless, but defines
our worth as transitional. We are more than we were, but less than
we might become, and the higher fulfillment of ourselves as humans is that which we should seek. The *Übermensch* is not the
blond beast. The blond beast remains behind, hopefully forever.
The *Übermensch* lies ahead.

Fine, one says, let us proceed. But what are we specifically to do?
The mere injunction to be better will hardly help a child who has
no idea in what being better consists. He perhaps knows only that
some of the things he has been doing should no longer be done.
Perhaps he stops doing some of them. That may make him better,
but the *Übermensch* is surely not a matter of stopping only what
we have been doing, it is a matter of starting in a fresh direction.
But whither? And what is the destination? Nietzsche may be
blamed, perhaps, for leaving things so open. His sister assured
Hitler that *he* was what her brother had in mind by the *Übermensch*. Older readers were sure he meant some specific model, at
least, in the past. Nietzsche was an inveterate worshipper of heroes.
He held a high regard for Goethe, Napoleon, Michelangelo, Julius
Caesar and—more idiosyncratically—for Cesare Borgia. Well, of
course, he was hardly alone in his admiration of these men. They
are paradigm cases (with the exception of Borgia) of great men.
It would be a futile, empty gesture to say that our ideal is to be
like them. Save in only the most external regard, we could not
take a first step. Recently, at least, for every ascetic sent into a fit

of self-despising and deprecation in contrast with his hopeless vision of goodness, there are hundreds who have lamented the niggardliness of fate in not endowing them with the gifts of their great heroes. If the *Übermensch* is to be a nonascetic ideal, it must be an attainable one, and its entertainment must fill us with a sense of mission and of value. But in fact, it is not to the point to look to the past for exemplars, for there never have been any *Übermenschen* in our history. Nietzsche writes:

Sultry heart and cold head: where these join together, there the roaring wind arises, the "Savior."

Truly, there were those who were greater and more highborn than those whom people named as saviors—those violating, roaring winds.

Yet you, my brothers, must be saved from those greater than all the saviors, if you would find a way to your own freedom!

There never yet was an *Übermensch*. Naked I saw them both, the greatest and the least of men.

They were all-too-similar to one another. Truly, even the greatest I found—all-too-human.[7]

We may, if we wish, regard this as a formula of sorts. A sultry heart plus a cool head, minus the human-all-too-human. But this, divorced from the extravagant language and the rushing cadences of Zarathustra's singing, turns out to be a bland and all-too-familiar recommendation, rather squarely in a moralistic tradition. It says only that we should seek to keep our passionate as well as our intellectual life in our command, not to deny one at the price of the other, and that we should not be petty and "merely" human. It is something of an irony that Nietzsche is least original where he has been most influential. Here is an ancient, vaguely pagan ideal, the passions disciplined but not denied, in contrast with the life and attitude of guilty celibacy which has been an official moral recommendation until rather recent times.

The *Übermensch*, accordingly, is not the blond giant dominating his lesser fellows. He is merely a joyous, guiltless, free human being, in possession of instinctual drives which do not overpower him. He is the master and not the slave of his drives, and so he is in a position to make something of himself rather than being the product of instinctual discharge and external obstacle. Beyond this Nietzsche says little in detail, except to render some implicit praise of those whose passions are turned to the production of scientific, artistic, and philosophical works. He left the idea of the *Übermensch* a variable and not a constant, to be given a value by those of us who are to achieve it. If the *Übermensch* has been taken to be a bully, whose joy is in the brute exercise of strength, Nietzsche has only himself to blame. His illustrations have obscured his principles. When he writes, in *Ecce Homo,* that one would sooner find the *Übermensch* in Cesare Borgia than in Parsifal,[8] he is not saying that Cesare Borgia *is* an *Übermensch,* or that he provides the model for one in any respect save the one in which he differs from Parsifal. But Parsifal is Wagner's late operatic hero, against whom Nietzsche holds two things: he is chaste and he is Christian. The contrast was in part meant to shock, but in part it is an instance of the subtle inversions and private allusions and jokes in which Nietzsche's writings abound. He never had the discipline to write for a true public, and one would have had to be privy to much of his biography not to have taken literally what was sometimes only a pun for initiates. His great misfortune has been the literalness with which even his more sympathetic critics have interpreted him. There is much in his writing that is merely personal, having nothing to do with philosophy at all. And, as he wrote to Jacob Burkhardt, "everything personal is really only comical."[9]

II

Nietzsche seems to have believed that the *Übermensch* ideal was not going to be automatically attained or realized through the natural course of events. His doctrine in this respect is anything but Darwinian. We know, in fact, that he believed it was the *unfit* who survive and prevail, and that more and more individuals, who are more and more alike, are going, in the course of time, to crowd out the exceptional individual who might break through to a new perspective and a more exalted form of life. He speaks at times as though the deterioration in the human material were so great, the unanimity of thought and outlook so widely instantiated, that further achievement and progress must be impossible: there must be a leveling off of the human type and a stasis in spiritual evolution. He warns, or Zarathustra does, of the dangers in the "Last man":

It is time that men set themselves a goal. It is time man planted the seed of his highest hope.

The ground is still rich enough for this. But one day the ground will be poor and tame, and no tree can grow high from it any more.

Woe! The time comes when man no longer hurls the shaft of his longing beyond mankind, and his bowstring forgets to twang. . . .

Woe! The time comes when man cannot beget a star. Woe! The time of the most despicable man comes, who cannot any longer despise himself.

Look! I show you the *last man!*[10]

This indeed sounds like a prediction of some increasing human entropy, if one may speak so, of a universal cooling off with no external source of energy to counteract and reverse the natural drift toward disorder, and the inevitable decrease in free energy. In fact Nietzsche did not believe there would or even could be a last man in this sense. There would and could not be a last state of mankind or of anything else. This, he felt, could be proved. If there could be a final state at all, it would already have been reached. If it had been reached, there would be no change. But there is change, and so no such final state has been reached, and so it never will be. "If the world had a goal," he writes in the *Nachlass*, "it must have already been attained. If there were an unintended final condition for it, this again must have been reached. . . ."[11] It has not, so there is none. This is a startling claim, a consequence of his most exotic doctrine: Eternal Recurrence. This is the second of his affirmations we must discuss.

Eternal Recurrence is the idea that whatever there is will return again, and that whatever there is, *is* a return of itself, that it has all happened before, and will happen again, exactly in the same way each time, forever. Nothing happens that has not happened an infinite number of times and which will not happen again, for all eternity, in exact iterations of itself. There is no beginning and end, and no middle either to the story of the world: there is only the monotonous turning up always of the same episode, time and again. Zarathustra squats beside a gateway with a dwarf, who is, in the allegory of that book, the personification of gravity. Zarathustra instructs him in this strange teaching:

From this gateway, called "Instant," a long eternal path runs back. Behind us lies an eternity.

Must not all things which *can* run *have* run already along this road? Must not everything which *can* happen *have* happened already, been done with, and flowed away?

But if everything has been here, what say you of this Instant, Dwarf? Must not this gateway already have been—here?

And are not all things so knotted fast to one another that this Instant draws after itself all things to come? Thus itself—once again?

For all that *can* run *must* run once again along this long road.

And this slow spider that creeps in the moonlight, and this moonlight itself, and you and I in the gateway whispering together, whispering of eternal things—must we not have been here already?

And returned again, and run down that other road before us—that long, terrible road? Must we not eternally return?[12]

In the same book, Zarathustra, convalescing now from an illness, speaks to his animal companions as follows:

You would say "Now I die and vanish." And "Now I am as nothing." Souls are as mortal as bodies.

But the knot of causes, in which I am tangled, returns again. And creates me again. I belong myself to the causes of eternal recurrence.

I come again with this sun, this earth, this eagle, this snake. Not to a new life or a better life or a similar life.

I come eternally again to this same life, in what is greatest and what is smallest, and teach again the eternal recurrence of all things.[13]

I have quoted this at length to show unequivocally that Nietzsche really was saying, not that similar things go on happening, not that there are always similar instances falling under the same law, not anything which ordinary common sense might suppose him to have meant: he meant that the very same things keep coming back again and again, *themselves* and not mere simulacra of themselves. He felt this to have been his most important teaching, and a terrifying idea, so terrifying, in fact, that he was reluctant to disclose it at all. Overbeck* tells us that Nietzsche spoke of it in whispers (as Zarathustra speaks to the dwarf) and alluded to it as an unheard-of revelation. Lou Salomé tells of the "unforgettable moment" when Nietzsche confided this teaching to her "in a low voice."† Nietzsche himself speaks of the precise time and place— in a place near a towering rock in Sils Maria during August, 1881, "six thousand feet beyond man and time"—that this idea, which he characterized as "the highest formula of affirmation that can ever be attained"[14] came to him with the apparent impact of a mystical experience. He was, according to Lou Salomé, reluctant to disclose it to the world until he could find the scientific confirmation he thought it must have if it was to be accepted. He regarded it as "the most scientific of hypotheses."[15] He came to believe he had a proof for it which was scientifically impregnable. I shall try to reconstruct a proof, based upon his argument, although very likely the exposition of his reasons for believing it true are less important for the understanding of his thought than his reasons for supposing the belief in it to be *important*.

III

Apart from the hermetic, poetical pronouncements of Zarathustra, and one or two mentions of it in *Beyond Good and Evil* and *Ecce Homo* (and some early hints in *The Gay Science*), the doctrine of Eternal Recurrence hardly appears in any of the pub-

* Carl Bernoulli, *Franz Overbeck und Friedrich Nietzsche* (Jena, 1908), II, 217.
† Lou-Andreas Salomé, *Friedrich Nietzsche in seinen Werken* (Vienna, 1894), p. 321.

lished works. Even when it does, it is announced and presented, but there is no attempt at argument or proof. There is in the *Nachlass*, though it is difficult to know how much weight to give it, a sketch for a book to have been known as *The Eternal Return: A Prophecy*. This was to have presented the theoretical presuppositions and consequences of the doctrine, its proof, its probable consequences in case it should be believed, and some suggestions as to how it might be endured, its role in history, and so on.[16] In fact the *Nachlass* is full of discussions, fragmentary arguments, and analyses, as though there is a book which lies unassembled in the literary remains. It is plain that Nietzsche thought hard about his teaching, and he worked at it throughout his most productive years in the 1880s. At one point he even considered resuming student life, to study the natural sciences in order to find more support for a doctrine he believed to be of the utmost importance.

There can hardly be anything like *evidence* for the doctrine in any simple sense of "evidence." We could not, for example, find in the world as it now is any *traces* of another and exactly resemblant world or world state. If they do *exactly* resemble each other, there would be no traces or scars left by one upon the other to differentiate them: any traces in the one would have identical counterparts in the other. No observer, again, could notice two worlds as exactly alike, because he himself would be part of the eternal recurrence, and his observations would be counted part of what takes place in a *single* total world episode; and just the same observations would be replicated in each world episode. It would be absurd to cast about looking for anything like *fossils* from a prior cycle. When two things are so exactly alike that they cannot in principle be told apart, nothing is to count as evidence that there are two things to be told apart. If they could be told apart, they would differ just at the point of differentiation, and this is ruled out by hypothesis. A simple-minded Verificationist could thus rule out the teaching as meaningless, but it would not be to anyone's profit to invoke a dubious principle of meaning here.

If the world is to be thought of as eternally repetitive, and if this is to receive evidential support, it must be through some evidential support of premises which then entail the doctrine of Eternal Recurrence. It was such a proof that Nietzsche sought:

If the world dare be thought of as a determinate magnitude of power, and a determinate number of power centers—and every other idea is indeterminate and hence *unusable*—it follows that it has run through a calculable number of combinations in the great dice game of its existence. In an infinite time, every possible combination would some-time have been attained: more, each would have been attained an infinity of times. And then, between each combination and its next repetition, all the remaining combinations must then be run through, and each of these combinations determines the whole sequence of combinations, so that a whole cycle of absolutely identical sequences results. The world is a cycle which has already infinitely repeated itself, and plays its play *in infinitum*.[17]

This is exceedingly garbled. The first half is hardly what Nietzsche wishes: it is little more than a statement of something like a frequency theory of probability—as the imagery of "dice game" suggests—where the probability of each of a number of alternatives approaches equality as the number of trials is infinitely extended. This hardly helps, because the question has to do not with the frequency with which different combinations come up but with the same combination coming up always—the whole run, as it were, repeating itself. The second half of the argument is simply out of the blue, even so far as it may be considered intelligible. A more nearly adequate account is this:

The total amount of energy [*All-Kraft*] is limited, not "infinite." Let us beware of such conceptual excesses! Consequently, the number of states [*Lagen*], combinations, changes, and evolutions [*Entwicklungen*] of this energy is tremendously great and practically immeasurable, but in any case finite and not infinite. But the time through which this total energy works is infinite. That means the energy is forever the same and forever active. An infinity has already passed away before this present moment. That means that all possible developments must have taken place already. Consequently, the present development is a repetition, and thus also that which gave rise to it, and that which arises from it, and so backward and forward again! Insofar as the totality of states of energy [*die Gesammtlage aller Kräfte*] always recurs, everything has happened innumerable times.[18]

I shall try to reconstruct this argument, and add any principles it seems to me are required to get the conclusion Nietzsche needs.

Let us list three propositions which this passage suggests Nietzsche believed to be true and interconnected.

1. The sum-total of energy in the universe is finite.
2. The number of states [Lagen] of energy is finite.
3. Energy is conserved.

These propositions are clearly independent. The truth of (3) is compatible with the truth *and* falsity of (1), and conversely. And (2) might be false even if both (1) and (3) were true. Nietzsche seems to regard (2) as entailed by (1), but it is not. To be sure, he has not specified how the term "state" is to be used, so it is somewhat difficult to say whether (2) is true or false. Yet it is plain that one could give a wholly natural interpretation of *Lagen* in which (1) and (3) are true and (2) would be false—so that entailment collapses. Imagine a conservative energy system with a finite amount of energy. For the sake of simplicity, let us say that the amount is equal to a finite number, 6. Suppose some of the energy is kinetic. Suppose again that as the kinetic energy increases, the potential energy decreases; the rate is such that the latter approaches 0 as the former approaches 6. These limits could be approached indefinitely without being reached. Now let *Lage* mean "the amount of kinetic energy plus the amount of potential energy at any given instant. There could be an infinite number of *Lagen*, then, and no *Lage* need ever recur. On such a model, (1) and (3) would be true, and (2) would be false. So (2) is independent of (1) and (3).*

But how do (1) through (3) entail that any *single Lage* occurs an infinite number of times? The answer is that they do not. We need also:

* The ancient theory of cosmic return sometimes maintained that since there is a finite number of atoms, there is a finite number of combinations of atoms. Hence each combination, etc. Nietzsche, however, rejected atomism as a fiction, though it has been suggested that Dalton's atomic theories made eternal recurrence plausible in the nineteenth century. See M. Capek, "The Theory of Eternal Recurrence in Modern Philosophy of Science," *Journal of Philosophy*, LVII (1960), 290. This makes Nietzsche's theory puzzling. It incidentally does not follow from the fact that a sum is finite that there is a finitude of parts. The series $1 + \frac{1}{2} + \frac{1}{4} + \frac{1}{8} \ldots$ sums to a finite number, 2. But there is not a finite number of members in the series.

4. Time is infinite.

5. Energy has infinite duration.

Now, (5) says that there has always been energy, and (3) assures us that there has always been the same amount of energy, while (1) assures us that this amount is finite. Suppose, in interpretation of (2), that we assume there are three distinct energy-*Lagen*, A, B, C. Suppose that each of these occurred for a *first* time a finite time ago, say at t-3, t-2, and t-1. Let us suppose that A had the first occurrence at t-3. Then, before t-3, there were *Lagen* for which our model allows. But from (5) it follows that there must have been energy before then, from (4) it follows that there was a "before then" for there to have been energy *in*, and from (3) it follows that the amount of energy before and after t-3 was the same. But on our hypothesis, at least *one* of the three *Lagen* must have existed before t-3 or, what comes to the same thing, there can be no first occurrence for each of the *Lagen*. Hence at least one of these *Lagen* must have occurred an infinite number of times, but we do not know which of the three it is. It is still possible that *two* of the *Lagen* could each have occurred a finite number of times.

Suppose A had occurred an infinity of times before B's first occurrence. B would mark a cut-off point temporally behind which stretches an infinitude of occurrences of A. But now (and here we are invoking principles unlisted in our premises), what sense would it make to say that A occurs an infinite number of times though nothing else occurs? Would it not be more appropriate to speak of one event of infinite duration? Nietzsche would rule this out as constituting an equilibrium state, and he is correct that an equilibrium, once reached, would endure forever. If there were only A through an infinity, nothing could bring about a change, for there is nothing but A, and to bring something in from outside would violate (3). So would it violate (3) if nothing were to happen between any given pair of A-occurrences. Let us then add a further premise, roughly to the effect that

6. Change is eternal.

The simplest sort of change would be an alteration of a pair of *Lagen*, A and B. With our model and propositions (1) through (6) we can prove that at least *two Lagen* have occurred an infinite number of times. This is still compatible with the remaining *Lage* occurring a finite number of times. Now imagine we have an infinity of alternations . . . A-B-A-B-A-B-A- . . ., and at a new cut-off point *C* occurs. Thus *C* had a first occurrence a finite time ago. Nothing, unfortunately, is so far incompatible with this. But if we add

7. Principle of Sufficient Reason

we can now rule out a first occurrence for *C*. That is, there must be a sufficient condition for *C*. But this must be either *A* or *B*, for this is all our model allows. Since each of these has occurred a finite number of times, *C* too must have occurred a finite number of times. So *C* can have no first occurrence either.

We can increase our model to any finite number, and by repeated applications of the argument just given we can demonstrate recursively that no *Lage* can have a first occurrence. This argument has gone through without any reference to space, so I think we may regard spatial considerations as irrelevant. Nietzsche seems to have felt that if space were infinite, a stasis must be reached—and hence it would already have been reached, so that space must be finite.[19] This is logically irrelevant, though there might possibly be spatial consequences of some of the premises required. The argument, as I have constructed it, can of course not be counted as a proof *against* the possibility of creation *ex nihilo*, for that has pretty much been assumed with (3), (4), and (5).

With this mélange of metaphysical and scientific theorems, including the First Law of Thermodynamics, we are able to deduce a proposition which is pretty much Nietzsche's theory, and which, in fact, is contrary to the Second Law of Thermodynamics. Nietzsche was apparently aware that if he was right, the Second Law was false: "If mechanics [*Mechanismus*] cannot escape the consequence, which William Thomson deduced from it, that there must be a final state, mechanics is thereby *refuted*."[20] In fact, there are some theorems in statistical mechanics, the Ergodic Hypothesis, for instance, whose compatibility with the Principle of Entropy is difficult to determine. Poincaré proved, in 1890, a doctrine of "phases" according to which a mechanical system satisfying a set of conditions specifiable within statistical mechanics must, in a sufficiently long period, pass infinitely close to any given state of itself an infinite number of times. But "infinitely close" is too far for Nietzsche's doctrine to have the point it is required to have. The scientific development came after him, and at any rate it lies outside the compass of this book and the competence of its subject.

IV

Scientific discoveries, or scientific theories, have at times brought sorrow or joy to philosophical souls. Believers in the freedom of the will suffered under classical mechanics, and took pleasure under quantum mechanics, thinking that here was scientific justification of their cherished belief. The Second Law of Thermodynamics, with its implication that the universe as a whole is cooling down, and that, since no external source of heat is available, it must in a finite time achieve a state of maximum disorder which is final, has saddened optimistic spirits despite the remoteness of this predicted result. This was the case especially in the early years of the twentieth century and the later years of the nineteenth when, perhaps, optimism ran higher than it does now and had a cosmic aspect. Even today, there are men who shudder at the idea. The relationship between science and philosophy is complex, and the validity of inferences which run from one to the other is utterly vulnerable to attack. Nevertheless, men have often sought for philosophical assurances in science or responded in a psychological way to scientific teachings, which then led them to seek philosophical interpretations. It was thus with Nietzsche's teaching.

His initial response seems to have been one of great horror. Even if his revelation was of a mystical order, mystical experiences need not always be exhilarating: "Wait until you've had one, dear reader," as E. M. Forster wrote. Nietzsche's later attitude toward the doctrine was disproportionately manic. Mingled feelings are expressed in this statement from *The Gay Science*:

What if a demon were to creep after you one day or night, in your loneliest loneness, and say: "This life which you live and have lived, must be lived again by you, and innumerable times more. And there will be nothing new in it, but every pain and every joy and every thought and every sigh—everything unspeakably small and great in your life—must come again to you, and all in the same sequence and series. . . . The eternal hourglass will again and again be turned—and you with it, dust of dust!" Would you not throw yourself down and curse the demon who spoke to you thus? Or have you once experienced a tremendous moment, in which you would answer him: "Thou art a god, and never have I heard anything more divine!"[21]

The justifiability of horror at this idea might be due to a number of things. There would be room in a given *corso* for only a finite number of combinations, each repeated to the smallest detail in each *ricorso*, and each *ricorso* repeated infinitely. There is no possibility for any ultimate novelty in the universe. It has all been thought of before (if only by yourself), and will all be thought of again (if only by yourself). This might cause some consternation: one might recall Mill's sadness at the idea that there is only a finite number of musical combinations, so that all the musical possibilities would someday be exhausted. The pleasure of anticipating great new compositions would be lost. The idea of finitude seemed inimical to, and incompatible with, the possibility of true creation:

The world, as power, may not be thought of as unlimited because it *cannot* be thought of that way. We are forbidden to use the concept of *infinite* power because this is *inconsistent with the concept of "power."* Thus—the world fails to have a capacity for eternal novelty.[22]

Not only is there to be an eternal monotony, with not the possibility of anything new under the sun, but everything *old* under the sun is going to keep coming back, time after time, forever. This means that, Zarathustra's imprecations notwithstanding, the smallness of mankind will always be with us.

Ach! Man eternally returns. The little men return eternally!

Once I saw them each naked, the greatest and the smallest. All-too-similar to one another—all-too-human, even the greatest!

All-too-small, the greatest. That was my disgust with man. And the eternal return of the smallest! That was my disgust with the whole of existence!

Ach! Sickening, sickening, sickening!—Thus spake Zarathustra, who sighed and shuddered.²³

There is then, this frustration together with the monotony.

Nietzsche felt, however, that there were some overwhelming compensations. By far the most important was that the world must give the lie to any proposal that it had a goal, or purpose, or meaning, or end-state of any kind. That which is always the same is obviously never different. So there is no ultimately higher condition for which we may hope or to which we may aspire. "It is a corrective against a whole set of possible world hypotheses,"²⁴ he says at one place in the *Nachlass*, and at another, "[it is] the highest form of Nihilism—meaninglessness eternally!"²⁵ In another respect the doctrine was encouraging as well, which was the obverse of the absence of any higher condition. There could be no lower condition, or no lowest condition that could be final. There would be no drying up, no dying away, no fatally disordered universe, eternally arrested in its abiding death.²⁶ Each thing, great and small, comes back. Each thing, in effect, is eternal. For there is no final passing away of anything if everything returns. Whatever is might just as well be said always to have been, and always must remain, virtually immortal.

Each emperor constantly asserts the transitoriness of all things, in order not to assign them too much *importance*, remaining in tranquility, thus, amidst them. To me, on the other hand, everything seems worth too much to be so fleeting. I seek an eternity for each thing. Does one dare to spill the costly wines and ointments in the sea? It is my faith that whatever there was is eternal. The sea throws it all back.²⁷

In the end, there is no passing away and no true becoming in the world. There is an eternally frozen mobility—a view strangely anticipatory of the gelid metaphysics of Eliot's *Four Quartets*.

Without a goal, there is no meaning to life. And, by parity, there is no meaning to the universe if it has no end. So man must give it one. The doctrine of Eternal Recurrence entails the meaninglessness of things, and the doctrine of the *Übermensch* is a response to that significance which man is obliged to will. These two ideas hang together in this way. In the scheme of things, Zarathustra always comes back

To this self-same life, in great and small, to teach the eternal recurrence of all things.

To speak the word of the great noontide of earth and man, to tell, once again, of the *Übermensch*, to mankind.

I spoke my teaching, and broke upon my teaching: thus wills my eternal fate. . . .[28]

It does not matter that we pass away and return and pass away again. What counts is what we eternally do, the joy in overcoming, whatever our task may be, and the meaning we give to our lives. And all of this for the sake of the thing itself, not for any consequences: for it leads to what it has led to and always will. What we do either has intrinsic meaning or it has none. It is we who give value together with significance. This we must accept if there is to be meaning to our life (for we could not change it if we wished to): we must affirm ourselves in our fate. This is a third affirmation of which we must take note. "My formula for greatness in men is *amor fati*: that one should not wish things to be otherwise, not before and not after, in the whole of eternity."[29] "My doctrine states," he amplifies in a posthumous note:

So live that you must desire to live again. This is your duty. At any rate, you will live again. He for whom striving gives the greatest feeling, let him strive. He for whom rest gives the greatest feeling, let him rest. He to whom order-following and obeying gives the greatest feeling, let him obey. He must only be clear as to what gives him the highest feeling, and be shy of no means! Eternity is worth it.[30]

Stated as an imperative: So act (or so be) that you would be willing to act exactly the same way (or be exactly the same thing) an infinite number of times over. Heeding this, men might stop feeling *ressentiment*. In existentialist terms, it is a plea for authenticity. It rules out the possibility of another life, in heaven or hell, only an immortal returning to what we are in this life. In place of the vision of another world, think how liberating this vision is. "Let us stamp the form of eternity upon our lives,"[31] he asks. Think "what effect the doctrine of eternal damnation has had!" "*This* life is your eternal life."[32]

EIGHT

The Will-to-Power

I

I HAVE felt forced from time to time to use the expression "Will-to-Power" in exposing this or that doctrine of Nietzsche's. Any other expression would have misrepresented his thought, and I felt it better to use his phrase, albeit unclarified, and let the implications of context serve for the stipulation of its use. Now I must try to explicate this central expression or the concept which it connotes. Like the Eternal Recurrence theme, this expression appears spontaneously in Nietzsche's writings without much explanation of what he means by it or, for that matter, any indication of the importance it had come to assume in his thinking. The *Nachlass*, however, is filled with passages, some of them extensive, devoted to the elaboration and articulation of the theory of Will-to-Power. Although his sister Elizabeth has been criticized for using *Der Wille zur Macht* as the title of a posthumous aggregate of aphorisms, there is some justification for her having done so. This was one of the titles he had for projected books, and although the collection of aphorisms published under that name could hardly have been *the* book he meant to write, there is no looser a fit between the title and the content of the collection than in most of his published writings. Nietzsche hoped to write a truly systematic work, and this certainly was not it. Nevertheless, it is plain that his most creative thinking during the later years of his foredoomed sanity was devoted to the analysis of the Will-to-Power concept. Will-to-Power was to have been the constructive idea with which he was to replace all of what had heretofore passed for philosophy and much of what had passed as science. It was to have provided the key to his own thought and to the way things are. Will-to-Power, together with the teaching of Eternal Recurrence, *Übermensch*, and *Amor Fati*, was to have been an affirmation.

It must be a pitfall for the casual or the superficial reader to assume that the Will-to-Power designates merely a power drive on the part of blond beasts and Borgias—something which some men have and others do not. It is, in fact, a trait (if, for the moment, I may call it that) which is invariant to us all, weak and strong alike. It is a generic trait of living creatures and, more important, it is not a drive *alongside* others, as for example the sex drive: the sex drive, the hunger drive, whatever drives there might be, are but modes and instances of Will-to-Power. One of Nietzsche's singular insights is that sex is pursued not primarily for either pleasure or propagation, but for power: the act of love is a power struggle, and sex is a means of domination and subjugation. So Will-to-Power, we might say, is the fundamental drive, standing to the other drives as (in the old metaphysical idiom) *substance* stands to *accident*.

It is hardly avoidable that we think of Will-to-Power in almost exactly the terms in which men once thought of substance, as that which underlies everything else and was the most fundamental of all. For Will-to-Power is not something we *have*, but something we *are*. Not only are *we* Will-to-Power, but so is everything, human and animal, animate and material. The entire world is Will-to-Power; there is nothing more basic, for there is nothing other than it and its modifications.

Plainly, then, Will-to-Power is an elemental concept in Nietzsche's thinking, a concept in whose terms everything is to be understood and to which everything is finally to be reduced. It is a metaphysical or, better, an ontological concept, for "Will-to-Power" is Nietzsche's answer to the question "What is there?" We must, therefore, try to understand this idea.

II

Nietzsche's methodology, insofar as we speak of him as self-consciously in possession of one, is more or less a principle of parsimony: "The commandment of method is the economy of principles."[1] Given any pair of allegedly distinct things, one must always seek to find some connecting principle in virtue of which one is licensed to treat them alike, so that in place of distinct kinds of things, we may suppose there to be just one kind. Repeated in connection with each pair of allegedly distinct pairs, we press toward a single principle in connection with which all may be treated as of a piece. This is Methodological Monism, as one might term it. We are not to acquiesce in the ultimacy of "several kinds of causality" until "we have driven to the utmost limit (to absurdity, I might say) the effort to get along with only one."[2] This, Nietzsche adds, is "the morality of method."

Let us assume as granted that we are creatures of desire and passion and instinctual drives. If we take for granted that any of our behavior, or any part of what we are, may be explained with reference to these basic drives, then the Principle of Methodological Monism directs us to endeavour to explain *all* of our behavior, and everything that we are, in terms of the same set of factors which at least have some partial explanatory relevance. Suppose, then, as Nietzsche does, "that nothing is 'given' as real other than the world of our desires and passions."[3] We might regard our conscious processes as indices of this passional life, to be explained in terms of it. We might regard our moralities as "sign languages" for the passions. And we might understand our perspectives in terms of our moralities. This we have seen as Nietzsche's program: step by step we reduce all problems to psychological ones; and reduce all psychology to a psychology of the unconscious, instinctual life, which courses on fundamentally in the same way, however it may be modified for this or that form of conscious life. Now suppose this program is fulfilled, and that we can see all that is of philosophy, morality, science, religion, art, and common sense— the whole of civilization and all of human behavior—explicable in terms of instinctual drives and passions. What of the nonhuman world, the world of physical events and material activity? Can we make a further appeal to our methodological principle, and see whether we are able to explain this in terms of drives as well? If Nietzsche has been at all successful, distinctions of all sorts will have collapsed—real and apparent, mental and material, inner and outer. Why not try, as consonant with the morality of method, to regard *all* processes as of a piece, to regard ourselves and whatever we distinguish ourselves from "as belonging to the same range of reality" [*als vom gleichen Realitäts-Range*]—"matter" being now understood "as a more primitive form of the world of affects, in which everything which is later to branch out and elaborate into organic processes is still bound together in a more powerful unity."[4] The physical world would then be a "preform [*Vorform*] of life" just as life would be a ramification of physical process. We then would have opened the way for a unifying principle, cutting across the main distinctions we have found it important to make. It was the function of Will-to-Power to close the gap and to provide an ultimate explanatory principle for whatever there might be.

It is important to remember that Nietzsche qualified all of this as simply a hypothesis, as an "experiment" which he could not refuse to try. I say this because he sometimes urged Will-to-Power with a blind and driving urgency, which is so characteristic of him, as though he were flailing his readers with a weapon. By now we must understand this tendency in him as a cry for attention and an attempt to secure a hearing. As philosophers, we must take him at his most circumspect and *au sérieux*. As to his hypothesis, which is but one of many possible ones his methodological principle might endorse, let us assume, with Nietzsche, that the will is causally operative. I must remind the reader that this hypothesis is not contradicted by his polemic against the concept of the will as explanatory. In a sustained analysis, he contests the idea that men catch causality in the act when they introspect the working of their own will. If, indeed, men *do* believe this, then Methodological Monism would direct them to think of will as the only form of causality. In effect, if we did this, we would be committed to a doctrine not very remote from his own. But his notion of *will* is not purely psychological; the psychological volition, if we suppose it to be real, must be explained in terms of it.

Enough: one must risk the hypothesis that wherever "effects" are recognized, will must work upon will, and that all mechanical occurrences, insofar as a power becomes active therein, are just Will-power, the effect of will. Suppose, finally, that we succeeded in explaining our entire instinctual life as the development and specialization of a basic form of will—namely the Will-to-Power, which is *my* thesis—and that all organic functions could be reduced to this, and the problems of generation and nourishment (which is one problem only) solved in terms of Will-to-Power, *then* we would have earned the right to define all effective energy as *Will-to-Power*.[5]

Of course this is a bold and ambitious idea, and it would be too much to suppose that it could be carried through in any save the most programmatic manner. It does, nevertheless, give some idea of the unifying, systematizing, and integrative power which this concept was to have had for Nietzsche's main philosophical statement. I shall try to sketch some of his ideas for its establishment.

III

Mechanics, which Nietzsche understood as more or less synonymous with physics, including thermodynamics, was, as he saw it, a fiction through and through. It was a convenient arrangement of the world, but it did not touch upon fundamentals:

Mechanics formulates sequences of phenomena, for semiotic purposes, by means of expressions which relate to the senses and to our psychology, e.g., that every effect is a motion; that where there is motion, something moves, etc. It does not touch upon the [real] causal power.

The mechanistic world is imagined in the only way in which the eye and the touch can make a world understandable to themselves (i.e., as moved). And, so that it may be calculated, causal unities are invented, "things" (atoms) whose effect remains constant. . . .

These are illusory: the mixing in of numerical concepts, thing concepts (subject concepts), activity concepts (separation of causal entities from effects), the concept of motion. In all of these are our visual and psychological [prejudices].

If we eliminate all these trimmings, there remain no things, but [rather] dynamic quanta, in a relationship of tension with all other dynamic quanta. Their being [*Wesen*] consists in their relationship to all other quanta, in their "effect" upon these. The Will-to-Power is not a being, and it is not a becoming. It is a *pathos*. This is the most elementary fact out of which an effect, a becoming, first results.[6]

This extended passage typifies the way in which the Will-to-Power doctrine was being worked at in the notebooks. Although it is broken and allusive, it is intelligible enough to a sympathetic reader, and one who is familiar with the larger shape of Nietzsche's thought. It must be a difficult doctrine to render wholly intelligible—and here we are back to a familiar point—because the terms of intelligibility for us are precisely those which the theory cannot fit. To explain the doctrine in our language is to tolerate a fiction which one wishes to overthrow. So one needs a radical new language. Then the question remains, How is this to be learned, and how might one learn to cope with the world by means of it? I do not think this is Nietzsche's problem just here, however. Indeed, one might suppose him to be thinking in a way not unfamiliar to students of seventeenth-century thought, in terms of a distinction between primary and secondary qualities similar to that which was insisted upon by thinkers like Galileo, Newton, and Locke. Secondary qualities were unreal, and primary qualities could not be explained in terms of them, but our language, for the most part, is based upon acquaintance with secondary qualities. Perhaps the theorists of primary qualities believed these were intuited as an act of pure reason. At any rate, they did not worry much about how they should be learned, a problem, after all, hardly obvious until one begins to work out empiricism in detail. Perhaps Nietzsche used the word "will" so as to permit an analogy between it and our ready-made psychological concept, the use of which (assuming it has a legitimate use) would not be learned via visual and tactile predications.

Whatever the case, we are to think not in terms of "things" any longer, but in terms of dynamic quanta. Nietzsche has an argument in the *Nachlass*[7] that a thing is simply the sum of "its" effects, so that if we eliminate the effects, hoping to isolate the thing as it "really" is, we will have nothing left. There is, as it were, no isolated thing which can be thought of on its own; there is only a community of effects, and, accordingly, the *Ding an sich* is an empty word. This gives us a world of effects, but not effects *of* anything. And effects are not entities, detachable, as it were, to be studied on their own. If we regard effects as connected with Will-to-Power, we could regard them as effects of Will-to-Power, but Will-to-Power would not be an entity separate from them: they would *be* Will-to-Power. An effect might be regarded as the impact of will upon will, not the shock of thing upon thing. We might find it hard to grasp this idea, but Nietzsche would attribute this to the repellent power of our subject-predicate grammar. It would be difficult to put it in a sentence which would not mislead, because of the sentence structure, if nothing else.

Perhaps we might work toward a more intuitive notion by taking a different passage from the *Nachlass*:

My idea is that each specific body strives to become master over the whole of space, and to spread out its power—its Will-to-Power— repelling whatever resists its expansion. But it strikes continually upon a like endeavor of other bodies, and ends by adjusting itself ("unifying") with them. . . .[8]

Here we are employing the suspect concept of a body. Let us replace it with the notion of an outward force (pragmatically we might regard a body as nothing more than an outward force anyway). A force will tend to move outward forever until some external force impedes its dilation. We might think of this as the "First Law" of Nietzsche's theory. Were it not resisted, a body (force) would occupy the whole of space. But there are other forces, each endeavoring to do the same. Each force occupies a territory (an area of space) and is pretty much what it is as the result of counter-forces meeting and opposing its territorial expansion. We now might identify these outward forces as power centers [*Kraftzentrum*], as Nietzsche sometimes calls them, or *will points* [*Willens-Punktationen*], "which continually either increase their power or lose it."[9]

A power quantum is defined through the force which it exerts, and which it resists. There is no neutral state [*Adiophorie*]. . . . It is essentially a will to overpower and to resist being overpowered. *Not* self-preservation. Each atom effects the whole of being. It is thought away if one thinks away this radiating of will-power. Hence I name it Will-to-Power.[10]

A strikingly similar view was held, with some pertinacity, I believe, by Kant, who subscribed to a dynamical theory of matter. He was opposed to the Cartesian physics (which must have had some advocates for Kant to have so insisted upon his theory), according to which everything is to be explained with reference to the geometric properties of matter. The Cartesians' basic physical concept was *extension*. Kant counters that it would not be through extension that body occupies space, but through *intensity*. Kant wrote:

Matter is the movable [*das Bewegliche*], so far as it fills space. To fill a space means to resist all movables which, through their movement, strive to penetrate a given space.

Matter fills a space, not through its bare existence, but through a particular moving force.

The universal principle of the dynamics of material nature is: everything real which is an object of the external senses, and which is not merely spatial determination (position, figure, and extension), must be regarded as moving power. Whence it follows that so-called solidity or impenetrability is an empty concept, to be outlawed from science, and replaced with the concept of repelling power.*

Kant was covertly appealing to this doctrine in the puzzling discussion of intensive magnitudes in the section "Anticipations of Perception" of the *First Critique*:† Mass is defined in terms of the intensity of matter filling a given space.

I mention Kant's views not so much to suggest an influence—it is altogether likely that there was none—but rather to suggest a kind of anti-Cartesian physical tradition (of course Newton was explicitly anti-Cartesian), some of the teachings of which might have been in the air when Nietzsche was writing. There was a good deal of speculation in the nineteenth century regarding the correct system of mechanics, and Nietzsche may have had some idea of a theory of energetics. It is difficult to say, and irrelevant to my task.

* Immanuel Kant, *Metaphysische Anfangsgründe der Naturwissenschaft.* Zweites Hauptstück: der Dynamik. The passages cited are from Erklarung 1, Lehrsatz 1, and Algemeine Anmerkung zur Dynamik, respectively.

† See R. P. Wolff, *Kant's Theory of Mental Activity* (Cambridge: Harvard University Press, 1963), pp. 232–233. It is through Professor Wolff's book that I learned of Kant's curious work on physical theory.

It provides a context which, if only through analogy, might better suggest what he had in mind.

It is difficult to know to what extent the doctrine might be cast into scientific terms, or to what extent, say, a theory of energetics might be thought to confirm it in any way. After all, Nietzsche has throughout contested the claim that science tells us anything about reality or the invariant causal principles which may be operative therein. He seems to doubt the possibility of law in any description of actuality:

If something happens this way and not that, there is still nothing of "law," or "principle," or "order," but only the working of power quanta, whose nature consists in exercising their power upon every other power quantum.[11]

The logical structure of science, at least science as we know it— "matter, atom, gravity, action, and reaction"—is nothing but "interpretations with the assistance of psychistic fictions."[12] Apart from the bare *assertion* of power striving, there appears to be little one can say about the world which is not interpretation; and interpretation is imposing of fictions.

Scientific possibilities notwithstanding, it is important to stress the content of the doctrine of Will-to-Power in the light of its notoriety. Here Nietzsche is more to be excused than blamed, for this part of his idea was never sufficiently far advanced to receive a place in his published work while he was in his mind.

IV

If we move a step higher in the direction of complexity (without pondering the criterion or principle of ascent), life, however it is to be distinguished from inanimate existence, is, differences notwithstanding, Will-to-Power.

A plurality of powers, bound together through a common nourishment process, we call "life." To this nourishment process, as a means to its possibility, belong all the so-called feelings, ideas, thoughts, i.e., (1) a resistance against all other powers; (2) an adjustment of the same in accordance with form and rhythm; (3) a valuation with respect to assimilating or eliminating [*Einverleibung oder Abscheidung*].[13]

Here we begin to move back to familiar territory. Our conceptual structures are instruments in the service of life itself. Our appraisals and tables of value derive *their* value from their facilitation of life. Because "life is Will-to-Power,"[14] concepts and values are expressions of the will and means for the exercise of will upon will. A living organism is apparently a collection of point-forces, operating in unison; the mental processes of higher organisms are but elaborations of dynamisms lower down which are the primordial prototypes of valuing and thinking. Degrees of complexity aside, the *function* remains the same throughout.

Here I must pause to mention Nietzsche's views on Darwinism, which I touched upon earlier in a different context. Aside from his dogged insistence (the result of a blind spot in his philosophy to which I have more than once adverted) that the *unfit* survive and the *fit* perish—a claim as susceptible to Huxley's famous refutation as its obverse—it is hard to see why Nietzsche wished to count himself an anti-Darwinian. He enjoyed, quite as much as the Darwinian popularizers, brandishing a picture of natural strife and struggle before the horrified eyes of a genteel audience, disposed to think of Nature as more benign. It turns out that his frequent anti-Darwinian utterances are based on virtually a pun.

Although it may well be that a living creature is a chorus of harmonizing power centers, engaged as one, so to speak, in a struggle with other organic aggregates, the struggle is not, as Nietzsche sees it, for self-preservation. The Will-to-Power is not to be explicated through the old concept of *conatus*—the drive to remain integrate. Nor is life to be understood, in putatively Darwinian terms, as a struggle for existence—that is, to find a foothold in the world where one may survive and propagate. Whether or not one preserves oneself has *nothing* to do with the blind exertion of Will-to-Power which characterizes each thing at each instant. Something survives and prevails only insofar as it is victorious in the struggle of wills, but it does not struggle in order to survive—if anything, it would be the other way round. "Above all, a living being will give vent to its force—life itself being only Will-to-Power —and self-preservation is merely an indirect, if frequent, consequence of this."[15] There will not and cannot be, then, in the nature of the world, rest after the battle. At every moment, we are what

we do; and at every moment, so far as we are alive, we are holding
the rest of the universe at bay while it seeks to claim for itself the
quantum of power which is us:

> As regards the famous struggle for existence [*Kampf ums Leben*], it
> seems to me that this is asserted rather than proved. It takes place, but
> it is the exception. The general aspect of life is *not* need, nor starva-
> tion, but far more richness, profusion, even an absurd prodigality.
> Where there is struggle, there is struggle for *power*.[16]

This is the pun to which I refer. The word "existence" is slightly
twisted from its usage as in connection with "living" to its usage
in connection with "living well" or "living poorly"—from a philosophical to an economic sense. So the twist misleads. It suggests
that we should not so much try to continue in life ("to exist") as
to sacrifice ourselves for something else, perhaps power, life not
being worthwhile on any other terms. But there *is* no life without
power, on his theory, and he is plainly not suggesting some heroic
course. It goes without saying that creatures strive to persevere in
existence. It does not follow that they strive to persevere in a
marginal existence. It would be the latter that he is attacking, but
then no one ever really held to such a view. It would at best be an
idea connected with nineteenth-century economics, with doctrines
of marginal yield and the iron law of wages and the Malthusian
principles. These, to be sure, were involved in the discussion of
Darwinism—what was not in the nineteenth century?—and Darwin was stimulated by a reading of Malthus. But there is not the
slightest implication in Darwin that the species strive for *marginal*
existence. It is difficult to justify the title of so many of Nietzsche's
aphorisms which are headed "Anti-Darwin," or words to that effect.
As with much of the discussion of Darwinism, his polemic was
ideological rather than scientific, and it had scant bearing on the
true interest and importance of Darwin's theories. Strictly speaking, then, there is no excuse for an extended discussion of Nietzsche's views of Darwin. He had some views of a private image he
thought to be Darwin.

A more relevant consequence of his Will-to-Power theory is the
thesis that *happiness* is not the goal for which we truly struggle.
Men, like the rest of the universe, pursue power. They have done

so with remarkable success, having mastered many natural forces and displaced order after order of living creatures. They plainly have a considerable amount of power, and this has nothing to do with happiness. Happiness, as far as it is relevant, is not separable from the struggle for power, for pleasure is simply the conscious reflection of the ascendancy of our strength. The "Last Man," who thinks in terms of 'peace' and happiness, is thinking in inconsistent terms. There is no happiness without struggle.

It is particularly illuminating to substitute for "happiness" (toward which everything that lives is supposed to strive) the term "power." Thus "They strive for power, more power." Pleasure is only a symptom of the feeling of power achieved, a consciousness of difference. They do not strive for pleasure; pleasure comes in when they achieve what they strive for. Pleasure is an accompaniment, not a motive.[17]

The banal characterization that men *seek* pleasure and *avoid* pain is wrong. Not merely men but "the least part of a living organism" seeks incrementation of power, and pleasure or pain are consequences of this "primitive affect-form." To seek power is to seek obstacles to overcome, and this in effect is to pursue pain [*Unlust*], for it is as *Unlust* that obstacles to one's Will-to-Power are experienced. So pain is the "normal ingredient of every organic event."[18] With this interpretation, one can hardly hope to eliminate pain from the nature of things. *Pleasure* is the experience of overcoming an obstacle:

What is pleasure but an excitation of power-feeling through an obstacle [*Hemnis*], which is all the stronger if there is a rhythmic obstruction and resistance which increases the excitation. Thus pain is inherent in all pleasure.[19]*

* The sexual implications here are unmistakable, and are made explicit elsewhere in the *Nachlass*. "There are cases where a kind of pleasure is determined by a rapid sequence of little pain-excitations. Therewith a very rapid increase in power-feeling, in pleasure-feeling, is attained. This is the case, for instance, in tickling, as well as by sexual tickling as in the act of coition, where we see pain as an active ingredient of pleasure."[21] This is doubtless fraught with psychoanalytically interesting suggestions regarding the psychosexual personality of Nietzsche himself, especially in view of his complicated and singularly unsuccessful relations with women. On the same page is the *philosophically* interesting suggestion that pleasure and pain are not precise opposites. Pleasure, as in sex, comes from a series of "small pains" but pain never comes from a series of small pleasures. This is an odd reason, but an interesting one, for supposing an asymmetry.

That a person should suffer pain is not an index of a decrease in his vitality. Obstacles, experienced as *Unlust*, are stimuli to Will-to-Power and preludes to pleasure.

There are, he goes on to say (thus sounding his familiar theme), two sorts of pain, one of which does indicate a decrease or depression of the Will-to-Power. This is *exhaustion*. There are pains that stimulate power, and there are pains that mark a falling-off of power and a lessening capacity to withstand the counterpressures of the invading world. There are two corresponding pleasures—the pleasures of victory versus the pleasures of sleep. The "exhausted" want "rest, repose, peace, and quiet—which is the happiness of the nihilistic religions and philosophies." The "rich and vital want victory, vanquished enemies, the feeling of power flooding over a wider area than ever."[20]

We have once again a wide and narrow use of a term, which is so characteristic in Nietzsche. But here, as elsewhere, it is the cause of confusion as well as of conceptual stimulation when the wider use of the term is meant in a context in which only the narrower use should apply. It is misleading and absurd to counter programs for the elimination of pain with the broad statement that *life* is pain and struggle, so that the program in question is contrary to life.[22] The incapacity to see the fallacy in this accounts, as much as anything does, for Nietzsche's peculiar blind spot with regard to social reform. I should regard as both cruel and stupid a man who remarks, upon being asked to help someone in his struggle with a stuck window, that *life* is struggle and goes on to berate, in the name of life, someone who comes in aid. The tragicomic impertinence of Nietzsche as the apologist for brute strength and the excuser of cruelties is based upon this surd.

V

If we dropped the matter here, however, we should not have seen the full extent to which Nietzsche believed Will-to-Power to have been a unifying concept found, in this or that form, at every level of existence. The form in which it appears at the level of *spiritual* life is that of the interpretations men give of life: art, science, religion, and philosophy exemplify Will-to-Power here. Once again, it is important to recognize that we are not distinct from what we do. We *are* Will-to-Power, and Will-to-Power is imposing one's force outward, and interpreting is a mode of imposition. Interpreting is, then, not something we do but what we are: we *live* our philosophies; we do not merely have them. "One must not ask 'Who does the interpreting?' since interpreting itself, as a form of Will-to-Power, has existence (not as a being [*sein*] but a *process*, a *becoming*), and as an affect."[23] "Interpretation" must be construed more widely than we are accustomed to doing: "Interpretation is itself a means by which to become master over something or other (organic processes continually presuppose interpreting)."[24] Our whole conceptual scheme is an interpretation and, on Nietzsche's view once more, not something we have but something we are, for with it we have created ourselves as well as ordered the world. All our categories of thinking—thing, attribute, cause, effect, reality, appearance, and the rest—are interpretations to be understood "in the sense of Will-to-Power."[25]

The Will-to-Power is the desire for freedom in those who are enslaved, it is a will to dominate and overcome others in those who are stronger and more free. But, "In those who are strongest, richest, most independent, and most courageous, [the Will-to-Power] appears as love of mankind, or of the people, or of the Gospel, or truth, or God. . . ."[26] This would be a strange and deviant statement to someone who knew Nietzsche only by his reputation. But to the one who has followed this discussion it will plainly have reference to the Ascetic Ideal. It is the self-discipline of the Will-to-Power. The strongest men, he wrote in *Beyond Good and Evil*, have always been fascinated by the saint because they intuited in him a power which was engaged in a self-trial, an autostruggle, exhibiting its strength through self-discipline. "They honored something in themselves when they honored the saint," he wrote. "They had something to ask him. . . ."[27] He is the step that must be taken toward a higher civilization.

In the end, the Will-to-Power teaching is one we have found throughout the writings of the philosopher we have been examining. It is the teaching that the world is something we have made, and must remake, and it has no structure and no meaning other than what we can impose upon it. To recognize that this is so, he would say, is to have gone a stage beyond the ascetic ideals to the view that what they hold out as a true reality is only form which they give to chaos and nothingness, that there *is* nothing there which corresponds to this form, but only the blank senselessness of reality.

The belief which holds that the world, which *ought* to be, *is* real, is a belief of the unproductive, of those who will not create a world as it ought to be. They imagine that it is there, and they seek ways and means to attain it. The "Will-to-Truth" is the impotency of the will to create.[28]

Nietzsche's was the will to create, and he felt this should be the same in all philosophers. Philosophical criticism, of which so much of his writing is made up, is only part of philosophy, an instrument and a means. Philosophical critics, as long as they remain only that, are instruments in the service of a philosophical Will-to-Power, but they are not philosophers as yet:

The real philosophers are commanders and lawgivers. They say, "It shall be so!" They determine the whence and the wherefore of mankind. They make use, thereby, of the preliminary labors of philosophical workmen, the overpowerers of the past. They grasp with creative hands toward the future, and everything which is or was becomes their means, their tools, their hammers. Their knowing is creating, is lawgiving, and their Will-to-Truth is *Will-to-Power*.[29]

Will-to-Power is related to Nihilism, in the mature phase of Nietzsche's philosophy, in much the same way as the Apollinian was related to the Dionysiac in its early phase. Here, as in his conception of art, both forces or concepts are required. Nihilism is needed to clear the way for creativity, to make it plain that the world is without significance or form. And Will-to-Power imposes upon that unshaped substance the form and meaning which we cannot live without. There is no *specific* form or meaning without which we cannot live, however. How we shall live, and what we shall mean, is up to us to say.

Nachwort

SUCH was the philosophy of Nietzsche, so far as I have been able to make it out. I have sought to elaborate it with as much system as I think it admits of, which is considerably in excess of what it is commonly thought to have. I have tried to show the disproportion between the role that the notorious moralistic theses play in his system, and their role in his reputation. In his system, they are either heavily capitalized particularizations of general principles to which he subscribed or, as I have suggested, lurid, expressionist illustrations for texts which were more philosophical and abstract. His only editors to speak of, when he was still in his own mind, were enthusiasts, like Peter Gast, who were interested in the illustration rather than the principle. Therefore he was allowed, and indeed encouraged if not incited, to indulge his appetite for fantastic anthropology and invective. The neglect his work met with, the silence which even his loudest shouting failed to dispel, perhaps reinforced the irresponsibility of his style.

It is time to scrutinize and then decide for or against his philosophical teachings with a more mature restraint than he was able or inclined to exercise in presenting them to the world. I hope that I have not merely imposed my own will-to-system upon the galaxy of fragments and aphorisms of which his work is composed—a corpus which critics sometimes think of as an immense literary deposit left by a philosopher who *expressed* himself in shards, so to speak, there never having been a parent body to which they all once belonged. The reader may turn to the fragments themselves, however, to see whether I am wrong or right in my construction. I should not be dismayed (although I have arguments against such a view) were someone to say that any construction is misguided, that Nietzsche was a topical writer, an aphorist, unformed or un-dominated by the systematic specter of philosophy. I should be amazed only were one to find a system *different* from the one I just sketched.

More than this I cannot say. A more detailed analysis than the one I have given belongs either to the professional philosophical journal or to a more refined and circumscribed study. In these last pages I wish only to raise once again the obvious question regarding the status of Nietzsche's philosophy in terms of its own conception of philosophical activity. Was his philosophy, too, a matter of mere convention, fiction, and Will-to-Power? To put it sophomorically but no less vexingly, was it his intention, in saying that nothing is true, to say something true? If he succeeded, then of course he failed, for if it is true that nothing is true, something is true after all. If it is false, then something again is true. If, again, what he says is as arbitrary as he has said, critically, that all of philosophy is, why should we accept him if we are to reject the others? And if not arbitrary, how can it be right? How can what he says be true if he has said what the truth is? Nietzsche was alive to these difficulties, I believe. As he wrote in *Beyond Good and Evil*: "Supposing that this, too,. is only an interpretation—and one will be eager enough to raise this objection. Well—so much the better."[1] I suppose he would say that we are to judge him by the criterion we have in fact always employed, our philosophical ideologies notwithstanding: by whether his philosophy works in life. He might continue: If you do not care for the form I give to things, you give things your own. Philosophy is a creative business, and the way is always open. Philosophy is a contest of will with will. Insofar as you oppose my philosophy, you illustrate and confirm it.

I doubt that everyone would be satisfied with such an answer, for I am not even certain that it *is* an answer. But I have no other to offer. We find ourselves here at the limits which every system reveals when we must talk about, rather than within, the system itself. What licenses a point outside a purportedly comprehensive system for use as a fulcrum? How can there be such a point? I will say this, appealing to another passage in the book from which I have just cited: "Every philosophy hides a philosophy; each opinion is also a concealment; every word is a mask."[2] There are assumptions of a profound philosophical nature behind Nietzsche's system, sunk so deeply into the form of his thought that he perhaps never became conscious that they were there. To what extent these are false, or to what extent their being so would affect the remainder of his philosophy, are hard queries to answer. I shall mention just one assumption.

In several places where the Will-to-Power is discussed, Nietzsche claims, in so unvarnished a manner as to suggest that he is voicing an undeniable truth, that *will can only act upon will*.[3] This is the sort of statement one learns to be sensitive to in philosophical writing, and in this example it can hardly be said that Nietzsche is representing usage. Those who have invoked the will in a causal capacity have done so, typically, to account for something they found puzzling—the action of a mind upon a body: we move an arm through an 'act of will.' This theory has been the object of virtually a massive philosophical attack in recent years; and one would like to enlist Nietzsche as an early skirmisher in this conceptual offensive. How odd it would be if he were an ally when *his* attack was motivated by his strange, complacent thesis that will can act only on *will*—"and not upon matter," as he adds. Why can will act only on will? Why, if there is such a thing as will at all, cannot it act upon other things as well? What *justifies* this dark and difficult thought?

I shall try in a few words to suggest what Nietzsche had in mind, although I offer it as a hypothesis which I see no way of verifying at present, except to the extent that it helps make sense of a statement otherwise either opaque, or silly, or wrong. Perhaps the following suggests the philosophy behind the philosophy, the meaning masked by the words. I think that Nietzsche thought of wills both as the most elementary things there are and as the only *active* things there are (using "thing" in the most noncommittal sense possible). He believed this, I submit, roughly in the way in which Bishop Berkeley believed that spirits were the only active things in the universe. Berkeley's ontology consisted in spirits and ideas, and he maintained that ideas were inert, were caused by spirits, and owed their entire existence to being entertained by spirits, so that without spirits, *they* would not exist, and hence *nothing* would exist. Nietzsche similarly holds that there are wills and interpretations, that interpretations have no validity except in relationship to a will, that in a special sense wills *cause* interpretations, and that without wills there would be nothing. He always seems to have understood acting, however, in the sense of *acting upon*, not as some isolated volitional performance. A Nietzschean solipsist would be a will which acts upon itself; but, if there are only wills, and there is no acting but only acting *upon*, then nothing can be acted upon but a will. Wills act upon wills, and the mode of their so doing is imposing a form, giving a shape which, in the highest level of life, consists in giving or imposing an interpretation. The wills, in other words, are formless antecedents to being *given* a form; and Will-to-Power is the general description of this conflict of wills, in which the victor imposes the form. Having no intrinsic form, a world of wills would be formless, which is the Nihilist doctrine we have been discussing. But since wills are always acting upon one another, form is always imposed.

It doubtless seems strange to couple Berkeley and Nietzsche in this manner, or to think of Nietzsche as holding to a version of idealism. If it is idealism at all, it is *dynamic* idealism to which he was committed. But having made this interesting idea explicit, I shall say nothing further about it or, in this book, about the philosophy I have labored to describe.

Aftertexts

1

The Tongues of Angels and Men

Nietzsche as Semantical Nihilist

On se fait une idole de la verité même.
—PASCAL, FRAG. 582

All that philosophy can do is to destroy idols. And that means not
making any new ones—say out of "the absense of idols".
—WITTGENSTEIN, MS 213, 413.

Donald Barthelme's mock disquisition "On Angels" begins with
the following piquant remark: "The death of God left the angels in a
strange position. They were overtaken suddenly by a fundamental question
. . . . The question was 'What are angels?' " Poor, forsaken angels: "New
to questioning, unaccustomed to terror, unskilled in aloneness, the angels
(we assume) fell into despair." A spokesangel had, however, this to say:
"For a time, the angels had tried adoring one another but had found it, finally, not enough . . . . They are continuing to search for a new principle."
And Barthelme, as angelologist, observes: "It is a curiosity of writing about
angels that, very often, one turns out to be writing about men." Angels, in
their essence, are adorers, which casts doubt on the outcome of their
search for a new principle. For adoration is adoration *of*, requiring an object, since transitive. The death of God, if seriously intended, ought then to
have meant the death of angels, if indeed he died of pity for them, for it is
cruel to deprive adoration of its intensional object but leave the state of
adoration unaffected, now as an insatiable kind of ontological hunger. The
angels now seek what one might call a "God substitute" in order to go on
fulfilling their angelic essence. They themselves are "not enough" as objects of adoration, so clearly what is required is the extirpation of the
hunger and hence the essence defined in terms of it. And the "strange position" the death of God leaves angels in is this: What, given that they were
designed to adore, is it to be an angel without adoration?

I take it that what God pitied angels for—what he pities us for—was him. But what is the good of dying out of pity if the appetite remains and fastens onto some other object before which we prostrate ourselves? Were it not for the perniciousness of the appetite, God might just as well have remained alive, lending color and hierarchy to the universe and doing no great harm, at least none of the kind of harm Nietzsche inveighs against. But given the way angels and men evidently are, mere ontological subtractions and additions count for very little. God may have reasoned that he could not exist without being adored, and, finding adoration somehow pernicious for the adorer, a kind of pathology, God, out of love and pity, died. But what then if angels and men now seek something to relate to in the same way in which they had related to God, prostrating themselves before *that*? The problem is evidently then not ontological but psychological, and the task not to smash idols but the propensity to idolize. Moses took the molten calf the Children of Israel had set up as a god and "burnt it in the fire and ground it to powder, and strawed it upon the water." But that was what one might call ad hoc iconoclasm. Another will take its place the moment the back is turned unless a radical cure is invented. What makes Nietzsche a *philosopher* rather than a prophet is that he sought just such a radical cure. Zarathustra merely proclaimed the death of God and announced the death as due to pity. What is instructive about angels and Israelites is that they forthwith seek to put something else in God's place—one another or a molten calf. Nietzsche said that we shall not get rid of God until we have gotten rid of *grammar*. When we change the grammar, we eliminate the place. We make reference to the place unintelligible, and unable to express what is required as an object of adoration, we are unable to adopt the posture of self-debasement for want of a term.

So Nietzsche's is not the "there is no god" of the village atheist or the freethinker, a term Nietzsche employs with contempt. The death of God only illustrates the kind of object freethinkers think they have gotten rid of when in fact they have put something else, functionally equivalent to God, in God's place. To be sure, Nietzsche rather encourages the view that he was a freethinker in this sense, being at once antichrist and an unweaver—what it is irresistible to call a deconstructionist—of the fabric into which the concept of Christ, or of God, is logically woven, and since these two postures are assumed in different texts, it is not difficult to take as canonical the denunciatory rather than the dissolutive text. After all, the old grammar has not been dismantled nor the new one made available for speech, and even in our own day we will find philosophers continuing to defend their beliefs and attack the beliefs of others, despite an eliminativism to which they are dedicated in which the claim is made that one day the whole idiom of beliefs and reasons will vaporize into nothing as all of us speak naturally in a neurophysiological discourse in which the very notion of beliefs cannot so much as be expressed. Or, to use a perhaps more natural analog to Nietzsche, it would be like attacking "philosophical questions and propositions," to use the phrase Wittgenstein's *Tractatus* employs, declaring them nonsense, and to do this in the light of an envisioned ideal language in which those propositions are unstatable and those questions incapable of being put. And, the ideality of the language is altogether a function of these incapacities. So in the same breath one condemns as nonsense what in ones grammatical heart one also believes is inexpressible to the point where one cannot so much as say what is nonsense. The philosophers, recall, stumble into nonsense because they do not understand grammar, and we shall not get rid of philosophy until we are rid of grammar. Needless to say, both Wittgensetin and Nietzsche were religious personalities, but I do not think that, so to speak, goes with the territory.

A lot of analytical philosophy, in the heyday of its visionary agenda, consisted in showing how certain fragments of language, deemed objectionable, could be paraphrased away and thereafter used with impunity since we can in principle always retreat into the shelter of a canonical discourse. So we learn to translate in principle physical-object terminology into sensedatum terminology, psychological discourse into behavioral discourse, sentences about societies into sentences about individuals, the language of numbers into the language of sets and thence into the regimented theorems of *Principia Mathematica*—and thereafter we can talk about tables, feelings, societies, and numbers with the vulgar. I have no clear sense that this would be a satisfactory agenda for Nietzsche, but I think not. For it would imply that no harm is done in speaking with the vulgar, since we can scoot into our cumbersome but acceptable discourse whenever we need to. All that is lost is a certain convenience, the tradeoff being ontological impeccability. Whereas I think Nietzsche thought this led to positive harm in the discourse rather than inconvenience, that it was pernicious and finally crippling. Look at the example of the angels, or, for that matter, look at the example of men and women whose deep moral pathologies reflect the fact that they speak a language, employ a grammar, that encourages them to "continue the search for a new principle" when the search itself is evidence of the same crippling grammatical pathogen that leads them to want to worship God or who- or whatever occupies the place of God after Zarathustra opened his big mouth.

So he is going to hit the present placeholder with everything he has while he preaches like Moses of a Promised Land where one cannot even talk about God, cannot even say that God is dead. Perhaps because he has a psychological thesis that claims that no one can say that God is dead without this engendering pain, hence one cannot simply say there is no god or there are no gods, the way we say there are, really, no angels, or that if there are angels, they are where they are the way finches are where *they* are. A young Chinese acquaintance, fresh some years ago from the mainland, watching my wife trim the Christmas tree, that emblem of her Swedish ancestry, asked, innocently, What are angels?—Barthelmes's question—as if they were to be found in the West the way pandas are to be found in the East. In any case, my interest is not in Nietzsche in this prophetic guise, as "antichrist," the way Walter Kaufmann's triune designation, "philosopher, psychologist, antichrist," has it. Rather, my interest is in the other two persons of this trinity, those who endeavor to deconstruct the system that has a place for God because of the psychological injuries from living under a grammatical system that has such a place in it, whatever happens to occupy it. The last book of the *Genealogy of Morals* is a litany of pernicious such placeholders, from God to Truth, idols all, which render us dysfunctional even in the act of iconoclasm, which presupposes there is an idol to smash. The situation is severe if even "the absense of idols" is an idol, as Wittgenstein proposes.

There is a form of what we might call logical adoration, which consists in laying down in God's name whatever maximal predicate it occurs to us might partially capture his magnificence: omnipotent, omniscient, omnificent, infinite, perfect, self-caused if caused at all, necessarily existent—a being, in brief, a greater than which or whom cannot be conceived. Reciprocally, of course, this puts the adorer in a position self-portrayed as impotent, ignorant, passive, finite, imperfect, contingent—a lesser than whom or which it is impossible to conceive. It is as if we cannot adore him without diminishing ourselves. But the logical aspect of reciprocal adoration leaves untouched the poetic, and thence the psychological aspect of being in relationship to the bearer of all that overwhelmingness. The poetics consists in finding more emotional ways of elevating God by lowering ourselves: we are worthless, are worms, weak, born between feces and urine, as Saint Augustine puts it, small, mean, human-all-too-human, to use Nietzsche's phrase. Contemplation of the moral vastness of the divine being goes hand in hand with sustaining a sense of our own diminishment and, as we say on the lip of the Grand Canyon perhaps, or in gazing at the starry heavens above, with a sense of our smallness and insignificance. And that is the psychological correlative of what begins as logical adoration. Consider the poetry of human awfulness for a moment. Think just of the infant born as Augustine says we are: stinking, puking, crying, drooling, greedy, messy, vulnerable, sucking, and selfish. A better poet could do a harsher portrait. And now thinking of that magnificent being entering under the miracle of enfleshment the vile body of the human babe, spiffed up in Renaissance adorations, equipped with an aura, which compromises the enormity of the sacrifice in which the Christian miracle consists. We celebrate the miracle by degrading the flesh, conceptually in prayer, actually in asceticism. We cannot adequately exalt God without in the same breath sufficiently loathing ourselves.

Nietzsche was a master of the religious psychology that goes with this, and his brief against Christianity in particular focuses upon the immense amount of energy turned back against the adorer in a transport of self-torture that would be comical were it not tragic in its consequences. It is tragic in the way of gifted and otherwise intelligent neurotic employing the considerable gifts at his or her disposal against himself or herself in gratuitous and objectively absurd self-punishment. Nietzsche's ascetic saints, in terms of the energies available to them but perverted, are, from the perspective of the pagan healthiness he so celebrated, heroes deflected from the bright course open to them by a misdirected vitality whose product is anguish and hopelessness. There is a marvelous portrait of such a figure in the character of Goetz, in the penultimate act of Sartre's Nietzschean play *Le diable et le bon Dieu*. The great soldier Goetz, military leader, ruthless, I suppose in every way a superman, goes ludicrously ascetic, fasting, tormenting himself with the sound of water he denies himself, living as an anchorite, all the great store of his energy turned back against its source—and the greater the power the greater the self-perception of evil—of *Böse*—and proportionately the greater self-aggression needed to keep it in line. When will the liberator mind get turned around so that that energy should flow outward and Goetz move with the joy of Achilles through the ranks of the enemy like flame through dried stalks? None of us—I think this must be Nietzsche's point—is as great a man as Goetz, but we are less than we might be because we have internalized the disproportions of logical adoration and feel something of guilt, and correspondingly of worthlessness.

The ascetic, in the narrow religious sense, as perhaps exemplified by Saint Bernard of Clairvaux who liked to intimidate by displaying his mortified neck—gaunt, drawn, and scarred—as the emblem of his devotion, the ascetic in this sense is but an exemplar of a more generalized human type. It is a type instantiated by men and women who may think of themselves immeasurably advanced in terms of moral enlightenment beyond the *penitente*. These are individuals who tend to depreciate themselves inversely as they appreciate some external and transcendent ideal in whose service they are enlisted: the state, the race, the revolution, the family, sisterhood, art, science, or, at last, the Truth. There is a painting by Rubens, at the entryway into the salon in which he depicted the truth as she wanted it depicted of the life and hard times of Maria de Medici: it is called *The Triumph of Truth*, in whose crusade Maria de Medici and certainly her great artist saw themselves as enlisted. "Even we knowing ones of today, we godless and antimetaphysical ones," Nietzsche wrote in *Die Frohliche Wissenschafft*, "Even *we* take our fire from a torch which a belief a thousand years old has kindled, that belief of Christ's which was also Plato's belief, that God is truth, that truth is divine." And then he adds a passage so inconsistent with this if one regards it as a pious utterance, as it was indeed read by Walter Kaufmann who omitted it from his text when he printed the passage as a kind of philosophical prayer, "What if this were increasingly unworthy of belief, what if nothing any longer proves itself divine? What if God [read *truth*] turns out to be our most enduring lie?" Of course, if a lie it is one in that *aussermoralischen Sinn* Nietzsche wrote of in his early and never published essay on truth and lies, the one that has become, at the hands of Jacques Derrida, the canonical work of deconstruction, with its view that language is entirely metaphorical, *literal* usage consisting of worn metaphor.

There is a short way with this striking claim, of a piece with Hume's short way with attacks on the concept of reason. It consists in asking whether the claim that all language is metaphor is itself metaphorical, and hence, using Nietzsche own "extra-moral" sense of the term, "a lie." If so, there is no reason to believe it, but then if it is not a lie, through being metaphorical, it is, simply, false. And there is again no reason for believing it. The foundation of deconstruction self-deconstructs, leaving, of course, the serious question behind of which are the metaphors and which are not metaphors at all. But my interest does not lie in this sort of quibble. It lies, rather, in Nietzsche's shattering idea that the concept of truth plays a role in secular life that is parallel and comparable in its attendant distortions upon those who believe in truth to that the concept of God played in explicitly religious life. It is, as he puts it, our "most enduring lie." Of course, it is possible to believe in truth without worshipping it, or so it would seem to me. But Nietzsche's argument, if I grasp it, is that it is difficult to posit truth without idolizing it, without, as Pascal says, making of truth itself an idol. So the question is whether, if indeed Truth is a value of a variable of which God is yet another value—and the "Ascetic Ideal" section of the *Genealogy* itemizes a number of other such values—we can eliminate the variable by changing the system in which it occurs. And this then would be the motive for revising grammar, supposing it true that we cannot rid ourselves of God (only for example) until we rid ourselves of the grammar which has a variable for Godlike values.

That really is the subject of this essay. Of course, Nietzsche did not really construct a novel grammar, but he did argue for a revision of our attitudes toward language, in which we give over thinking of it as representational and more and more think of it as instrumental. This tack has been taken in our time by Richard Rorty, for whom language is simply a practice, and the neopragmatism of his philosophy refuses to allow the Question of Truth to arise. And I suppose it was a tack of Wittgenstein and his followers as well, thinking as they did of meaning as use and of language as a set of games. One can find in the Wittgensteinian literature claims such as this, that praying is among the many uses of language, something we do, for which there are well-marked rules. There is no less a practice of adoration. So why should the death of God especially discomfort those whose essence is adorational?

The angelic orders can chorus "Adoremus" with as much feeling as ever, given that its use is also its being. The question is, why would they continue to play that language game if God is dead? Would we continue to use the language of science and history if truth, in parallel, were dead? Rorty would say, of course, that truth really has reference only to what works, and truth marks this fact of working. Why do we resist that, if we do? Is it because we are resistant to a grammatical revision in which the mind aches for something more connected to reality than instrumentalism allows? For something with which to "hook" language to the world, to use Rorty's metaphor? Can we really live without truth? And in saying this, are we not just agreeing in advance with Nietzsche, who wants to say that we ourselves are a product of our grammars, so that *we* may not be able to envision ourselves living without truth because *we* are what our grammar has made us? But what of those shaped by a different grammar? How plastic after all can we suppose ourselves to be?

There is in Nietzsche the thought that we are *absolutely* plastic in this respect, that our ways of representing ourselves and the world is the product of a long evolution in which what he cleverly calls "the genius of the species" was imposed upon its members as a condition of their survival. Thus the way our minds work is but the will-to-power of the species read off by its members as the ways things deeply are. I suppose the personality who most deeply internalized this view was Foucault, who truly saw the world as a kind of prison and who experimented with breaking out of it through extreme sexual conduct, through drugs, through a kind of romantic politics, and through writing intended to crack the confining walls of thought and practice. Foucault's recent biography has him distinguishing between what he terms "*enquête*" and "*épreuve*," which in turn imply two different notions of truth—so different that there is no way in which they can come into conflict. There is the truth which is the outcome of an enquiry and the truth which is the outcome of an ordeal, a *trial*, where one flings oneself against one's limits to see what it is like to penetrate them. One thinks of Ghandi's title, *My Experiments with Truth*, and though he and Foucault would have been very different characters, the truth of either is not that of Tarski's T-rule or what the correspondence theory of truth means to explicate. Both lived the life of the ordeal, but Foucualt's was an ordeal of escape from certain hated limitations he—talk about the empowerment of metaphor—saw as prison walls. So, in a way, did Nietzsche, who saw us confined by grammar (understood, to be sure, broadly), in the sense that it is at least thinkable that there are other ways of representing or organizing experience, even if *we* cannot think them. This is tantamount to saying, I suppose, that they are synthetic a priori, a priori because we are constituted by them, synthetic because their denial is consistent even if unimaginable in concrete terms. We cannot think them but they are thinkable. And if we could live under them, well, we might be rid of God and truth. Of course that might leave unaffected the truth of *enquête* as opposed to that of *epreuve*. And then the question remains whether we cannot talk, unhysterically and unidolatrously, about the truth of inquiry's outcome, viz where the denotation of the subject term falls within the extension of the predicate term. Even Foucault needed this much just to get his views stated.

But the question I want to raise, and tentatively answer in the negative, is whether a change in grammar would entail a change in reality as we are constrained to think of it, speaking the languages we do. I want to answer in the negative because it seems to me that the structure of our language, which grammar represents, has no descriptive content of its own. It casts no shadows on the blank face of reality. Ours at least does not, and there is therefore no good reason to want it changed, for neither would the grammar of the languages we exchanged it for. In fact, even the more restrained attempts to exchange it for an instrumentalism are far more constraining than a descriptive view of language could be. And in the concluding pages of this essay, I shall endeavor to give some reasons for this view.

225

Semantical realism is the thesis that in order for language to fit the world, the world must fit language and hence must be structured the way language itself is structured. I am not altogether happy with the term, but the symptomology is reasonably well defined, and it is virtually coextensive with philosophy, for a great deal of philosophy has been generated under its auspices. The most familiar recent exemplar of semantical realism is the

Tractatus of Wittgenstein, which defines the world composed of facts—of facts, remember, and not of stars and flowers, molecules and genes—and as where a fact has a logical structure or form that enables propositions, of course possessed of logical structure or form, exactly to mirror it. It is an ideal language because there is a pictorial function that connects proposition with fact as mutual isomorphs: they are pictures of one another. Another example might be, though I am not as certain of it as I would like, Spinoza's dictum that the order and connection of ideas is the same as the order and connection of things, where again the realist premiss is that ideas can represent reality only if they have the same form, like hand and glove. This means that reality must have a linguistic structure, and that it fits language only because it does: language is the world *put into* words. My sense is that Nietzsche himself accepted the premiss of semantical realism but in fact believed that the world lacks the required structure. Instead, however, of moving to the unexceptionable conclusion that language does not require the world to have a linguistic structure in order to fit it, he drew the conclusion that since the premiss fails, language does not fit the world at all. This is semantical nihilism, and it unhinges language from its descriptive offices so completely that it becomes an open matter what language we choose to use. The motive for changing languages lies in the fact that our actual language, on his view, projects a structure that is not there and that holds us prisoner. What is not there, of course, is a preexisting structure of the kind semantical realism requires. From his recognition of this, Nietzsche flew to the conclusion that there is no structure there at all, that the *world* is infinitely plastic, when of course it has whatever structures it does have, but these are not the structures of language at all.

The more adequate language would be one, he sometimes suggests, where there are only verbs rather than substantives and where we have to be careful not to infer, from impersonal verbs, that there are agents for every process, that lightning, to use his favorite example, need not be something that stands apart from and performs the flashing: lightning is the flashing, rather than something that does it. And so as well with us, who are not separate from but one with our actions. Or he talks about other creatures whose sensibilities are finer than our own and so cannot see the similarities we see and hence find general terms unintelligible. I think of the character in Borges's story "Funes the Memorious" in this connection:

> Locke, in the seventeenth century, postulated and rejected an impossible language in which each individual thing, each stone, each bird, and each branch, would have its name. Funes once projected an analogous language, but discarded it because it seemed too general to him, too ambiguous. Funes in fact remembered not only every leaf of every tree of every wood, but also every one of the times he had perceived or imagined it. He decided to reduce each of his past days to some seventy-thousand memories, which would then be defined by means of ciphers. He was dissuaded from this by two considerations: his awareness that the task was interminable, his awareness that it was useless.

"The two projects are senseless," Borges concluded, "But they betray a stammering grandeur." A language composed of so many proper names that only a memorious being could master it, and one, moreover, that referred in any case only to his memories, would subvert the true purposes of language. It would be like the entirety of experience dissolved into pixels. But so does Nietzsche's vision of a language made only of verbs. "Why does lightning flash?" is a coherent question, for even if we knew what lightning was—an electrical discharge—the question still remains worth asking as to why an electrical discharge flashes. The world is the way it is. And language is the way it is. Do we need to remake language in order to forestall ideas we evidently can explain perfectly in the language that is ready-to-hand? And will we get rid of God when we have gotten rid of a subject-predicate grammar and replaced it with a grammar all of verbs? Will there not under that dispensation be room for God as Be-ing, the actual verb denoting the activity? Can revising language as language really prevent anything at all? And what is the point of such revision if there is no real way anyway language as language forecloses on our view of how the world is?

A last word on the matter of instrumentalism, which Nietzsche inclined to with his version of the pragmatic theory of truth, and which, I think, is Richard Rorty's view, and certainly Wittgenstein's. My own thought on it is that if sentences in fact are tools, instruments, then we have to learn their uses the way we learn the uses of tools. Certain sentences will open doors; certain others will close them. Our language, then, if it consists in such as system of uses, locks us into a form of life, consisting specifically of those uses. Learning life consists in mastering a phrase book, a list of what to say when. Now forms of life in fact are revolutionized all the time without language itself being revolutionized in that way. Words get added, to be sure, and meanings change. But sentential structure is not indexed to social practice. Our truth-conditions make us free.

2

A Comment on Nietzsche's "Artistic Metaphysics"

When Joseph Beuys declared, in the 1970s, that everyone is an artist, he effectively meant that anything can be art—a proposition made possible though the particular history of art to which Beuys himself contributed, but which would have been unthinkable a century earlier, when, in his 1873 opuscule *On Truth and Lie from an Extra-Moral Point of View*, Nietzsche declared that we are all artists. Obviously, Nietzsche did not and could not have meant that we are all artists in the received sense of that term, but that certain activities, which define us as a species, are, abstractly considered, best understood as artistic. We are poets through the mere fact that language as such is metaphorical. This thesis required as radical a reconsideration of language as Beuys's did of art, with the difference that whereas Beuys's thought fit into a widespread pattern of artistic revolution, Nietzsche's was more or less original with him. His thesis was that the initial impulse of language is to make metaphors, which means that in its initial phase language is poetry. Metaphor gives rise to language, rather than being something language is merely capable of—an embellishment of speech, or speech used ornamentally.

Nietzsche was of his time in thinking of language from the perspective of vocabulary rather than grammar, and his formulations were initially paradoxical: "All expressions are metaphors" flies in the face of the fact that "metaphorical" presupposes "literal," hence if everything is metaphorical, nothing is literal, and so nothing is metaphorical either. His genius was to have introduced implied temporal indices: what we call literal was once metaphorical but its poetical origins have been forgotten and it has become stale and used. Nietzsche even felt this way about his own "written and painted" thoughts. In *Beyond Good and Evil*, he wrote:

> Not long ago you were so variegated, young and malicious, so full of thorns and secret spices, that you made me sneeze and laugh—and now? You have already doffed your novelty, and some of you, I fear, are ready to become truths, so immortal do they look, so pathetically honest, so tedious. (296)

The antonym of "true" for him is not "false" but "fresh," and the criteria are aesthetic—"young and malicious" against "honest and tedious." There is no semantical difference, and both the true and new are simply "lies"— Nietzsche's rather incendiary assessment of metaphor, fresh or stale. There is no effort to explain how things become true—no "genealogy" of truth of the sort Bernard Williams attempted to write before his recent death, according to which telling the truth is part of what holds society together.

Why lies? The answer is that Nietzsche thinks we don't know what really happens in the body when we have an "idea"—he uses the classical term of modern epistemology, according to which ideas are mental representations. There is a "nervous impulse" that gets translated into an "idea"—he says "picture" or "image," which he counts as itself a metaphor for the nervous impulse. Perhaps the idea is thought of as a metaphor because the relationship between it and the subjacent nervous impulse is thought of by him as translational, but it is a reckless step in his case, since nobody knew then, as nobody knows now, what the relationship is between psychology and physiology. It seems a strange basis for calling us "artists," but that is his basis; quoting from his 1873 text: "A nerve stimulus is first translated into a picture. First metaphor. The picture is transformed once again into a sound! Second metaphor." It is this that makes Nietzsche at once so seductive and infuriating as a writer, giving us handsome philosophical compliments—"You are all artists!"—that turn out to be high-flown redescriptions of quite ordinary processes: in the present case certain hard-wired neurological processes that take place when we undergo perceptual experiences that in no obvious way resemble the neurological processes that un-

230

derlie them. In part, it is this in which our being artists consists. He is interested in the stream of experience in which the "dream" of conscious life consists and in the fact that it is an epiphenomenon, something that merely accompanies the underlying shuttle of ionic interchange at the neurophysiological level. It relates to reality the way fiction does.

What are the consequence for ethics of this aestheticized picture of human existence? My sense is that the answer must be that there can be no consequences. Ethics is part of life, or part of the dream, since Nietzsche leaves us no internal basis for discriminating one part from another in point of truth or reality. Though he may say that the only values he recognize are aesthetic, in truth we have already, however it has happened, woven all other sorts of values into the fabric of life, and we have allowed ourselves no standpoint for their removal. There are philosophies in which values are noncognitive, but Nietzsche has a noncognitivist account of cognition, hence no way of segregating any part of the fabric from any other. If everything is a lie, it is no criticism of morality that it is a lie. True, if we accept the picture that life is a work of art of which we are the creators, then full recognition of this yields the option of becoming better and better artists. But that is not the same thing as becoming better and better people. And it is difficult to see how to put this into action, since everything takes place beneath the threshold of consciousness—it does so for just the reason that the sources of consciousness are outside consciousness—and there are no entry points for us as conscious beings below the threshold of what makes us conscious. Whatever we are capable of doing must be within consciousness—within the dream—and presumably we are doing that already. So we cannot really get better at what we do. The kind of artist we have to be for Nietzsche's aesthetic metaphysics to function leaves no real room for improvement. But that is the price of his inflationist definition of being artists. It is the metaphorical use that Locke appealed to when he asked, rhetorically, "Whence comes [the mind] by that vast store which the busy and boundless fancy of man has painted on it with an almost endless variety?" Nietzsche speaks of "forgetting that [we ourselves are] *artistically creating subjects.*" This is not something any of us have forgotten. We would never have known it had Nietzsche not told it to us. It could never have been something we would have known without him.

A COMMENT ON NIETZSCHE'S "ARTISTIC METAPHYSICS"

In the final paragraph of his text, however, Nietzsche somewhat withdraws the compliment in favor of singling out the artist as a type—the Intuitive Man—who stands "side by side with another type—The Rational Man." The former counts as real "only that life which has been disguised as illusion and beauty." Again, this would not be something known to the person of whom it is true. It is a drive of which the person who possesses it is essentially unaware. Nietzsche projects a theory to the effect that when, under rare and favorable conditions, the Intuitive Man prevails, then "a culture can take shape and art's mastery over life be established." He thinks this may have happened in ancient Greece. And he conjectures, "Neither the house, nor the gait, nor the clothes, nor the clay jugs give evidence of having been invented because of a pressing need." This is a fascinating idea, that there is an aesthetic supplement superimposed on the practical solutions in which a culture consists, when a certain human type prevails. All cultures need houses, garments, vessels, but these become art just when the conditions of life are mastered and something more, beauty, for example, is wanted. He might have added that all cultures need an ethics as well but that there is an artistic mode of moral life that takes the form, say, of a sort of courtesy in certain cultures. Nietzsche was a cultural critic, and my sense is that he felt that the rational, practical type of human held ascendancy rather than the artistic type: hence his shrillness in certain of his scarier texts. Here I think he himself forgot the difference between lies in the moral and in the extra-moral sense of his text. His famous moral passages are self-conscious lies, through and through.

Beginning to Be Nietzsche

On *Human, All Too Human*

> Yet they ought at the same time to have accounted for error also;
> for it is more intimately connected with animal existence and the
> soul continues longer in the state of error.
> —ARISTOTLE, *ON THE SOUL*

> All human life is sunk deep in untruth.
> —FRIEDRICH NIETZSCHE, *HUMAN, ALL TOO HUMAN*

Human, All Too Human must be judged quite differently, depending upon whether we view it retrospectively, in the light of the masterpieces that followed it, or prospectively, from the perspective of the author whose first philosophical work, properly speaking, it was. When Nietzsche wrote it, he had behind him the extraordinary *The Birth of Tragedy out of the Spirit of Music* (1872)—a work of speculative philology—and four of a projected suite of thirteen pamphlets of cultural criticism, published as *Thoughts out of Season* (1873–76), to use the poetic Edwardian translation of their overall title. These works show evidence not only of philosophical literacy but of extraordinary philosophical imagination, but in them Nietzsche did not confront, directly and as a philosopher, the canonical questions of philosophy. This he began to do in *Human, All Too Human*, but he had other intentions as well, which in some way screened the depth and daring of its philosophical thought.

In *The Birth of Tragedy*, Nietzsche appropriated from Schopenhauer the tremendous distinction between Will and Idea, which he mythologized as opposed but complementary aesthetic principles associated with the deities Dionysus and Apollo and embodied, respectively, in music and sculpture, whose joint offspring was tragedy and, ultimately, opera. But *The Birth of Tragedy* was at the same time an exercise in late-romantic visionary social philosophy. It postulated a form of artistic practice in which an entire community participated and in which individuals were (and this was an appropriation from Hegel) negated and transcended, brought onto a higher redemptive plane of communitarian existence by being taken up into a dramatic action in which the distinction between audience and actors was overcome: what had been audience became chorus, and what had been actors became vehicles through which gods were felt to make themselves manifest to all. If this indeed happened in the past, it could in principle happen again, under the auspices of Wagnerian opera, appreciated as the rebirth of tragedy. Opera, enacting myths that would be internalized by viewers, would achieve for modern men and women what tragedy had achieved for the ancients. It would dissolve and then reconstitute at some exalted level the bonds of the society. We would become chorus, then celebrants, then participants in some overwhelming, uniting revelation.

One might read *Thoughts out of Season* as an effort to vindicate a book like *The Birth of Tragedy* and to suggest reforms and revisions in German educational practice that would put the enhancements of life as the center and criteria of scholarship. In a sense, Schopenhauer and Wagner were the Apollo and Dionysus of Nietzsche's thought—they embodied, as it were, Idea and Will, respectively, so that just as tragedy was the product of the arts of form and frenzy, Nietzschean thought might be the product of philosophy and of opera. So inevitably there was a pamphlet on Schopenhauer (as educator) and on Richard Wagner (as artist and social transformationist). And there was a marvelous pamphlet, still worth reading, on the use and abuse of history for life, in which the kind of history that *The Birth of Tragedy* exemplified—bold, imaginative, vivid, and humane but hardly capable of being pegged, like Gulliver tethered by the Lilliputians, footnote by footnote, to the plane of reality—is contrasted with archival history—respectable, responsible, irrelevant, and dull—by whose standards the philological exuberance of *The Birth of Tragedy* had been anathematized by the establishment. So in a way, *Thoughts out of Season* was a blueprint for remaking German culture over in his own image, redeeming the culture by getting himself accepted as its model, playing a role in culture analogous to that played by the hero in tragedy or in (Wagnerian) opera.

Alongside these ambitions, philosophical achievement and distinction is decidedly of lower consequence and at best of compensatory value, especially if, as Wittgenstein was later to say, philosophy leaves the world as it found it. And in truth it is not clear that Nietzsche saw *Human, All Too*

234

Human as a philosophical work. Judging from its sour title, it would certainly be a book which differed from its visionary and Utopian predecessors. "Human, all too human" is a kind of sigh in the face of the intractability of the human material to the projects of moral sublimity. It is the spiteful verbal reflex of a disillusioned man, the way "Women are all alike!"—or *Cosi fan' tutte*—would be the thin salve applied to injured sexual pride by a man let down, as he views it, by a woman who forsook him. It is the effort to seek comfort in a sad universal—a "What can you expect?" It is the cheapest kind of philosophy, exactly the weary, cynical, jaded, and pessimistic *consolatio* that a weary, cynical, jaded, and pessimistic person might offer someone whose hopes for something better from humankind had just been dashed. To say that humans are human-all-too-human is in effect to say there is no heroic hope for them—for us—and for someone like Nietzsche, who had held the human sufficiently plastic as to be candidate for redemption through art, it is a bitter saying. So one feels that a book with that title was intended to injure his chief injurers. Richard Wagner is nowhere mentioned—not until Nietzsche added a preface to the book a decade after its publication. But one feels that he is the title's target—and in a way the book's target. Wagner is submerged in the generic category of artists, and art has, so to speak, lost its capital *A*. Artists are not redeemers and thaumaturges; they are, whatever their pretensions, human, all too human, absurd players in the *comedie humaine trop humaine*: "Not without deep sorrow," he writes, wiping away a crocodile tear, "do we admit to ourselves that artists of all times, at their most inspired, have transported to a heavenly transfiguration precisely those ideas that we now know to be false" (220).

235

Still, the title is meant universally, as if Nietzsche is going to portray the common clay out of which Wagner, even Wagner, is made. So the title promises a contribution to what in the nineteenth century was designated philosophical anthropology. It is going in a way to be a philosophical portrait of human beings as human. But think of that title against the great sequence of philosophical titles in which the word "human" appears: *Essay Concerning Human Understanding*, by John Locke; *A Treatise Concerning the Principles of Human Knowledge*, by George Berkeley; *An Enquiry Concerning Human Understanding* and *A Treatise on Human Nature*, by David Hume; *The Analysis of the Human Mind*, by James Mill; *Human Nature and*

Conduct, by John Dewey. In all of these, the word "human" is used neutrally and descriptively: human beings are represented as understanding, as having knowledge, as possessing a mind, a nature, a character, a mode of conduct. The titles pass no judgment, save in the respect in which it is implicitly a commendation to attribute knowledge, understanding, the possession of a mind to someone. As a title in this sequence, *Human, All Too Human* feels like an interjected sneer. It is as if one were to mutter in the deflationist iterations of Yiddishized English, "Human schmuman." If the book is to be philosophy, it is not to be an analysis, an enquiry, a treatise, an investigation, but a diatribe of some sort, where the subject—us—is not neutrally specified but deprecated and possibly despised. And the book is in some way to be punitive. In any case, it is difficult to imagine any of the books I mentioned dedicated in a subtitle to "free spirits," that is, those who have in some way seen through humanity and risen above the smallness, meanness, vileness of the human, all too human—who can say, with Hamlet, "Man delights not me."

Feeling oneself addressed by the subtitle, one might have picked the book up in 1878 for the pleasure of malice as promised by the title: it is, whether the free spirit sees it that way or not, human, all too human, to want to read a book by the name of *Human, All Too Human*—simply because we like to see our fellow beings portrayed in moral shortfall. And to a degree this appetite would be gratified, especially in the compilations of aphorisms, which constitute an address to a worldly reader from a writer whose stance is cosmopolitan and even jaded. "Ah," one imagines the speaker saying as he leans back and blows an indolent smoke ring, "Man is *dot-dot-dot*. Whereas Woman must *dash-dash*." The aphorisms are short enough for us to memorize them and just outrageous enough that one waits for the right moment to retail one in mixed company, for the pleasure of seeing the males slap their knees and the females prettily protest. There is just enough misanthropy to balance the misogyny. Nietzsche was a B-plus aphorist, but how many aphorists of any grade do we encounter? His auditors and correspondents must have encouraged him, perhaps urging him to publish them. I do not know the compositional history of the book, but the title and the collections of aphorisms seem to me to go sufficiently together to imply an intention. The intention would be to print, for free spirits of course, a little volume of applied psychology in which readers might see hu-

manity portrayed in its true colors—small, vain, selfish, envious, hypocriti-
cal, greedy, lubricious. Not *evil*! But, to use the term as he was later to define it, *bad*, or *Schlecht*. Indeed, in the transformation of moral vocabulary
that was to be the high point of *The Genealogy of Morals* (1887), "good"
was the human-all-too-human way of being what free spirits would call
bad. A free spirit might very well be capable of evil, but not of badness.
Badness was a constellation of little vices and large weaknesses. But in
1878, Nietzsche had not quite risen to this vision. The psychology is not very
deep, but one would not expect aphorisms, which are one step up from
clichés, to be very deep. Occasionally something gets said which does strike
us as deep, as in 491:

> *Self-observation.* Man is very well defended against himself, against his
> own spying and sieges; usually he is able to make out no more of himself   237
> than his outer fortifications. The actual stronghold is inaccessible to him,
> even invisible, unless friends and enemies turn traitor and lead him there
> by a secret path.

This sounds familiar, in a way, to ears that have been trained on Freud. If
491 is true, a very complex theory of the mind and of self-knowledge is
true, and Nietzsche in fact is in possession of something like such a theory—that is why Freud was to express such admiration for him as a
thinker—but it is really not yet accessible to him. It is even invisible in his
writings as of 1878. The "secret path" will be the unfolding of his philosophy, which is a lot deeper than the tissue of tittering truisms out of which
the aphorisms are woven. Later, as the philosophy becomes visible or partially visible, the aphorisms are going themselves to deepen. They will carry
on their tips the toxins of a theory of another stripe altogether from the psychology he and Doctor Paul Ree bandied with one another, and they plant
themselves inextricably in the flesh of the mind. Still, the first innocent readers of *Human, All Too Human*, wanting nothing more than a recreational
shudder at the writer's daring, will have found themselves entangled in
something more ingenious and really unprecedented. And the book, as Nietzsche, lightheartedly casting himself as a philosophical Papageno, por-
trays it in the preface, is set with "snares and nets for careless birds, and an
almost constant, unperceived challenge to reverse one's habitual estimations

and esteemed habits." One of the snares consists in thinking there is only one kind of net or snare to worry about.

For in the end there are two books here, one in the grand tradition of Locke, Berkeley, Hume, genuinely but revolutionarily philosophical and antiphilosophical, and the other a book of surface observations, a hashwork of little woundings to the human pride in being human from which—and what would one expect of something human, all too human?—nobody was going to bleed to death. Whatever the surface intention, something else was getting written as the book evolved. Nietzsche could not have formed the intention to transcribe his extraordinarily original philosophy because that philosophy itself was only half-conscious—if it was even as conscious as that. I am not sure Nietzsche himself knew what sort of book he was writing: I am not sure he himself saw the difference between the two kinds of truths. How, after all, could he? What was invisible to him is what we, from our perspective in history, can see vividly: Nietzsche as philosopher. The great originality that took over in the earlier books took over here, but it was the originality of a powerful philosophical vision, which was only to be worked out, book through book, over the remaining literary life of the author.

Part of my reason for thinking that Nietzsche did not really know what kind of book he was writing is the fact that he printed, "in lieu of a preface," a passage from Descartes's *Discours de la methode*. I do not merely mean to infer—from the fact that he relinquished the opportunity that a preface affords a writer to address the reader directly about the book at hand, explaining what he had sought to do and what he achieved, so far as his powers allowed—that he was not clear about what he had achieved. His lack of clarity follows even more strongly from the fact that he let Descartes—Descartes of all writers!—speak for him in that confessional passage in which the latter speaks of discovering "something new, which seemed to me sufficiently important, and not at all familiar to other men." This passage simply does not fit the psychological part of the book—the part that deals with the human, all too human—for there is nothing new there, it is familiar to everyone, it is the core curriculum of everyday life, composed of the small betrayals, of others and of self, that constitutes growing up as human, all too human, in society.

But neither does Descartes fit what *is* new, what *is* important, and what *is* unfamiliar in this book. For what is new, important, and unfamiliar is precisely a set of philosophical theses defined by their opposition to everything for which Descartes argued. If, in the somewhat annoying locution of adolescent patois, one were to say "not" after asserting each of the propositions in the great fourth book of the *Discourse*, one would have Nietzsche's philosophy in a nutshell. As a philosopher, Nietzsche is exactly the Anti-Descartes. Everything that Descartes says about thought, self, God, knowledge, certainty, morality, error, and mind is something that Nietzsche is going to argue—is already beginning to argue in this book—is as false as what artists "at their most inspired" have raised to the highest spiritual power. Descartes is credited with beginning modern philosophy. Nietzsche must therefore be credited with ending it. And the whole of *Human, All Too Human* is larded with philosophical denials of a kind it is fair to say had never been written, certainly never written down in the sustained and relentless way in which we find them highlighted in the text. But those highlights are projections from the privileged historical position from which the whole of Nietzsche's philosophy lays exposed and articulated to someone who has all the later books to consult. And I do not think that Nietzsche saw the difference between the passages that philosophical retrospection would highlight and the rest. What he says about human nature, construed philosophically, probably did not strike him as different at all from what he says about the human, all too human, as construed from the posture of the aphorist. When this did begin to be visible to him, he had deepened his views of ordinary humanity and had come to see that philosophical falsehoods are falsehoods of a special order. They are not the kind of falsehoods in which the human, all too human, shows its shabby duplicities. The falsehoods of philosophy are not the human, all too human: they are the human as such. They call for another kind of critique altogether. When Nietzsche reprinted the book a decade later, he had a far clearer picture of what he had achieved in it, and of course he dropped the passage from Descartes and wrote a preface of his own.

In his own preface, Nietzsche puts into the mouth of a wounded reader the concerned reaction to this book: "What's that? *Everything* is only—human, all too human?" The consternation expressed is that morality itself is

239

just another way of being human, all too human, when one would have hoped morality provides a remedy against precisely that. After all, the aphorist wraps the sadism of his description in the vestments of the moralist: by holding up the mirror, the hope is to trap the conscience of human beings who, seeing themselves painfully deficient, might undertake to mend their ways. But if the mirror itself is human, all too human, simply another mode in which human beings exert power over one another, then there would be a kind of futility in moralizing—like someone using language to correct language when language itself is in some irremediable way flawed. Still, we do improve and enhance language in various ways for various individual and institutional purposes, and if, beyond that, there may be some deep philosophical sense in which language as language is flawed and imperfect, those flaws and imperfections are of a different order from the ordinary vagueness, ambiguity, woolliness, and ungrammaticality with which this or that person's use of language is flawed. Using for the moment Chomsky's distinction between competence and performance, there is a distinction to be drawn between misperformances and incompetence, where the latter would be something deep in the nature of language itself that someone with a certain kind of philosophical vision might decry. Misperformances are to language what bad manners are to morality: they are capable of piecemeal modification. And the human, all too human, is of this order. Incompetence is another and deeper matter, and beyond remedy. It might consist, for example, in language being thought to have no purchase on reality—something we hear a lot about from poststructuralist writers. It might consist, in the domain of morality, in morality's having no grounding in truth. That is a philosophical position on morality, and one very close to Nietzsche's heart. It has little to do with moral misperformances—selfishness, greed, vanity, and the other elements in the aphorist's armory. The deep flaws in the human material are not the kinds of flaws the aphorist could hope to correct. They are beyond his range. But those are the kinds of flaws Nietzsche *as philosopher* deals with all the time. Where he differs from Descartes is here: Descartes thought those flaws could be, within limits, removed—treated so to speak as mere misperformances. For Nietzsche they define what we are. We are, from the Nietzschean perspective, incompetent at our core.

Descartes understood human beings as flawed or, as he put it, imperfect beings. And since he defined human beings as essentially thinking substance—as what he termed *res cogitans*—he naturally saw our imperfection to consist in certain pathologies of thought: we are prey to muddled thoughts or, in his language, to "ideas" which lack clarity and distinctness. Not all our ideas lack clarity and distinctness, and in his *Meditations*—as well as in book 4 of the *Discourse*—he thought there are a certain number of clear and distinct ideas at which each of us can arrive regarding our own existence, the existence of God, and the immortality of the soul. Our idea of God is an idea of a perfect being, and indeed it is only by contrast with the perfection we conceive of God as necessarily possessing do we know ourselves to be imperfect. Any idea we grasp clearly and distinctly is, Descartes held, true beyond serious question, and beings capable of discovering such deep truths as he felt himself to have established must be capable of redemption from total cognitive darkness. So he proceeded to rid himself, systematically, of as many errors as he could by using his criteria of clarity and distinctness: any idea (we would say: any proposition) grasped with clarity and distinction is true. Such truths are the foundations of knowledge. And with them as our base, we may build with care, assigning to each proposition only that degree of confidence its clarity and distinctness underwrite. We *have* perfect control over assent and dissent, and indeed, this is what freedom for a thinking being consists in. Within limits, we can (as Spinoza, writing in the Cartesian spirit, put it) "improve the understanding" and achieve the maximum degree of happiness to which a finite being may aspire.

241

Plainly, there is a considerable difference between freedom as Descartes defines it and the free-spiritedness Nietzsche assigns to his ideal readers. To begin with, there may be no free spirits, as he says: he invented them to keep himself company, to hold philosophical loneliness at bay. They are a kind of willed fiction. But then what is not a willed fiction? "Truths" are just the lies we tell ourselves to enable us to get on in life when those lies happen to work. Nor are we to exchange lies for truths, step by Cartesian step, as we lay down foundations for knowledge. We are products of the lies— lies to be sure in what, in a precocious essay, posthumously published, he described as "an extra-moral sense," or, in another of his famous phrases that served as a title of his masterpiece, as "beyond good and evil." There are lies that are—beyond truth and falsity. The whole question of truth and falsity is really a question of what kind of creature it is that a certain number of "lies" enables to prevail—and what kind of creature might result if the lies that define our world were to be exchanged for another set? The whole of Nietzsche's anti-Cartesianism is contained in aphorism 11 of this book, under the section "Of First and Last Things": "Very belatedly (only now) is it dawning on men that in their belief in language they have propagated a monstrous error"; "*Logic*, too, rests on assumptions that do not correspond to anything in the real world"; mathematics "would certainly not have originated if it had been known from the beginning that there is no exactly straight line in nature," and so on. And again, in aphorism 16: "That which we now call the world is the result of a number of errors and fantasies, which came about gradually in the overall development of organic beings . . . and [are] now handed down to us as a collected treasure." It *is* a treasure—"for the *value* of our humanity rests upon it." Can we get rid of this error without, as it were, getting rid of ourselves? Such falsehoods are not imperfections—they define the only kind of being we can imagine for ourselves. "*Error about life is necessary for life*," he says, summarily, at 33. So the problem is not to get rid of falsehood but to discover what falsehoods we need for life and to understand that we need them.

242

The propensity to lie is not just another smutch in the catalog of the human, all too human. The propensity to lie is what makes life possible. It is who we are. My imagined reader, who picked the book up for an evening's moral entertainment, who anticipated the kind of pleasure someone might derive from perusing a book about, say, snobs, might find the first and second section, and given nineteenth-century attitudes toward religion, the third section on religious life, rather deeper water than that reader meant to splash about in. All at once, such readers would be in over their heads. This was not an ordinary book about vanity, but neither was it an ordinary book of philosophy. It strikes off on philosophical paths nobody had ever taken before—paths so novel that it is excusable in the author that he might have thought he was writing the sort of book my imagined reader thought he was about to read. The book is A-plus philosophy disguised by the B-plus aphorisms. The writer is a metaphysical genius who appears to have the ambitions of a feuilletonist.

That is why the book looks so different from the perspective of its future than it had to have looked in the perspective of its present. The great philosophy to come highlights its anticipatory passages for us, and we can read it as a first, tentative statement of one of the great philosophical visions. Its first readers lacked that clarifying vision and so did its writer. Who could have understood the extraordinary discussion in aphorism 45—"Double prehistory of good and evil"—the way we now can, in the backward light of *The Genealogy of Morals*? The problem of the book lies in its divided intentions: the intention to revise philosophy and the intention, as it were, to revise humanity as a moralist rather than an analyst of the deep nature of morality itself. But as a writer, Nietzsche was always defined through divided intentions. He did not want at any time to give up his critique of the human, all too human, as he continued all the while to build the great philosophical account of human nature that in less gifted hands would have been a treatise, an essay, an enquiry, a dissertation. He tried to practice philosophy in the way he thought of history as being practiced when in the service of life rather than in the production of academic scholars. His divided intentions very nearly queered his philosophical reputation, inasmuch as philosophers since his time have pretty largely just been academic philosophers, trained by codes of expressions Nietzsche fails to follow, whereas we might now see in him a model for how to do philosophy when we want to be taken seriously in the academy and at the same time effective in life. *Human, All Too Human* is a marvelous place to begin for readers with that sort of ideal, as it was precisely the right way for the writer to begin to be who he became.

Nietzsche's *Daybreak: Thoughts on the Prejudices of Morality*

It was Peter Gast, Nietzsche's copyist, claque, practical nurse, and constant correspondent, who gave this book its epigraph from the *Rig Veda*: "There are so many days that have not yet broken." It may have been a fateful ornament, since *Rig Veda* 1:113 (To Dawn) chants, "She, first of endless morns to come hereafter, follows the path of morns that have departed," and the doctrine of eternal recurrence struck Nietzsche with the force of a revelation later that year—1881. But it in any case suggested the title *Eine Morgenröte* to Nietzsche. "There are so many gay and particularly red colors in it!" he wrote Gast in February, but the "*Eine*" was dropped in proof, on grounds of pretentiousness. Gast regarded the new title as pretentious, preferring the original *Die Pflugschar* (The ploughshare) whose vivid connotations perhaps better suited his, and for that matter Nietzsche's, perception of the kind of book it was: turning over the caked and stubborn crust of moral custom preparatory to fresh growth. In a late preface, Nietzsche writes, "In this book you will discover a subterranean man at work, one who tunnels and mines and undermines." This metaphor was with him from the beginning: "I go on digging in my moral mine," he wrote to Gast in 1880, "and sometimes seem to myself wholly subterranean." And in the pages devoted to *Morgenröte* in his strident and exclamatory apologia, *Ecce Homo*, ploughing and mining give way to fishing: "Almost every sentence in the book was first thought, *caught*, among that jumble of rocks near Genoa, when I was alone and still had secrets from the sea."

Bringing something unsuspected out of the depths may characterize the *labor* of the book, but *Morgenröte*—felicitously translated by R. J. Hollingdale as *Daybreak* rather than *Dawn*, or the redundant and vapid *Dawn of Day* of the first English translation in the Oscar Levy edition—expresses Nietzsche's hope for the historical position of the book. "This book is what one calls a 'decisive step,' " he wrote his dour publisher Ernst Schmeitzner on February 23: "More a destiny than a book." To his mother he wrote, "I have brought forth one of the boldest, loftiest, and most self-possessed books ever born from human heart and brain." To his friend and colleague Franz Overbeck, he says on March 18 that "This is the book on which my name will probably depend," and, in August, claiming that the effect of his book will be like that of the strongest spiritual drink, he writes, "It is the beginning of my beginning." "With this book," he wrote again in *Ecce Homo*, "my campaign against morality began." *Morgenröte* was published in July 1881, without anyone much noticing it. A cautious acknowledgement came from Jacob Burkhardt, who only had had time to leaf through it. The predictable epistolary handshake came from Overbeck. "It's all very decent and well-intended, what they write me," he laments to Gast on August 14, "but distant, distant, distant." Mostly it was silence. Crazed that summer with physical pain—"Five times I have called for Doctor Death!"—the most original mind in Europe, the best philosopher of his time, the finest writer of his own language, led a crank's life. He walked, watched his diet, eked out his pennies, moved restlessly from pension to pension, sought a possible climate, maintaining throughout an adorable cheerfulness and an incredible literary energy. By 1882 he was sending a new book to Schmeitzner. And book after book followed until his breakdown in 1889 and his almost simultaneous global fame.

The book is composed—or compiled—of 575 short "thoughts," some no more than a single line, none much more than three pages, grouped into five "books." Each component piece has a title of its own, but none of the five books does, so it is unclear what, if any, principle of organization may have applied. The "thoughts" of one book seldom relate more closely to the other thoughts in it than they do to those in other books, though on occasion we get a suite of thoughts on the same topic, for example, pity. Many of the later thoughts, on the other hand, are aphoristic rephrasings of thoughts treated more expansively in early pages, as though a constant

246

process of distillation were taking place. Though less sharply structured than *The Genealogy of Morals* or *Beyond Good and Evil*, for which it is a precursor, it is considerably less sprawling than *Human, All Too Human*, which preceded it by three years, which suggests that he was beginning to find his way to a somewhat more architectonic exposition and that he wanted something more than tiny bits, however striking and bright. The pieces treat of The Artist, The Lover, The Philosopher, The Christian, The Jew, The Greek, The Roman, and The German—and of women, animals, death, marriage, genius, feelings, morals, and the structure of the mind. "A book such as this is not for reading straight through or reading aloud," Nietzsche says in thought 454, "but for dipping into, especially when out walking or on a journey." So the absence of headings from the five books, the small format of the individual components, as well as the abrupt shift from topic to topic, *could* be devices for slowing the reader down. But 454 247 could also be a lame effort at making a virtue of the fact that he had not yet found himself able to work with larger forms and even was not yet clear on where he was heading. "I feel that I may have found the main gallery," he told Gast in 1880, "but that is a belief one can form and reject a hundred times." *One* price of being subterranean is that one is in the dark. And in any case Nietzsche then lacked what we now possess, namely his own later works, in the light of which we can discern the deeper themes already sounded in *Morgenröte*, but too softly yet to hint at the systematic structures which were at last to emerge. The great Nietzschean formulations lay ahead: Eternal Recurrence, Will to Power, Superman, Antichrist, Master and Slave Morality, the Death of God, Nihilism, and the Transvaluation of Value. Without the structural benefits of the whole system, it would be difficult, as it would then have been impossible, to appreciate the book as a contribution to moral theory rather than to moralistic literature, though of an uncommonly high order, or to see a great philosophy being born. One could not, for instance, have read 501—"On Mortal Souls"—as presaging a consequence of accepting eternal recurrence, or 502 as an anticipatory gloss on the *Übermensch*.

The stance of the moralist, all the more so the stance of the moralist who insists on aphorisms, is commonly to hold the human, all too human, delinquencies up against a background of received moral notions. His aim is to describe moral weakness, expose hypocrisy, and depict, like Hogarth, the varieties and degrees of vice. He is reminding his readers of what they already believe and in a way seeking to deepen that belief. There is a strain of moralism in Nietzsche, but mainly it is the very principles moralists take as givens that *he* terms moral "prejudices" and puts in question. So his attitude to deviants from these principles is somewhat complex: they really are, so to speak, sinners, even though the dogmas that define them as such are in fact merely prejudices. What makes the work profound, however, is that he is beginning to impose onto moral codes as a class a structure of interpretation that is quite original with him. He is at least as original as those other interpretative strategists of the nineteenth century, Marx and Freud, with whose thought his shares a kind of logic. They sought to reveal both the choices men make and the patterns of justification they use to validate those choices as expressing a set of underlying material causes of which the agents are in general unaware—are explicitly unconscious on Freud's analysis. These I call "deep interpretations," and they are more and more the form of what pass for theories in the so-called human sciences. Nietzsche in this sense is giving deep interpretations of moral conduct and moral reasoning together: his question is what are we *deeply* doing that shows up on the surface as moral existence.

Deep interpreters typically claim that their theories are ultimately liberating. Once we understand the underlying dynamics, we shall be in a position at last to make our own history, in the case of Marx; and once we see what underlying conflicts get transformed into irrational behavior, we shall be freed from the latter and at liberty to work and love, in the case of Freud. Nietzsche too believes his theory to be liberating not so much from morality as such but from misperceiving the function of morality through not understanding the subsocial forces that express themselves in the medium of moral codes, and so putting us in a position to choose the values we want to live by. "In us there is accomplished—supposing you want a formula— the *self-sublimation of morality.*" The German phrase is *die Selbstaufhebung der Moral.* "Self-sublimation" will pass as a bare translation of *Selbstaufhebung*, but *aufheben* is one of the legendary terms of German, especially Hegelian philosophical vocabulary, meaning: to negate, to preserve, and to transcend—*all at once*; a translator or editor ought to give a warning footnote to this effect. "It goes without saying," he writes in 103, "that I do not deny—unless I am a fool—that many actions called immoral ought to be avoided and resisted, or that many called moral ought to be done and encouraged—but I think the one should be encouraged and the other avoided *for other reasons than hitherto.*"

What morality as morality deeply expresses, I suppose, is the power—he will later say the will to power—of a group, internalized as a kind of form through which the individual perceives others and perceives himself, so that a distorting screen of self-interpretation interposes itself between our awareness of ourselves and ourselves. Diagnostics to one side, it is here that Nietzsche sounds most contemporary, philosophically speaking, since his moral psychology is so resolutely anti-Cartesian. It *had* to be anti-Cartesian, since his critique of morality entailed the view that we do not really know what we are and Cartesianism is precisely the view that what we essentially are is something immediately present to consciousness, so that nothing is true of us psychologically of which we are not directly and noninferentially aware. The connection between his philosophy of morals and his philosophical psychology is but one example of how his work is finally systematic, the system only revealing itself late in the course of his working it out through his book, and only dimly discriminable here. It is as though the book itself exemplifies its teaching, that with regard to what goes on in our minds we are typically out of cognitive touch. The psychology in the book is dazzling and precocious, and it is fair to say that after several decades of intense analytical work, the discipline of philosophical psychology has only begun to pull abreast of Nietzsche's thought.

In the great prime of his literary prowess, Nietzsche's prose suggests the performative assurance of a marvelously gifted and intuitive lover. The text of *Morgenröte*, with its sudden shifts of rhythm and tone, at one moment lyrical and at the next moment earthy, its mock distance and its sudden intimacy, its sweeping playfulness, its jeers, sneers, jokes, and whispers—and its abrupt unanticipated kills—is a kind of eroticism of writing, and it requires of its reader a partnership in pleasure and intelligence. Nietzsche's voice has lost the professorial authority of the early writing and has not yet acquired the strident conviction of a prophet unheeded. And in none of his books, I feel, is there a more palpable sense of spiritual well-being. *Morgenröte* was put together at an especially quiet moment in Nietzsche's life.

"The whole book," he wrote later, "contains no negative word, no attack, no spite—it lies in the sun, sound, happy, like some sea animal basking on the rocks." For something finally so incendiary, it is a sunny book, and Nietzsche describes it that way at 553: "Whither does this whole philosophy, with all its circuitous paths, want to go? Does it do more than translate as it were into reason a strong and constant drive, a drive for gentle sunlight, bright and buoyant air, southern vegetation, the breath of the sea . . . ?" It was a time when the ideas he was mothering were still tender, did not yet show the savage power that would tear him along with them towards their terrible destiny, not loosing him from their grip till madness intervened just when history was about to take them up and put them to uses undreamt of as he clambered, half-blind, over the sea rocks near Genoa on his endless hopeful walks—when he still could write to Gast, "Nothing has happened to anyone because of me; no one's given me any thought."

250

Some Remarks on *The Genealogy of Morals*

The third essay of the three that compose *On the Genealogy of Morals* is, according to Nietzsche's preface to the work, a gloss on its prefixed aphorism, which reads: "Unconcerned, mocking, violent—thus wisdom wants us. She is a woman, and always loves only a warrior." What sort of warrior is unconcerned? One, I suppose, for whom the means is an end, for whom war making is not so much what you do but what you are, so that it is not a matter of warring for but as an end. There is, he tells us in the first essay, "no 'being' behind doing . . . 'the doer' is merely a fiction added to the deed." So the unconcerned warrior is perhaps best exemplified by the great archer Arjuna, in the *Bhagavad Gita*, instructed by Krishna that unconcern for consequences, hence disinterested participation in the battle, is the path to follow if release is sought from karma: it is not desisting from action, which is in any case impossible as much for the Gita as for Nietzsche, but a certain enlightened view of the metaphysics of action that wisdom loves.

If this is the recommended morality, what does the warrior mock? Clearly those still locked in the world of goals and purposes, who subscribe to hypothetical imperatives, who fight for causes, rather than those who are categorical fighters, for whom warring is for its own sake. So violence too is not instrumental but the moral essence of the warrior, not something he especially uses to terrorize, but a secondary effect of the martial art. Why should wisdom then love only the anticonsequentialist? The author of the Gita would answer this out of a moral metaphysics in which karmic transmigration is a form of hell, a view finally negativistic and, as we shall see, predicated on a kind of *ressentiment*, since we blame our suffering on karmic pollutions we ourselves are responsible for. These considerations scarcely would have daunted the discoverer of eternal recurrence, hence of the certitude of unending repeated Mahabharatas, in each of which Arjuna fulfills himself by drawing bowstrings and steering chariots; nor would they faze the prophet of *amor fati* for whom the evil to be avoided consists in trying to be something other than what one is. Kant, the other dominant anticonsequentialist, has a metaphysics of morals, in which it is true that an effort is made to derive our duties from our being, *except* that it construes derivation itself to be our characteristic form of action and our essence itself to be reason, and so entraps an opponent as a confirmer, since denial too exemplifies rationality.

So, if you are Nietzsche, you don't deny, you *reject*. And that is what is to be expected from a warrior whose campaigns happen to be philosophical and who philosophizes with a hammer: who does not so much love wisdom as is, like a warrior, loved by wisdom. So not Nietzsche as a philosopher but Nietzsche as *sophiaphilos*, whose weapons are words, sometimes used as hammers. (Erase the human, all too human, fraudulence of "the old artilleryman," as he referred to himself on occasion with an affected gruffness.) As one does not argue with an idealist if one does not want to be enmeshed in his web—one instead kicks a rock, or, to cite the practice of one of our most influential contemporary philosophic critics, one does not refute the thinkers one opposes but instead sneers at them. One puts metaphysics *on ice*, as Nietzsche says in another place: one *mocks*. Mockery is the violence of the metaphysician as warrior. And if one's writings are to be mocking and violent, hence meant to *hurt*, the aphorism is a natural, obvious form to use; for, piercing like a dart the defenses of reason, it lodges inextricably in the mind's flesh, where it sticks as a perpetual invasion: like a barbed arrow, it cannot be extricated without tearing its host.

This aphorism has a complex pragmatics, since it is at once used *and* used to demonstrate what it means to use language in this way, and the commentary, while it does not quite mitigate the pain to philosophical susceptibilities the aphorism may cause—wisdom does not love those who love wisdom—at least reduces the chance of such suffering as it may cause being smothered in the *ressentiment* it is also the task of that commentary to dissolve. And in some way its use is meant to have an effect quite opposite to the instillation of an ascetic ideal, as he generalizes upon that concept in the third essay, and so is not meant to transform one into a philosopher, since philosophers are the first to be discussed in that essay as falling under the balefulness of asceticism.

The aphorism is a special use of the language it is also *about*, and it is the second time in two books that he has drawn a joke from the grammar of gender, feminizing wisdom and truth, and both times in order to emphasize a difference between the way he uses language and the ways "philosophers" use it. In *Beyond Good and Evil* he observes that if truth has the attributes of femininity, then she is unlikely to yield her favors to the cloddish and clumsy idiom of philosophers who do not know how to seduce, as he, Nietzsche, does. But in the same way, the aphorism is the way to approach wisdom, epitomized as female in *this* aphorism: wisdom does not bestow herself upon writers who write as philosophers write, hence not from books that are read as philosophical books are read. Rather language must *implant* itself in the reader, and wisdom comes from an experience that is literary only in the sense that it is caused by a book. So it is language used in a way as to bypass the faculties used ordinarily in reading. "An aphorism," he writes aphoristically, "when properly stamped and molded, has not been 'deciphered' when it has simply been read."

In my address to the American Philosophical Association, "Philosophy as/and/of Literature," I argued that by treating philosophy in general as the sort of thing that can be expressed in articles of the sort through which we define ourselves professionally as readers and writers, we misperceive that vast diversity of literary forms the historical bibliography of our discipline displays. Each kind of book has to be read in its kind of way, and just possibly each kind of reader is to be transformed into a different kind of person—the sort of person the philosopher requires the reader to be if the philosophy is to reach him. So we have to realize that in reading Nietzsche we are being attacked; we need some kind of shield or the aphorism will *land* and we lose to the words. One way of fighting back *is* of course to treat him as a philosopher himself: the net, too, is a gladiatorial weapon in the skilled left hand of the *retiarius*. So to cage him into a system of repressive categories, to put his toxin on ice, to slip the manacles of asceticism onto his wrists, to locate him in the history of thought is like driving a stake through Nero's heart in order to keep his ghost stable.

There is a tendency to divide commentators on Nietzsche into those who portray a hard Nietzsche and those who portray a soft Nietzsche. But it is possible to acknowledge him as hard by treating him as though he were soft; so when Philippa Foot reviewed my book on him with a certain appreciation for the originality of treating him as a kind of linguistic epistemologist and then raised the question of why, if this was what he was *au fond*, anyone would be especially interested in him any longer, I felt I had won a kind of victory—as though I had transformed him into a minotaur by devising a maze. But certainly there is a Nietzsche who genuinely stands against philosophy rather than illustrating it and who is dangerous and even terrible: and in this essay I would like to acknowledge the virulent Nietzsche, not

this time examining his views on language but his use of language, to see what he must have intended by this use and what his beliefs may have been for such intentions to have been coherent. This approach too is a way of standing aside and at a distance.

The psychology of metaphorical address, since metaphor is a rhetorician's device, is that the audience will itself supply the connection withheld by the metaphor; the rhetorician opens a kind of gap with the intention that the logical energies of his audience will arc it, with the consequence that having participated in the progression of argument, the audience convinces itself. There is another but comparable psychology for the aphorism, namely, that once heard it is unlikely to pass from recollection, so its pointed terseness is a means to ensoul the message it carries and to counteract the predictable deteriorations of memory. So it is a natural instrument for the moralist. The whole great second essay of the *Genealogy* is precisely addressed to the role of pain in the forging of a moral memory. *Forgetting* is a dimension of animal health, a requisite of mental hygiene—"no mere *vis inertias* as the superficial imagine." Nietzsche writes: "It is rather an active and in the strictest sense positive faculty of repression." *Consciousness*, in which attention and memory or memorability coincide, is contrary to the animal nature and possibly even a sort of disease—one of the discontents of civilization—a disturbance against which forgetfulness is a preserver of psychic order and peace: "It will be immediately obvious how there could be no happiness, no cheerfulness, no hope, no pride, no present, without forgetfulness."

Nietzsche is speaking of what we might call deep forgetfulness here, a complete metabolization of experience rather than the repressive forgetfulness that Freud's later concept of the unconscious introduces into mental economy, where what is put there clamors to be made conscious and so is not *deeply* forgotten. In order, then, that this sustaining mental entropy should be arrested or reversed, some mnemotechnic is required. As Nietzsche puts it, "If something is to stay in the memory it must be burned in; only that which never ceases *hurting* stays in the memory." This, he continues, "is a main cause of the oldest (unhappily also the most enduring) psychology on earth." And, a moment later, "Man could never do without blood, torture, and sacrifices when he felt a need to create a memory for himself." Then, after a catalog of medieval cruelties, he concludes, "All this has its origin in the instinct that realizes that pain is the most powerful aid to mnemonics." We still talk of teaching someone a lesson as a synonym for administering a beating; we still say "this will learn you" as we land a punch. And we all admire Kafka's brilliant image in *The Penal Colony* where the inscription of the crime is the crime's punishment, since it is in the medium of the victim's agony. And, when one comes to it—as we shall in more detail—the entire office of religion has consisted in teaching us that our suffering has meaning, so that the chosen people spontaneously turns to its prophets to explain what lesson it is being taught through the suffering it has come to accept as the avenue of communication.

Nietzsche was too much the classicist not to know that aphorism and remembering are pragmatically complicated, or to be ignorant that the earliest collection of aphorisms was attributed to Hippocrates and constituted a kind of *vade mecum* of medical praxiology, a body of maxims pointed and polished in order to stick in the intern's mind. Since aphoristic form is prophylactic against forgetfulness and since pain is the prime reinforcer of retention, aphorism and pain are internally related. So this form spontaneously presents itself to a writer whose warrior violence must be turned against those he appears to admire: the healthy forgetters, the innocent brutes. So when, in the second essay's discussion of the mnemonics of hurt, he writes, "In a certain sense the whole of asceticism lies here," he is being

255

disingenuous, inveighing against asceticism while using language specifically framed to scourge. Someone who uses ascetic practices to kill asceticism is engaged in a very complex communication, supposing he is coherent at all, and he would be right that we are missing what is taking place
when we merely *read the words*. An apologist for paganism, for the happy
instinctive unconscious life of the spontaneously unremembering beast, has
no business creating a moral memory in the course of such apologetics,
leaving a scar of consciousness against the easy viscosities of the mental life
he celebrates: so the apology for paganism must itself be a moral stab, and
self-conscious paganism is logically unlivable. So the remarks on paganism
are *meant to hurt* in a way in which the memory of happiness becomes, in
Dante's scale, the *maggiore dolore* in a general context of torment: it is as
though the entirety of the *Genealogy* is a cell of inflictions and an instrument of ascetic transformation and a very rough book.

256

"Even those who suppose, erroneously, that *Beyond Good and Evil* is a
collection of aphorisms that may be read in any order whatever," Walter
Kaufmann wrote, having in mind by "those" specifically me, "generally recognize that the *Genealogy* comprises three essays." This in his view brings
the book closest to what we Anglo-American philosophers expect philosophical writing to be, all the more so in that "Nietzsche's manner is much
more sober and single-minded than usual." But the manner of the essayist
is a marvelous camouflage for the sort of moral terrorist Nietzsche really
was, as the essay itself is a kind of literary camouflage for the sharpened
stakes of aphorism he has concealed for the unwary, making this in a deep
sense the most treacherous book he ever compiled, one almost impossible
to read without being cut to ribbons. Flaying alive—"cutting straps"—is
itemized in his inventory of ghastly interventions that at last instill "the kind
of memory by the aid of which one comes at last to reason!" For how precisely is one to forget what he writes about Jews, slaves, justice, seriousness; about barbarism, morality itself, sensuality, torture, cruelty; about war,
women, and will?—even if the book also seems to provide passages of
modulating analgesis, enabling him to say, soothingly, that he did not exactly mean what he said, enabling his commentators to reassure us that
those who took him at his word had taken him out of context—as though
he was, after all, just to be read. It is like saying the lace handkerchief is
the context for the stiletto it hides or the wine the context for the powdered

glass or the rose an attenuation of the thorn. A man cannot write this way and then stand back in mock innocence and point to the fine print, to the footnote, to the subtle conciliatory phrase written in all but invisible ink, or say that one had expected we were subtle enough to read between the lines!

This book was not written for Nietzsche scholars, capable of handling even deadly poison with the long forceps of *Wissenschaft*. And often Nietzsche tells us as much. At the very beginning, for example, he talks about the English moral psychologists whose interest for us in part lies in the fact that they have written uninteresting books, the question being what were they *doing* by writing such books—"What do they really want?" He hopes we will be clever enough to ask that of this book, take the hint, raise the query as to why he wipes away with his left hand the blood he has drawn with his right, and that we will not pretend that we are not bleeding or that it is our fault if we are. Just by printing on that package the warning against the contents, you have not provided prophylaxis. There is a passage in Wittgenstein in which he explains certain confusions about language as due to "the uniform appearance of words when we hear them spoken or meet them in script or print." "It is like looking into the cabin of the locomotive," he goes on to say: "We see handles all looking more or less alike." But what shows a greater uniformity of appearance than *books*? *The Genealogy of Morals* is of about the shape and heft of *Utilitarianism* or *Foundations of the Metaphysics of Morals*—or for that matter the *Imitatio Christi*. But that does not mean that they are all to be treated the same way or that reading is a uniform matter—"especially," as Wittgenstein writes, "when we are doing philosophy." To treat the *Genealogy* as though it were precocious analytical philosophy is to have swallowed a bait without having yet felt the hook. After all, the subtitle is *Eine Streitschrift*. So *à la guerre comme à la guerre*: one had better study one's defenses!

In fact the *Genealogy* is in some ways the least analytical of Nietzsche's books, though it contains one of the subtlest discussions of moral predicates I know. For the question must be raised as to who the readers were to be, what was to bring them to this book, and what particularly were they to get from it. And this returns me to the Hippocratic model of the aphoristic collection. Such collections, our sources claim, were regarded as suitable for dealing with subjects to which no scientific or methodical treatment had been as yet successfully applied, such as, in particular, medicine. I want to claim that the *Genealogy* is in this respect a medical book: etiological, diagnostic, therapeutic, prognostic. I want to underscore *therapeutic* here, for the book is not for other practitioners of the caring art so much as it is for those who suffer from the diseases it addresses. So the assumption must be that the intended reader is sick, if typically in ways unrecognized by him: one learns the nature of one's illness as one reads the book. And part of the reason the aphorism is so suitable a form is that the language has to get past the defenses we bring to the book, since the defenses are in a way part of the disease, as in neurosis according to the classic analysis, where the repression of the pathogen is part of the pathogen. As in analysis, a task of the therapist is to bring to consciousness the mechanisms of disassociation and, if there is such a word, of disconsciation. So the reader is, as it were, being treated as he reads, and a condition of therapeutic success is that he be kept continuously conscious of the disorder the book means to drive out: as Hippocrates says, the practitioner is to be "seconded by the patient." And in a way the patient, or reader here, must be helped by the practitioner to cure himself. In a way, I suppose, there is an analogy to Socratic maieutics, here the point being that only the sufferer can solve the problem of his suffering, the doctor's role consisting in showing him that he is sick. So the book has to be painful. And arguably the cure is more painful than the disease, with which, after all, we have grown comfortable.

It scarcely can pass notice how frequently and characteristically Nietzsche here employs the vocabularies of pathology (it would be an interesting scholarly enterprise to see the degree to which the same vocabularies occur in all the main books in this way, or whether each book has its paradigm lexicon, from which the mode of literary address can then be inferred). The period of Nietzsche's great productivity was the great age of German physiology. Johannes Müller, Justus von Liebig, and Karl Ludwig had made Germany the center for physiological investigation in the form it has had ever since, and though in no sense myself a historian of medicine, I am certain that a suitable scholarship would discover among their procedures certain ones that Nietzsche adapted, transforming them of course through his own special genius. It is still difficult, and it must in Nietzsche's time have been all but impossible, to draw a careful distinction between physiological and physiognomic differences and to suppose that a certain blue-eyed blondness might not connote a physiological distinctiveness of some importance: or that shortness of stature might not be a physiological defect.

The physiologization of moral concepts, the proposal that in the end moral differences must be physiological differences or that a certain physiognomical paradigm must be a paradigm of health, all other variants being sick, are among Nietzsche's most reckless and dangerous conjectures. But the shock of Darwinism was still being felt, and he was not immune to the moralization of natural selection that almost defines nineteenth-century thought, which can lead to the view, as we know, that those with different moral beliefs may be contagious, ought to be segregated at least, and at worst may have to be eliminated in the interests of moral sepsis. And these ideas can lead, in the other direction, to the view that those who are physiologically distinctive, and for that matter different, must fall under a different moral order and need not be treated in the way we treat one another. I imagine that the great movements toward equal rights, equal no matter what one's age, sex, color, competence, or creed, constitute an effort to make physiological differences irrelevant to moral considerations. And while we must not be dismissive since, as Hippocrates says, "art is long, life is short," and there will always be more to find out than we can possibly hope, and no one knows whether criminality is chromosomal—or for the matter generosity genetic—it remains unclear how such discoveries should be responded to morally. It is also doubtful that reading a book of *this* sort could be regarded a significant intervention if it turned out that a certain moral difference *were* a physiological one in that way. But neither would Nietzsche have supposed it *were*—so the question is for what sort of disease could it have been that he might have thought the book *was* significantly interventive? And here I can say perhaps most of what I have to say about this work.

I think the answer must lie in a distinction between what I shall term extensional suffering and intensional suffering, where the latter consists in an interpretation of the former. As I see Nietzsche's thesis, it is this: the main sufferings human beings have been subject to throughout history are due to certain interpretative responses to the fact of extensional suffering. It is not clear that Nietzsche believes he can deal with extensional suffering. But

259

he can deal with intensional suffering, thus helping reduce, often by a significant factor, the total suffering in the world. For while extensional suffering is bad enough, often it is many times compounded by our interpretations of it, themselves often far worse than the disorder itself.

Consider the example of impotence in the human male, in certain cases genuinely a physiological symptom of an underlying sickness with no clinical identity of its own, due, say, to diabetes, prostate disorder, and the like. For most men, and doubtless for most women sexually involved with men, it is a pretty appalling symptom. But to explain why it is refers us to the complex of ideas connected with the male self-image of adequacy and power and the extreme vulnerability in the male ego that sexual incapacity opens up. It can lead, it has led, to suicide, depression, despair, divorce. So if we subtracted all this suffering from the sum total of suffering, the actual symptom might not amount to very much in the scale of human agony. Compare it to the other symptoms of diabetes: polyuria, polydipsia, retinopathy, renal malfunction, circulatory problems, propensity to gangrene, susceptibility to fungus, to heart disease, acidosis, coma—and a merely flaccid penis seems pretty minor. But knowing the male temperament I am certain that this morally overcharged symptom would be singled out as the most intolerable effect of this disorder. Very few, I think, attach much significance to the mere fact of hyperglycemia or would commit suicide over that or regard themselves as flawed—or sick. It is a good example of moralized physiology, but in any case the disorders addressed by Nietzsche in this book, and that it is his enterprise to help us cure ourselves of, are interpretations of suffering that themselves generate suffering.

They are due, one and all, to bad philosophy, bad psychology, to religion—which in Nietzsche's scheme does not have a *good* form so as to make "bad religion" nonredundant—and of course bad moral systems, such as the one that takes as its primary value opposition the distinction between good and evil. All of these are in a way modalities of *schlechtes Gewissen*, which I shall persist in translating as "bad consciousness." Bad *conscience*—in English usage at least—is more or less the same as guilty conscience, but guilt is only one of the modalities of badness. Bad consciousness is consciousness of badness, which of course may be illusory, as when someone good falsely seems bad to himself. Any suffering due to

260

false moral beliefs about ourselves is due to bad consciousness, when there is nothing bad about us *except* our consciousness of being bad. And the book might then in part be addressed specifically to the cure of this sort of suffering.

Though at times Nietzsche speaks as though only the extensionally strong and healthy are subject to bad consciousness, in truth it is difficult to see how anyone in our civilization can have altogether escaped it; even those who in his view really do suffer, really are in his sense "bad"—that is, bad specimens of the species *human*—typically also suffer from misinterpretations of this disorder and no less than the good may be for this reason subject to bad consciousness. It is possible, of course, that Nietzsche's psychohistorical account is correct and the particular form bad consciousness takes may be traced back to the pathogens of what he terms *ressentiment*, to which the extensionally bad are subject; even so they themselves suffer from the epidemics of bad consciousness that define the subsequent history of our civilization, that is, not to be coy about it, from Christianity, if he is right. So even the bad might profit from dissipation of this sort of intensional suffering, leaving extensional suffering to be treated by those whose specialty it is. After all, identification of the real disease is the first step in medicine.

Let us attend, for a moment, to the concept of *ressentiment*. Nietzsche more or less assumed that anyone in a state of *ressentiment* must also be in some state or other, in his scheme, of actual physiological suffering, for what *ressentiment*—which is only distantly connected to the English word *resentment*—amounts to is a certain sort of interpretive explanation of suffering in the mind of the sufferer. In actual fact it would not matter if the suffering in question were real, that is, physiological, or only believed to be real, as in cases of what used to be called hysteria. Nietzsche's point is put into what one might term an a priori of suffering:

> Every sufferer instinctively seeks a cause for his suffering; more exactly an agent . . . some living thing upon which he can, on some pretext or other, vent his affects, actually or in effigy: for the venting of his affects represents the greatest attempt on the part of the sufferer to win relief, *anaesthesia*—the narcotic he cannot help desiring to deaden pain of every kind.

This, which Nietzsche glosses as "the actual physiological cause of *ressentiment*, vengefulness, and the like," could easily have formed a section in the Hippocratic collection. And the implication is clear: sufferers tend to *moralize* suffering by holding someone or something responsible for it: as though mere suffering, undeserved only in the sense that it makes no sense to speak of it as deserved, is simply unintelligible. "Why me, Lord?" is the spontaneous response to sickness; "What did I do to deserve this?"—as though there were no unearned suffering, as though suffering were in every instance a *sentence* of some sort. "Someone or other must be to blame for my feeling ill," Nietzsche puts in the mind of the sufferer—a kind of reasoning "held the more firmly the more the real cause of their feeling ill, the physiological cause, remains hidden." And Nietzsche adds at this point a parade of medical opinion that reflects the state of knowledge of the time, or his state of knowledge, as well as the intention of the text:

262

> It may perhaps lie in some disease of the nervus sympathicus, or in an excessive secretion of bile, or in a deficiency of potassium sulfate and phosphate in the blood, or in an obstruction in the abdomen which impedes blood circulation, or in degeneration of the ovaries, and the like.

Readers of Nietzsche's letters appreciate the degree to which he was a dietary crank, but in any case, amateur diagnostics notwithstanding, it is perfectly plain that the disease he was addressing was not of the sort itemized here but a metadisease that requires of the sufferer that his illness, as Susan Sontag has phrased it, be metaphorical. In any case *ressentiment* consists in re-feeling suffering as the *effect* of a *moral* cause one may also *resent* if one feels it is undeserved. As in the case of Job, whose classic posture is exactly that of resentment in this form, since he can see no *reason* why God should be causing him to suffer. But even if he did feel he deserved the boils and losses, this would still be a case of *ressentiment* because he moralized his suffering.

Religion, save the rather rare case of Job, abolishes all possibility of resentment, but it scarcely abolishes all possibility of *ressentiment*, since in fact it depends upon it for existence: for what does religion do except to teach us that the suffering we endure we also deserve. Religion redirects *ressentiment*, as Nietzsche puts it, by making the patient the very agent he seeks, informing us that we have brought it on ourselves. Consider the Black Death, which swept Florence and Siena in the fourteenth century. Of course it was physiological, but men alive at that time had no way of knowing how: *b. plagus* was not an available concept. But they immediately assumed they were at fault (as they doubtless were in matters of elementary hygiene), chiefly through their arrogance vis-à-vis God, as shown in their treatment of human subjects in painting after Giotto! So the most rational thing, under prevailing theory, was to change the styles of representation, which have been traced for us by Millard Miess. I don't say this was wholly silly, and the consequences could be benign, as when an outbreak of some epidemic in Venice moved the governing body to commission a church from Palladio. True, this did not help any sufferers, but nothing they knew how to do would have done that anyway, and *Il Redentore* still stands. Religion, then, makes suffering intelligible—but only in the framework of a scheme that makes search after its true causes unintelligible. And this is true even in those cases where we ourselves *have* brought on our own suffering, as in the case of gout or obesity or venereal disease or cirrhosis of the liver or chronic drug addiction: these disorders are the consequences of, not *punishments* for, the excesses that led to them.

Interestingly, Nietzsche observes that "this plant blooms best today among the anarchists and the Anti-Semites." That is, blaming the Jews, or blaming the bourgeoisie, for all social ills, rather than looking more deeply into the social structure for proper etiology, parallels the classic forms of the a priori of affect. Admittedly, we may know about as much regarding what affects society as Florentines knew in the Cinquecento of what affects the human body, and often in our ignorance we attack as cause what may only be another effect. I tend to think that certain accounts by feminists, in which men as men are blamed for the suffering of women as women, must ultimately yield to a finer analysis in which what coarsely is considered a cause of feminine agony is itself a symptom of the same sickness from which they doubtless suffer. I have often thought no better specimen of *schlechtes Gewissen* can be found than the sort of self-castigation shown by men, say in the weekly column "For Men" in *The New York Times* magazine section, where men boast of their degree of feminization. I have no criticism of this, and nothing but criticism of its opposite, where men vaunt the paraphernalia of machismo: but it is a good

SOME REMARKS ON *THE GENEALOGY OF MORALS*

case of self-despising to illustrate that term in Nietzsche's moral psychology. Nietzsche condenses his general insight in one of his profoundest aphorisms: "What really arouses indignation against suffering is not suffering as such but the senselessness of suffering." And if there is any single moral/metaphysical teaching I would ascribe to him, it would be this: suffering really is meaningless, there is no point to it, and the amount of suffering caused by *giving* it a meaning chills the blood to contemplate.

I of course am not talking about suffering we cause under the name of punishment, where some complex balance must be struck between the suffering caused by the culprit and the suffering the culprit must undergo in order to restore equilibrium. That is a model of justice that must be debated on grounds other than any I want to advance here. What Nietzsche objects to is not so much this model but its total generalization, making *every* suffering a punition and the entire *world* a court of justice with a penitentiary annex. If I am right that this is his view, the final aphorism of the *Genealogy*, "man would rather will the *nothing* than *not* will," does not so much heroize mankind, after all. What it does is restate the instinct of *ressentiment*: man would rather his suffering be meaningful, hence would rather will meaning onto it, than acquiesce in the meaninglessness of it. It goes against this instinct to believe what is essentially the most liberating thought imaginable, that life is without meaning. In a way, the deep affliction from which he seeks to relieve us is what today we think of as hermeneutics: the method of interpretation primarily of suffering. And when he says, in so many places and in so many ways, "there are no facts, only interpretation," he is, I believe, finally addressing the deep, perhaps ineradicable propensities of *ressentiment*. Meaning, *si je peux aphoriser moi-même*, is demeaning.

There is an obverse, which is that in order to accept the consolations of religion, the dubious gift of meaning, as it were, one must accept the anthropology that alone makes religion applicable in the first place, namely, that we are weak, defective, and almost defined through our propensity to suffer. The limits of man are emphasized such that we are unable to release ourselves save through the mediation of a being whose power is adequate to the salvation. Of course, with religions in general, the salvation is often from suffering we would not know we had were it not revealed, to a state abstractly defined through the absence of revealed suffering, by means we again would not understand but for revelation. Who would know we were contaminated by Original Sin, for instance, that we need to be saved from it, and that the means whereby this might be achieved is for God to take on a form whereby he might purge our suffering through his? Which leaves everything as it was so far as life itself is concerned, since the suffering we were told was ours was not felt and the redemption we have been given does not connect with release from any felt suffering. And the limits are finally limits only relative to the scheme of suffering and relief erected alongside the actual schedule of human agonies and joys that the scheme itself does not penetrate. Whatever the case, the picture of man as limited and weak, if believed, goes hand in hand exactly with *schlechtem Gewissen*. And to release us from that is to release us from the picture: and that is the therapeutic task of the *Genealogy* and of Nietzsche's philosophical work as such.

Let me return to hermeneutics. I would concede to the continental theorists that it is the fundamental fact of human being and hence must be the final datum for the human sciences, that men cannot experience without interpreting and that we live in a world of intersignification. I am far from certain that the human sciences must themselves reflect the structure of their subject, that science itself is only a form of interpretation of a piece with the interpretations it is supposed to study: hence I am far from certain that there is a hermeneutical circle that somehow invalidates such a science: for there may be ways of representing interpretations that are not at all of a piece with the interpretations represented. Even so, we may accept the hermeneutical picture that our *esse est interpretari*. But then the contrast must be perfect between ourselves and the *Bestie*, and it is less their cheerful innocent savagery that Nietzsche applauds in the blond beasts than their absolute freedom from meaning. They live, as he says in his early book on history, as beasts do, "in a happy blindness between the walls of the past and the future." Human existence, by deep contrast, is "an imperfect tense that never becomes a present." It is not so much history as the philosophy of history that robs life of happiness, since the latter seeks perennially the significance of events it would be happiness instead merely to forget or, next best, to take as they came, at a kind of absolute magnitude, without forming a kind of text. Nietzsche's doctrine of Eternal Recurrence, itself the topic of so much speculation and scholarship, must be perceived by everyone, however otherwise divided on its cognitive status, as deeply contrary to any philosophy of history: iteration dissolves meaning, and infinite iteration erases it totally. It is a rock against which history as significance must shatter, and in particular religious history, the history of Fall, Covenant, Sin, Redemption, Trial, Judgment, and Hell, where it is an unrelieved anxiety as to where we stand and what we can hope for.

When Zarathustra announces the death of God, he goes on to say he died of pity. The implication is that what he pitied us for was him: pitied us for the hopeless disproportion between a being of infinite value and his creatures who must in relationship to him be incalculably worthless. By his disappearing, the ratio is broken and the disvalue that depended upon the disproportion itself vanishes. It is a beautiful gift, that of disappearance: Which of the parents among us is capable of it? By comparison, sacrificing even only begotten sons is easy: our world is full of gold-star mothers and fathers, proud of their distinction. With the death of God we are returned to what Kundera speaks of, alas as unbearable: a certain lightness of being. It is plain that God did not die in order that something else should take his place: rather, he meant for the place to die with the occupant. The genius of the third essay of the *Genealogy* lies in its inventory of disguises the ascetic ideal takes, so that often positions that define themselves as contrary to asceticism only exemplify it. As a class, these occupants of the position vacated by God impose on their subscribers a network of interpretation of suffering and project a kind of Utopian redemption: science, politics, art, and certainly much that passes for psychological therapy only change the name of the game. There are even ways of understanding the notorious concept of the Superman that vest themselves in the same demeaning armature that Christianity did, another disguise of asceticism. But this could not be Nietzsche's Superman if he has the least consistency. The Superman does not reside in a kind of *beyond* since it is precisely that kind of beyond that Nietzsche is bent on stultifying. The man of the future, he writes at the end of the second essay, is "this bell-stroke of man and the great decision that liberates the will again and restores its goal to earth and his hope to man."

I return to the aphorism I began by interpreting. The *unconcern* that wisdom is supposed to love clearly connects with the will. It is an unconcern with goals that imposes a program of choices on life, where these depend on schemes of meaning that it is the goal of Nietzsche's philosophy to demolish. It is not so much the extirpation of the will as its reeducation and redirection: its return to the goals of simply normal life. Nietzsche's philo-

266

sophical mood is one of lightness, cheer, sunniness, which was also his personal mood, heroic in view of his familiar sufferings. He complains of terrible headaches, nausea, stomachache: he was afflicted by the cold, the damp, bad food, and of course a sense of isolation and unrecognition. He sought like a cat for a comfortable corner of Europe, and the preposterous exultation of his discovery of the alleged salubrities of Turin are an index to his discomforts. He did not suffer, however, in the way in which, on his view, the bulk of mankind suffers: from meanings that truncate the lives they are supposed to redeem. When we contemplate the sufferings human beings have endured in the century since God made the supreme sacrifice, we wonder at the wisdom of that evacuation. If we were to subtract all the intensional suffering from the history of our century, we would subtract the history of the century.

But that is what Nietzsche would like to have achieved: to subtract all those schemes of disvaluation of the present by reference to an inflated valuation of a future; to make the world the place we live rather than pass through to some higher state; to restore the present to the present; to replace a morality of means with a morality of principle; to act in such a way as to be consistent with acting that way eternally; to stultify the instinct for significance. This is the posture of unconcern, and while it is unclear that it would make us altogether happy, it is perfectly plain that it erases most of what has made for human unhappiness through history: the martyrdoms, the crucifixions, the eggs cracked in the name of political omelettes, man as a means. Not surprisingly it is the only view consistent with human dignity, the only view of man as an end.

Notes

Listed below, in roughly chronological order, are the writings of Nietzsche to which I refer. This of course is not a complete list of his writings. I have made very little use of *Thoughts Out of Season* [*Unzeitgemässe Betractungen*] except for the essay on Wagner.

The letter or letters following the German and English titles indicate the abbreviation employed in the note section.

Zur Genealogie der Moral (1887)	The Genealogy of Morals	GM
Der Antichrist (1888)	The Antichrist	AC
Götzendämmerung (1889)	Twilight of the Idols	GD
Nietzsche Contra Wagner (1889)	Nietzsche Contra Wagner	NCW
Ecce Homo (1889)	Ecce Homo	EH
Nachlass	Unpublished Notes	NL

Much of the unpublished material was arranged and published posthumously under the title *Der Wille zur Macht* (*The Will-to-Power*). Professor Karl Schlechta, in his superb edition of Nietzsche's writings, *Nietzsches Werke in Drei Bände* (Munich: Carl Hanser Verlag, 1958), has used instead the noncommittal title "*Aus dem Nachlass der Achtzigerjahre*" ("From the Unpublished Work of the 1880's"). He has done so because of the notorious editorial liberties taken with Nietzsche's literary estate by his sister and those directly responsible to her in the Nietzsche Archives. These writings are difficult to date: they have no special order in the manuscript notebooks, and, pending some exacting philological reconstruction, they must be taken more or less as Professor Schlechta has given them to us. Certainly there was no book *as such* called *Der Wille zur Macht* which Nietzsche had in manuscript. It is far from clear how he would have arranged the vast number of unpublished opuscula.

In the notes all references to the *Nachlass* as published by Schlechta, are followed by the page number. Unfortunately, the reader who cannot follow the German will be unable to verify these translations or, more important, determine the context of the passages I cite. Certain statements about the doctrine of Eternal Recurrence have been taken from the Leipzig edition (1901) of Nietzsche's works because I could not locate them in Schlechta—the promised index to his edition has not appeared as yet. Except for the Nachlass, there are fair to excellent English translations of the remaining works. I have cited the references so that readers can locate the passages in any edition, in any language. In each citation the number reference will not be to a page but to an aphorism. Roman numerals refer to chapters where this information is relevant; for example, where Nietzsche starts renumbering his aphorisms at the beginning of a new chapter. Thus GM, II, 20 refers to *The Genealogy of Morals*, Chapter Two, aphorism 20. Nietzsche does not always give numbers to the separate parts, but he periodically begins to renumber the aphorisms. In such cases the Roman numeral indicates the part, the Arabic number is the aphorism. In *Thus Spake Zarathustra*, Nietzsche numbered the chapters, or parts, but he gave titles to the aphorisms. Aphorisms sometimes are a few pages long, so the reader may have to search a bit before finding the lines to which I refer. But a more precise citation would limit the flexibility which the numerous editions and translations demand. Finally, although Schlechta's third volume furnishes an ample selection from the correspondence, I have indicated Nietzsche's relevant letters by the name of the recipient and the date of the letter. Again, the passage can be sought out in the numerous places where his correspondence is to be found.

ONE. PHILOSOPHICAL NIHILISM

1. JGB, 296.
2. Letter to G. Brandes, May 4, 1888.
3. JGB, 56.
4. *Ibid.*
5. NL, p. 834.
6. FW, 347.
7. NL, p. 554.
8. *Ibid.*
9. *Ibid.*
10. NL, p. 677.
11. NL, p. 678. Suspended dots in text.
12. NL, p. 555.
13. NL, p. 834.
14. NL, p. 684.
15. NL, p. 853.
16. NL, p. 677.
17. NL, p. 727.

TWO. ART AND IRRATIONALITY

1. WL, I.
2. *Ibid.*
3. *Ibid.*
4. *Ibid.*
5. *Ibid.*
6. *Ibid.*
7. Nietzsche to Peter Gast, December 9, 1888.
8. NL, p. 421.
9. JGB, 296.
10. WL, II.
11. GT, Toward a Self-Critique [*Versuch einer Selbstkritik*], v.
12. GT, viii.
13. PTG, 7.
14. WL, I.
15. GT, 1.
16. *Ibid.*
17. NL, p. 788.
18. *Ibid.*
19. GT, 1.
20. *Ibid.*
21. GT, 2.
22. GT, 8.
23. GT, 2.
24. H.
25. *Ibid.*
26. *Ibid.*
27. *Ibid.*

28. GT, 2.
29. GT, 3.
30. Ibid.
31. GT, 25.
32. GT, 4.
33. Ibid.
34. Ibid.
35. Ibid. Cf. WL, II.
36. GT, 4.
37. GT, 17.
38. GT, 24.
39. GT, 7.
40. GT, 8.
41. Ibid.
42. GT, 7.
43. Ibid.
44. GT, 10.
45. GT, 12.
46. Ibid.
47. Ibid.
48. Ibid.
49. GT, 13.
50. Ibid.
51. GT, 14.
52. Ibid.
53. GT, 15.
54. Ibid.
55. Ibid.
56. GT, 18.

57. GT, 15.
58. GT, 14.
59. GT, 15.
60. WB, 4.
61. Ibid.
62. Ibid.
63. Ibid.
64. EH, III, iii, 5.
65. Nietzsche to Ritschl, January 30, 1872.
66. GT, Toward a Self-Critique, 3.
67. NCW, "We Antipodes."
68. MR, 50.
69. MAM, 146.
70. MAM, 147.
71. MAM, 148.
72. MAM, 151.
73. MAM, 154.
74. MAM, 159.
75. MAM, 160.
76. MAM, 162.
77. MAM, 166.
78. MAM, 220.
79. MAM, 222.
80. MAM, 223.
81. GT, Toward a Self-Critique, 2.
82. Ibid., 5.

THREE. PERSPECTIVISM

1. MAM, 109.
2. Ibid.
3. MAM, 153.
4. MAM, 29.
5. MAM, 24.
6. MAM, 16.
7. MAM, 10.
8. FW, 293.

9. MAM, 3.
10. JGB, 204.
11. NL, p. 692.
12. MAM, 16.
13. Ibid.
14. NL, p. 814.
15. NL, p. 915.
16. NL, p. 903.

17. NL, p. 705.
18. NL, p. 729.
19. NL, p. 903.
20. NL, p. 769.
21. *Ibid.*
22. MAM, 9.
23. MAM, 16.
24. MAM, 33.
25. MAM, 34.
26. MAM, 517.
27. MAM. The title of one of the *Unzeitgemässe Betrachtungen* was *Vom Nutzen und Nachteil der Historie,* "On the Use and Abuse of History."
28. GD, III, 3.
29. EH, "Human, All-too-Human."
30. MAM, 20.
31. WS, 55.
32. WS, 11.
33. MAM, 11.
34. MR, 47.
35. MAM, 11.
36. *Ibid.*
37. MAM, 519.
38. JGB, 20.
39. GD, III, 5.
40. GD, III.
41. *Ibid.*
42. NL, p. 776.

43. FW, 112.
44. JGB, 14.
45. NL, p. 896.
46. FW, 121.
47. FW, 110.
48. JGB, 20.
49. JGB, 11.
50. FW, 111.
51. *Ibid.*
52. NL, p. 727.
53. MR, 117.
54. FW, 265.
55. FW, 110.
56. WS, 2.
57. NL, p. 526.
58. MAM, 11.
59. NL, p. 726.
60. GD, "How the 'Real World' Finally Became a Fable."
61. *Ibid.*
62. NL, p. 704.
63. JGB, 12.
64. NL, p. 705.
65. JGB, 12.
66. MR, 121.
67. NL, p. 876.
68. NL, p. 501.
69. FW, 112.
70. JGB, 21.
71. FW, 109.
72. FW, 110.

FOUR. PHILOSOPHICAL PSYCHOLOGY

1. NL, p. 442.
2. JGB, 24.
3. MR, 117.
4. FW, 347.
5. JGB, 45.

6. NCW, "The Psychologist Speaks Up."
7. JGB, 23.
8. JGB, 12.
9. FW, 109.

10. NL, p. 537.
11. JGB, 23.
12. JGB, 54.
13. NL, p. 487.
14. NL, pp. 487–488.
15. JGB, 54.
16. JGB, 20.
17. GD, III, 5.
18. NL, p. 540.
19. NL, pp. 540–541.
20. NL, p. 540.
21. GD, III, 5.
22. Ibid.
23. JGB, 16.
24. Ibid.
25. NL, p. 577.
26. Ibid.
27. JGB, 17.
28. JGB, 16.
29. JGB, 19.
30. NL, p. 914.
31. JGB, 19.
32. Ibid.
33. Ibid.
34. GD, III, 5.
35. NL, p. 914.
36. JGB, 21.
37. NL, p. 776.
38. JGB, 21.
39. Ibid.
40. FW, 354.
41. Ibid.
42. NL, p. 666.
43. FW, 11.

44. NL, p. 499.
45. FW, 354.
46. NL, p. 587.
47. NL, p. 667.
48. FW, 354.
49. Ibid.
50. Ibid.
51. Ibid.
52. Ibid.
53. Ibid.
54. Ibid.
55. Ibid.
56. Ibid.
57. JGB, 268.
58. Ibid.
59. NL, p. 610.
60. Z, II, "The Child with the Mirror."
61. FW, 355.
62. Ibid.
63. NL, p. 732.
64. MAM, 13.
65. MR, 119.
66. MAM, 13.
67. Ibid.
68. Ibid.
69. MR, 119.
70. GD, Foreword.
71. GD, V, 4.
72. NL, p. 442.
73. NL, p. 673.
74. NL, p. 667.
75. MR, 48.
76. FW, 332.

FIVE. MORALITIES

1. JGB, 4.
2. Ibid.
3. Ibid.

4. JGB, 3.
5. Ibid.
6. JGB, 5.

7. JGB, 6.
8. NL, p. 499.
9. NL, pp. 517–518.
10. JGB, 9.
11. *Ibid.*
12. *Ibid.*
13. NL, p. 556.
14. JGB, 108.
15. GD, VI, 1.
16. *Ibid.*
17. WS, 19.
18. NL, p. 485.
19. NL, p. 480.
20. JGB, 4.
21. MR, 9.
22. MR, 16.
23. MR, 10.
24. MAM, 96.
25. MR, 19.
26. GD, VI, 1.
27. FW, 116.
28. *Ibid.*
29. GD, V, 6.
30. NL, p. 485.
31. GD, VI, 1.
32. Z, I, "Of the Thousand-and-one Goals."
33. *Ibid.*
34. JGB, 268.

35. JGB, 23.
36. GD, III, 1.
37. *Ibid.*
38. JGB, 188.
39. *Ibid.*
40. *Ibid.*
41. WS, 53.
42. JGB, 188.
43. WS, 37.
44. WS, 65.
45. GD, III, 1.
46. *Ibid.*
47. *Ibid.*
48. JGB, 36.
49. JGB, 188.
50. JGB, 201.
51. *Ibid.*
52. *Ibid.*
53. JGB, 260.
54. MAM, 75.
55. JGB, 260.
56. JGB, 258.
57. JGB, 260.
58. JGB, 293.
59. MAM, 81.
60. *Ibid.*
61. JGB, 260.
62. MAM, 40.
63. JGB, 259.

SIX. RELIGIOUS PSYCHOLOGY

1. Z, I, "Of the Thousand-and-one Goals."
2. *Ibid.*
3. GM, I, note.
4. NL, p. 710.
5. GM, I, 7.
6. *Ibid.*
7. JGB, 195.

8. GM, I, 10.
9. *Ibid.*
10. *Ibid.*
11. *Ibid.*
12. GM, I, 13.
13. *Ibid.*
14. GM, II, 1.
15. GM, II, 2.

16. GM, II, 3.
17. GM, II, 7.
18. MAM, 103.
19. GM, II, 6.
20. MR, 30.
21. *Ibid.* The examples are Nietzsche's.
22. *Ibid.*
23. MR, 112.
24. GM, II, 16.
25. *Ibid.*
26. *Ibid.*
27. *Ibid.*
28. *Ibid.*
29. MR, 113.
30. GM, II, 22.
31. *Ibid.*
32. GM, II, 23.
33. AC, 5–6.
34. EH, "Why I Am a Destiny," 8–9.
35. JGB, 293.
36. *Ibid.*
37. MR, 133.
38. *Ibid.*
39. JGB, 259.
40. JGB, 60.
41. *Ibid.*
42. GD, IX, 14.
43. *Ibid.*
44. GM, II, 16.
45. GM, I, 5.
46. GM, III, 28.
47. GM, III, 13.
48. GM, III, 28.
49. *Ibid.*
50. GM, III, 24.
51. FW, 344.
52. *Ibid.*
53. *Ibid.*
54. *Ibid.*
55. GM, III, 24.
56. GM, III, 25.
57. *Ibid.*
58. *Ibid.*
59. *Ibid.*
60. FW, 343.

SEVEN. ÜBERMENSCH AND ETERNAL RECURRENCE

1. NL, p. 826.
2. EH, "Why I Am a Destiny," 3.
3. Z, I, "Of the Thousand-and-one Goals."
4. Z, Prologue, 3.
5. Z, Prologue, 5.
6. Z, Prologue, 3–4.
7. Z, I, "The Priests."
8. EH, "Why I Write Such Good Books," 1.
9. Nietzsche to Burkhardt, August, 1882.
10. Z, Prologue, 5.
11. NL, p. 458.
12. Z, III, "The Vision and the Riddle."
13. Z, III, "The Convalescent."
14. EH, "Thus Spake Zarathustra," 1.
15. NL, p. 856.
16. NL, p. 873.

17. NL, p. 704.
18. *Werke*, Vol. XII, p. 51.
19. NL, p. 446.
20. NL, p. 704.
21. FW, 341.
22. NL, p. 459.
23. Z, III, "The Convalescent."
24. NL, p. 704.
25. NL, p. 856.

26. NL, p. 703.
27. NL, p. 680.
28. Z, III, "The Convalescent."
29. EH, "Why I Am So Clever," 10.
30. *Werke*, Vol. XII, p. 116.
31. *Werke*, Vol. XII, p. 124.
32. *Werke*, Vol. XII, p. 126.

EIGHT. THE WILL-TO-POWER

1. JGB, 13.
2. JGB, 36.
3. *Ibid.*
4. *Ibid.*
5. *Ibid.*
6. NL, p. 778.
7. NL, p. 502.
8. NL, p. 705.
9. NL, p. 685.
10. NL, p. 777.
11. NL, p. 776.
12. *Ibid.*
13. NL, p. 684.
14. NL, p. 480.
15. JGB, 13.

16. GD, IX, 14.
17. NL, p. 750.
18. NL, p. 712.
19. *Ibid.*
20. NL, p. 713.
21. NL, p. 714.
22. JGB, 259.
23. NL, p. 487.
24. NL, p. 489.
25. *Ibid.*
26. NL, p. 524.
27. JGB, 51.
28. NL, p. 549.
29. JGB, 211.

Nachwort

1. JGB, 22.
2. JGB, 289.

3. JGB, 36.

Index

belief, 15, 83, 112, 173; in moralities, 115–16; Nihilism and, 11–12
Berkeley, George, 213–14
Bernard of Clairvaux, 222
Bhagavad Gita, 251–52
Birth of Tragedy out of the Spirit of Music, The (Nietzsche), 1, 17–18, 24, 30, 35, 53, 62, 170; art in, 39, 42–43, 122, 233–34; failures of, 43–44; as late-romantic visionary social philosophy, 233–34; Nietzsche's stance toward, 46, 49
blond beast, 151–52, 155, 160, 162–63, 180, 196, 265
body, 63, 95–97
Borges, Jorge Luis, 227
Borgia, Cesare, 180, 182
Brandes, Georg, 5
Burkhardt, Jacob, 246

canonical discourse, 219–20
Cartesianism, 35, 203, 249. *See also* anti-Cartesianism; Descartes, René
causality, 90, 248; acts of will and, 91–92; consciousness and, 109–10; Perspectivism and, 62, 75–78; will and, 96, 199–200; will-to-power and, 204. *See also* imaginary causes
certainty, quest for, 83–84, 92–93
change, 187–91
chaos, 54, 78, 80, 106, 111
Chomsky, Noam, 240
chorus, 37–39, 124, 233–34
Christianity, 46, 87, 88, 117, 130–31, 164–65, 182. *See also* death of God; religion
cogito, 92–94
common sense, 58; language and, 65–66, 68; metaphysics and, 56–57; as perspective, 59–60; as perspective of herd, 60–61; scientific repudiation of, 73–74. *See also* Perspectivism

common-sense world, 55–57, 72–73
communication, 101–4, 123. *See also* language
communitarian existence, 233–34
compassion, 166–67
concepts, 21–23, 40, 49, 72
conditions of existence, 59–60, 69–70, 131, 145
consciousness, 231, 254; bad, 162–64, 172, 260–61; causality and, 109–10; drives and, 161; evolution of, 99–100, 123, 171; herd and, 126–27; individual, 125; psychological view, 98–104; self-consciousness, 98–99. *See also* thought
consolation, 235
Correspondence Theory of Truth, 15, 54–55, 57, 62, 80–81, 112, 174n, 225
creativity, 27–28, 210
cruelty, 33, 140–41, 159–60
culture, 66–67, 234
custom, 118–22, 126, 145

Darwin, Charles, 169–70n, 206
Darwinism, 205–6, 259
Daybreak (*Morgenröthe*) (Nietzsche), 47, 110, 245–50; self-sublimation of morality in, 248–49; spiritual well-being in, 249–50; structure of, 246–47
death of God, 173, 175–76; as due to pity, 167, 217–18, 266. *See also* God
deconstruction, 222–23
deep forgetfulness, 255
Derrida, Jacques, 222–23
Descartes, René, 30–31, 35, 64, 86, 238–39, 240–41; doubt, view of, 84–85, 92–93. *See also* anti-Cartesianism; Cartesianism
descriptive metaphysics, 104
determinism, 97, 144
deviant experiences, 21–23
diable et le bon Dieu, Le (Sartre), 221–22

German physiology, 258–59
God, 144, 227; as lie, 173–74; as perfect being, 241; suffering and, 159, 163–64. *See also* death of God
goodness, 124–25, 145; as negative, 149–50
grammar, 66, 78; motive for revision, 226–27; revision of, 218–19, 223. *See also* language
Greeks, 31–35, 41, 50, 164, 232
Greek tragedy, 37–39, 124, 233–34

happiness, 206–7
hatred, slave morality and, 149–50
herd, 59, 103, 105, 135; consciousness and, 126–27; individuals and, 124–26; Last Man, 179, 183; master and slave morality, 137–41; moralities and, 119, 120–21; perspective of, 60–61; spirit and, 169–70n
hero, 180, 234; art and, 40–41; outlaw, 134–35, 136; of tragedy, 38–39; warriors, 134–36, 251–52
Hippocrates, 255, 257, 259
Hitler, Adolf, 180
Hobbes, Thomas, 123, 149
Homer, 33
honor, 134–36, 156
Human, All Too Human (Nietzsche), 45, 48, 233–43; aphorisms in, 236–37, 239–40; development of Nietzsche's philosophy in, 237–38; as diatribe, 235–36; distinction between Will and Idea, 233, 234; historical context, 233, 242–43; prefaces, 238–40; Wagner in, 234, 235
human types, 137–38, 145–46
Hume, David, 75–76, 91–92, 117–18

idealism, 78, 214
ideas, 21, 123, 230, 233, 234, 241
idols, 108–9n., 220, 223

Iliad (Homer), 33
illusions, 35–36, 57; art and, 20, 34–35; truth as, 20–21
imaginary causes, 108–9, 119–21, 144. *See also* causality
imaging, 30
imperfection, 240–41, 242
incompetence, 240
individuals, 125; exceptional, 103, 105, 119, 125–26, 135–36, 167–68; society and, 122–26
individuation, 36–37, 98
instincts. *See* drives
instrumentalism, 81, 84, 223–24, 227–28
internalization, 161
interpretations, 56, 58, 88, 115, 118, 209; deep, 248; dreams as, 107–9; of suffering, 262–64. *See also* perspectivism
intoxication, 29–31, 46–47
intuition, 22–23, 24
Intuitive Man, 24, 232

Jews, 148–49, 168n, 263
judgment, 117–18
justice, 264

Kafka, Franz, 255
Kant, Immanuel, 22, 43, 70, 77–78, 203, 252
Kaufmann, Walter, 108n, 169n, 173–74n, 220, 256
knowledge, 43, 82; as false, 81–83, 106; of self, 98, 107, 109–11

language, 229; common sense and, 65–66, 68; conceptual schemes and, 22–23; culture and, 66–67; error in, 67, 242; falseness of, 78–79, 88; ideal, 25, 219, 226; as instrumental, 84, 223–24, 227–28; made only of verbs, 226–27; moralities and, 115–16,

282

283

suffering (*continued*)
  as meaningless, 264, 267; moralization
  of, 262–63; pleasure in, 155–56,
  158–59, 163; a priori of, 261–62;
  religion and, 171, 264–65
superego, 121
Superman. *See Übermensch*
survival, 71, 205–6

theoretical entities, 69
thermodynamics, 190, 191, 200
things. *See* objects
thought, 74–75, 88, 102; *cogito*, 92–94
Thrasymachus, 153–54
Thus Spake Zarathustra (Nietzsche):
  Eternal Recurrence, 183–95; on good
  and evil, 124–25; *Übermensch* in,
  178–83
Tractatus (Wittgenstein), 219, 225–26
tragedy, 32, 36–39, 61, 233–34
Triumph of Truth, The (Rubens), 222
truth, 14, 20–21, 25, 212, 230, 240;
  clarity and distinction, 241;
  Correspondence Theory of, 15,
  54–55, 57, 62, 80–81, 112, 174n,
  225; error, relationship to, 56–57, 71;
  as illusion, 20–21; as lie, 222–23,
  241–42; Nietzsche's use of term,
  61–63; as outcome of enquiry/ordeal,
  224–25; science and, 53–54
Turgenev, Ivan, 11, 12

Übermensch, 3, 16, 178–83, 193–94, 266
unconcern, 251–52, 266
unconscious, 255
understanding, 79–80, 103, 125
Urvermögen, 27–30, 35
Usener, Hermann, 46
utility, 140–42, 145

value, 14–15, 54, 117–18, 242
volitions, 91–92, 95

von Bülow, Cosima, 44
von Bülow, Hans, 32n.
von Wilamowitz-Moellendorff, Ulrich,
  45–46

Wagner, Cosima, 44, 148
Wagner, Richard, 18–19, 24, 43, 44–49,
  148, 182, 223, 234, 235
Wagnerian art, 43, 122, 234
warrior, 134–36, 251–52
will, 94, 233–34; acts of, 91–92, 95–97;
  causality and, 96, 199–200; contests
  of, 155–56; effect and, 200–202;
  free, 96–98; memory of, 156–57;
  psychology of, 90, 91–98; redirection
  of, 266–67
will-to-power, 3, 12, 88, 90, 154, 196,
  249; asceticism and, 209–10; causality
  and, 204; deflected by religion,
  171–72; as explanatory principal,
  199; happiness and, 206–7; matter
  and, 202–3; moralities and, 115,
  119, 132, 134, 136; pain and, 207–8;
  Perspectivism and, 62; self-overcoming
  and, 161–62; of the species, 224;
  spiritual life and, 208–9; struggle for
  existence and, 205–6
Will-to-Truth, 174
wisdom, 251–53, 266
Wissenschaft, as term, 49n.
Wittgenstein, Ludwig, 96, 103–4, 219–20,
  223, 225–28, 234, 257
world: apparent, 57, 72–73, 78, 109;
  common-sense, 55–57, 72–73; as
  infinitely plastic, 224, 226; inner and
  outer, 98, 102–4; language required
  to fit, 225–26; physical, 198–99;
  scientific picture of, 73–74; structure
  of, 225–26; as valueless, 14–15. *See
  also* Eternal Recurrence

Xerxes, 141